A Guide Through the Old Testament

A Guide Through the Old Testament

Celia Brewer Marshall

Westminster / John Knox Press
Louisville, Kentucky

Westminster / John Knox Press
Louisville, Kentucky

Unless otherwise indicated, Scripture quotations are from the Revised Standard Version of the Bible, copyrighted, 1946, 1952, © 1971, 1973 by the Division of Christian Education of the National Council of the Churches of Christ in the U.S.A. and used by permission.

Acknowledgment is given to publishers and copyright holders for permission to reprint excerpts or adaptations from the following:

Ancient Near Eastern Texts: Relating to the Old Testament, by James B. Pritchard, 3rd ed. with Supplement. Copyright © 1969 by Princeton University Press. Excerpt, pp. 93–95, reprinted with permission of Princeton University Press.

The text for "Abraham" and "Gomer" from *Peculiar Treasures: A Biblical Who's Who,* by Frederick Buechner, copyright © 1979 by Frederick Buechner. Reprinted by permission of Harper & Row, Publishers, Inc.

Out of the Past, by William O. Kellogg. Copyright 1969 by Independent School Press. Pages 116–28 used by permission of William O. Kellogg.

Understanding the Old Testament, by Bernhard W. Anderson, 4/E, © 1986, pp. 184–92. Excerpted by permission of Prentice-Hall, Inc., Englewood Cliffs, New Jersey.

The Graphic Bible, by Lewis E. Browne. Copyright 1928 Lewis Browne, renewed 1956 by Rebecca Tarlow. Pages 48–52 and 65 (map) used by permission of Macmillan Publishing Company.

A Shepherd Looks at Psalm 23, by W. Phillip Keller. Copyright © 1970 by W. Phillip Keller. Adapted material used by permission of Zondervan Publishing House.

A Shepherd Looks at the Good Shepherd and His Sheep, by W. Phillip Keller. Copyright © 1978 by W. Phillip Keller. Adapted material used by permission of Zondervan Publishing House.

"Have You Explored the Library?" by Celia Marshall, in *Adult Leader-DJF* 1983–84. Copyright 1983, Graded Press. Adapted material used by permission of Graded Press.

Library of Congress Cataloging in Publication Data

Marshall, Celia Brewer, 1954–
    A guide through the Old Testament / Celia Brewer Marshall.
        p.   cm.
    ISBN 0-8042-0124-2

    1. Bible.   O.T.—Textbooks.   I. Title.
BS1194.M344 1989
220.6'1—dc20   89-36883
                                        CIP

10 9 8 7

Printed in the United States of America
Published by Westminster/John Knox Press
Louisville, Kentucky

To Alfred, Anna, and Sally Spencer

Per aspera ad astra

Preface

Fortified with the best intentions and the strongest motivations, how many folk have attempted to read the Old Testament on their own, from cover to cover, only to find themselves confused and discouraged after the first few books? It is little wonder that they quit, overwhelmed by the sheer bulk of material and the strangeness of it all, vowing either to return to the project "when I have more time to figure it out" or never to try again!

The purpose of the *Guide* is to steer and direct the reader through the Old Testament, to point out key passages and themes, to provide the reader with the background knowledge necessary to read for sense and for meaning. The reader is asked to study selections from the Old Testament and to formulate answers to a wide variety of questions on these selections. You, the student and reader, will work hard as you complete these study guides. Each question is followed by room for written responses. The book will provide a record of your responses and reactions to the text.

This *Guide* is the product of a decade's work with high school students. When I first began teaching, fresh out of divinity school, I gave impassioned lectures to passive students. The Bible became for them (bless their hearts) another subject in which the teacher was the authority and their task was simply to take notes. To say, "Go home and read Genesis 1–11," would lead to confusion and discouragement, so I simply told my classes what I thought the text had to say. When it came time to grade responses to test questions, I realized that I was reading my lecture notes over and over again, and having to grade the students on their ability to remember what I had said in class.

And so this book evolved from study guides I developed as a "hands on," direct, and individualized approach to reading Scripture. The real work is now done by the student, independently. The classroom then becomes a place for discussion rather than lecturing. These study guides are the bases for group discussion and the chronicles of the students' own reaction to and dialogue with the Old Testament.

The *Guide* may be used in a variety of settings. It was written with a high school level Old Testament survey course in mind; as a supplement to the Bible it contains everything Old Testament students need to have in hand

(except tests and final exams!). Selected chapters might be used in World Religions or English classes, when times does not permit a thorough study of biblical literature but the teacher wishes to familiarize the students with some readings from the Old Testament. Sunday school classes for high school age on up to adult classes will find the book helpful, either in its entirety or in a concentrated study of a few OT books. Finally, the *Guide* lends itself to self-study and may be used by individuals who wish to read the OT with guidance. The book simply directs the reader through the OT, making it accessible and manageable.

I am deeply grateful to The Westminster Schools in Atlanta, Georgia, for generously awarding me a sabbatical year in which to write. The administration and faculty have been immensely supportive, particularly Donn M. Gaebelein, the schools' president; Merrilyn Eastham, head of the Bible Department; and John Roberts, who helped me put together a query package when I decided to find a publisher. Most of all I want to thank George Lamplugh, who used and revised much of the material when it was still in bulging manila folders and encouraged me to get it in print.

Celia Brewer Marshall

Contents

CHAPTER I

Introduction to the Old Testament

THE HOLY LAND: GEOGRAPHICAL FEATURES

"For the LORD your God is bringing you into a good land, a land of brooks of water, of fountains and springs, flowing forth in valleys and hills, a land of wheat and barley, of vines and fig trees and pomegranates, a land of olive trees and honey, a land in which you will eat bread without scarcity, in which you will lack nothing, a land whose stones are iron, and out of whose hills you can dig copper. And you shall eat and be full, and you shall bless the LORD your God for the good land [God] has given you." (Deut. 8:7–10)

In this way, Moses described to the twelve tribes of Israel the land that they were about to enter, the land first promised to their forefather Abraham centuries earlier. After years of bondage in Egypt and wandering in the wilderness, the covenant people would find a geographical and spiritual homeland in this place. It was the land of milk and honey, the land of God's promise, the Holy Land.

As its political status underwent momentous changes in ancient Near Eastern times, this region from the Mediterranean coast to the Dead Sea and the Jordan River valley went by a variety of place names. They are listed here in roughly chronological order:

1. It was originally called *Canaan* because the land was first inhabited by the Canaanites, polytheistic peoples who were invaded by the Hebrew tribes around 1200 B.C.

2. *Israel* was the name given to this area after the conquest, when the twelve tribes descended from the sons of Jacob (also known as "Israel") settled there. Later, *Israel* was used as the name of a separate kingdom in the region to the north of the Dead Sea, which existed from the time of Solomon's death (922 B.C.) until the Assyrian conquest in 722 B.C.

3. *Judah* was the name of the southern part of this region (Judah being the largest tribe in the south); it was also the name of the southern, Davidic kingdom, which existed from 922 to 586 B.C. Jerusalem, the capital of the kingdom, is the major city in this region.

4. The region was called *Palestine* in the Hellenistic era, because the Philistine (in Greek, *Palaistinē*) settlements on the coast were known to the Greeks before the interior, Jewish communities were known to them.

5. *Judea,* from which we get the word Judeans, or Jews, was the name given to the region by the Romans when this area existed as a province of the Roman empire.

No single feature unites the Holy Land geographically. Two long valleys run north and south, one along the Mediterranean coast and the other along the rift known as the Arabah created by the Jordan River. The Arabah valley is lush and tropical. From its origins around Mount Hermon in the north to its endpoint in the Dead Sea, the Jordan River descends 3,000 feet (1,000 meters). The Dead Sea, which has a salt content so high that no animals or plants can live in it, is the lowest place on earth. Its bottom is 2,600 feet (800 meters) below sea level. The two major valleys provide fertile farmlands that fit Moses' description in the Deuteronomy passage. Between these fertile areas are many small mountain ranges also running north and south. The range of craggy hills is broken in the north by several shorter valleys. Deserts lie to the east of the Arabah rift and to the south and west of the Dead Sea. The Mediterranean coast south of Mount Carmel has no natural harbors; thus neither the Israelites nor the Canaanites before them were seafaring peoples. The hills were suited to raising sheep and the valleys to farming in Old Testament times.

Thus the Holy Land comprises a wide variety of geographical features: mountains, valleys, and deserts. Its latitude is roughly that of Georgia or southern California. The seasons are only two: a cold, wet winter and a hot, dry summer. Summer temperatures averages in the coast and hills are 71–77° F (22–25° C). Around the Dead Sea, the average is 104° F (40° C). One particularly irritating feature of summertime is the sirocco—hot, dry winds that blow in from the east for two to three days at a time. The rains begin in September or October, the beginning of the agricultural year. This is the time for plowing and for the New Year of the Jewish calendar. The rains are heaviest in December or January and end in April, the time for ripening of the crops. The average rainfall in Jerusalem is comparable to that in London, but the rains are not scattered throughout the year. Jerusalem gets between fifty and sixty rainy days per year; northern Israel (the Galilee region) gets between sixty and seventy; the Negev desert in the south has only ten to twenty days of rain annually.

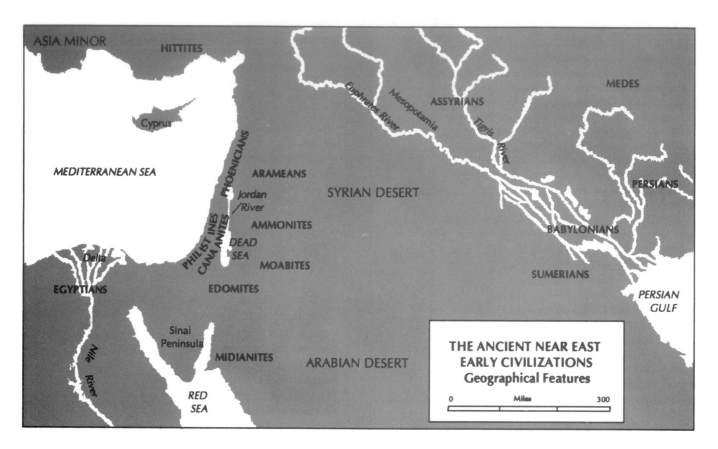

ASIA MINOR
HITTITES
Cyprus
MEDITERRANEAN SEA
MEDES
ASSYRIANS
Euphrates River
Mesopotamia
Tigris River
PERSIANS
ARAMEANS
SYRIAN DESERT
PHOENICIANS
Jordan River
AMMONITES
BABYLONIANS
PHILISTINES
CANAANITES
DEAD SEA
MOABITES
SUMERIANS
Delta
EGYPTIANS
EDOMITES
PERSIAN GULF
Sinai Peninsula
Nile River
MIDIANITES
ARABIAN DESERT
RED SEA

THE ANCIENT NEAR EAST
EARLY CIVILIZATIONS
Geographical Features

0   Miles   300

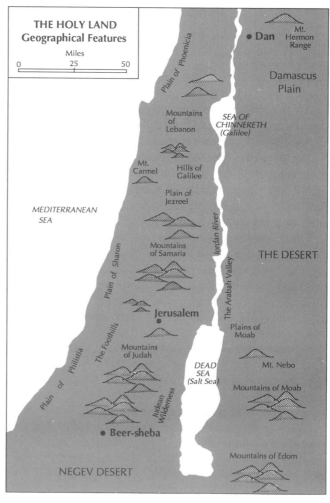

THE HOLY LAND
Geographical Features

Miles
0   25   50

Plain of Phoenicia
Dan
Mt. Hermon Range
Damascus Plain
Mountains of Lebanon
SEA OF CHINNERETH (Galilee)
Mt. Carmel
Hills of Galilee
Plain of Jezreel
MEDITERRANEAN SEA
Plain of Sharon
Mountains of Samaria
Jordan River
THE DESERT
The Arabah Valley
Jerusalem
Plains of Moab
Plain of Philistia
The Foothills
Mountains of Judah
Mt. Nebo
DEAD SEA (Salt Sea)
Judean Wilderness
Mountains of Moab
Beer-sheba
Mountains of Edom
NEGEV DESERT

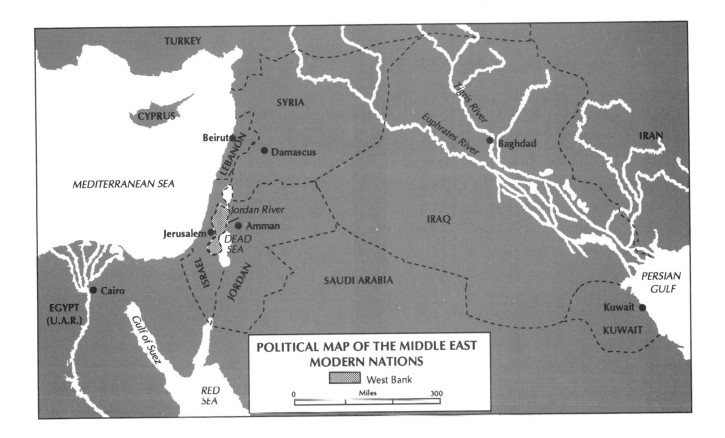

POLITICAL MAP OF THE MIDDLE EAST
MODERN NATIONS
West Bank

The distance from Dan to Beersheba, the traditional northern and southern limits of the territory occupied by the Israelites, is around 150 miles (240 kilometers). The area that they claimed as their promised land was roughly 10,000 square miles: the size of Vermont or one-fourth larger than Wales. In Old Testament times this tiny region was strategic. Mighty empires rose and fell to the west, east, and north of Israel. For Egypt to the west and the great Mesopotamian civilizations to the east, Israel was an important bridge between Africa and Asia. Being at the crossroads of so many power struggles meant that Israel was rarely at peace. Foreign infiltration was a constant source of troubles. Despite its precarious position as the coastal corridor for many hostile peoples, the Israelites never wavered in their belief that this little region was God's gift to them.

"And because [God] loved your [ancestors] and chose their descendants after them, and brought you out of Egypt with [God's] own presence, by [God's] great power, driving out before you nations greater and mightier than yourselves, to bring you in, to give you their land for an inheritance, as at this day; know therefore this day, and lay it to your heart, that the LORD is God in heaven above and on the earth beneath; there is no other. Therefore you shall keep [God's] statutes and [God's] commandments, which I command you this day, that it may go well with you, and with your children after you, and that you may prolong your days in the land which the LORD your God gives you for ever."

(Deut. 4:37–40)

HOW TO LOOK UP BIBLE REFERENCES

The method for looking up biblical references is standardized in the following way:

1. The name of the biblical book comes first, and it is often abbreviated (Genesis: Gen.; Exodus: Exod.; and so on).

2. After the name of the book, the number of the chapter will be given. Thus Genesis 1 (or Gen. 1) means the first chapter of the book of Genesis. If the reference is to more than one chapter, the notation will be written as follows: Genesis 3; 4 means the third and fourth chapters of Genesis (sometimes written Gen. 3—4 or Gen. 3, 4). Genesis 11—50 means chapters eleven *through* fifty of Genesis.

3. For specific verses within a chapter, a colon (:) will

follow the chapter number and precede the verse number. Thus Genesis 1:1 means the first verse of the first chapter of Genesis. A dash (—) means "read through" from one chapter to another: Genesis 3:2—4:1 means start at verse 2 of chapter 3 and read through verse 1 of chapter 4. A semicolon (;) means "stop and turn to a new chapter": thus Genesis 4:11; 6:7 means read verse 11 of chapter 4, then stop and turn to chapter 6 and read verse 7.

4. Sometimes a verse needs to be divided in half for special consideration. The first half of a verse is denoted by the letter *a* following the verse number; the second half is denoted by the letter *b*. Thus Genesis 2:4a refers to the first half of the fourth verse of chapter 2 in Genesis.

5. If reference is made to several verses beyond a particular citation, the symbol *ff.* is used. Thus Genesis 2:4 ff. means start at verse 4 of chapter 2 in Genesis and read several verses following.

6. When only one book is being considered in a study guide, often the name of the book will be omitted after the first reference.

7. When it is clear which chapter of a book is being considered, the chapter number is often omitted and verse numbers are given using the letters *vs.* for one verse, or *vss.* for more than one verse. Thus vs. 11 means the eleventh verse of the chapter being considered, and vss. 11—18 means verses eleven through eighteen of that chapter.

Practice looking up the following examples, using the explanations.

1. Exod. 6:7 (the book of Exodus, chapter 6, verse 7)

2. Lev. 19:18, 33 (the book of Leviticus, chapter 19, verse 18 and verse 33)

3. Num. 14:8, Exod. 14:14 (the book of Numbers, chapter 14, verse 8 and also the book of Exodus, chapter 14, verse 14)

4. Deut. 6:4—7 (the book of Deuteronomy, chapter 6, verses 4 through 7)

5. 2 Sam. 6:1 ff. (the second book of Samuel, chapter 6, verse 1 and several verses following)

6. Isa. 6:8, 30:15 (the book of Isaiah, chapter 6, verse 8, and also chapter 30, verse 15)

7. Jer. 30—32 (the book of Jeremiah, chapters 30 through 32 inclusive)

8. Jer. 31:33b (the book of Jeremiah, chapter 31, the second half of verse 33)

9. Ezek. 2:8—3:3 (the book of Ezekiel, chapter 2, verse 8 through chapter 3, verse 3)

Exercises

Look up and read the following biblical references.

1. Deut. 33:26—27
2. Pss. 8; 100; 104
3. Isa. 40:27—31; 55:9
4. Exod. 20; 32:16
5. Hos. 4:1 ff.; 6:4—6; 11:1—4
6. Jer. 23:23—24; 31:20, 33
7. Gen. 2:4b ff.

WORKING WITH B.C. DATES

In Hebrew public records, years were recorded in reference to some noteworthy event rather than by a system of formal numbering. Thus Isaiah records that his call to be a prophet occurred "in the year that King Uzziah died" (Isa. 6:1); he could not have written that it occurred in the year 742 B.C. as we know it today.

Julius Caesar established the Julian calendar of 365 days, with every fourth year a leap year. In 1582 Pope Gregory XIII made certain changes in the Julian calendar and used Jesus Christ's birth as the starting point for counting the years. This Gregorian calendar, or Christian calendar, is the system of dating used in the West. Dates after the birth of Christ are noted A.D. (*anno Domini*—in the year of the Lord). We count backwards or away from the birth of Christ to indicate dates before Christ, or B.C. When dealing with B.C. dates in the Gregorian calendar, dates get *smaller* as they get nearer to the time of Christ's birth. Isaiah began his prophetic career in 742 B.C., and his prophecy spanned fifty-three years; thus his career ended in 687 B.C. The following chart shows the relationship between B.C. and A.D. dates:

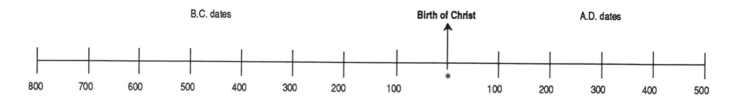

| B.C. dates | | Birth of Christ | A.D. dates |

| 800 | 700 | 600 | 500 | 400 | 300 | 200 | 100 | * | 100 | 200 | 300 | 400 | 500 |

When we speak of centuries (hundred-year units) and millennia (thousand-year units), the method is less obvious. The dates in the first century A.D. run from years 1 to 99; the second century dates run from 100 to 199. (Think of how you determine your age; you began your first year of life as soon as you were born, but you do not celebrate your first birthday until you have *completed* your first year of life.) The same system applies to millennia. The first millennium A.D. runs from year 1 to 999, and the second millennium runs from 1000 to 1999.

In working with B.C. dates, the method is reversed. The first century B.C. runs from 99 to 1 B.C., the second century from 199 to 100 B.C. The first millennium runs from 999 to 1 B.C., the second millennium from 1999 to 1000 B.C. The higher numbers are *earlier* in B.C. dates, because we are counting backwards. Thus if an event occurred "early in the eighth century B.C." it would be closer to 799 than to 700, while if it occurred "early in the eighth century A.D." it would be closer to 700 than to 799.

Many Old Testament dates cannot be established with certainty. We use the initial *c.* before a date to indicate that the event occurred "around" (*circa*) that time. Thus when we date Abraham's migration from Ur to Canaan c. 1750 B.C., we mean that it probably occurred around 1750 B.C., or some time in the middle of the eighteenth century B.C.

Use the following diagram to help you work the Exercise in Dating:

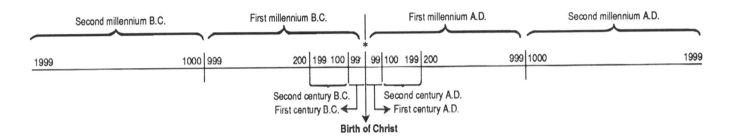

Exercise in Dating

1. Give the century, then the millennium, for each of the following dates:

A. 27 B.C. _____

B. A.D. 14 _____

C. A.D. 1492 _____

D. your birthday _____

E. 1290 B.C. _____

F. 3100 B.C. _____

G. A.D. 2000 _____

2. King David began his reign over Israel around 1000 B.C. and ruled until his death thirty-nine years later. When did his reign end?

_____

In what century would you place this date?

_____

What millennium?

_____

3. The Northern Kingdom of Israel fell to Assyria in 721 B.C. The Southern Kingdom of Judah lasted another 135 years, until it fell to Babylonia. What is the date of the fall of Judah?

_____

In what century would you place this date?

_____

Did the fall occur early or late in that century?

_____

4. If a person was born in the year 40 B.C. and lived for eighty-two years, what is the date of her death according to the Gregorian calendar?

_____

5. The Romans occupied Palestine from 63 B.C. until 324 A.D. How many years was Palestine under Roman occupation?

_____

For roughly how many centuries?

_____

High and Low Points in Old Testament History

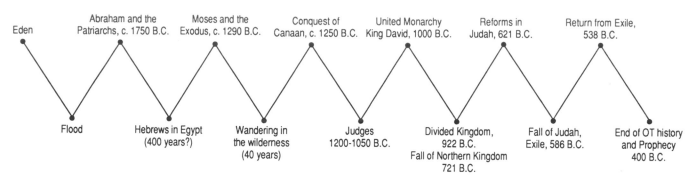

Timeline
The Patriarchs Through the United Kingdom

PERIOD	EGYPT	PALESTINE	MESOPOTAMIA
4000 to 3000 B.C.		First year of Jewish calendar: 3760	Growth of Semitic civilization in Mesopotamia; Sumerian civilization flourishes by 3500 Invention of writing, 3300
3000 to 2000 B.C.	Cheops builds Great Pyramid, 2600 Rise of Middle Kingdom, 2050		
2000 to 1500 B.C.	Hyksos invasion with horse and chariot, 1700 Period of Favor under Hyksos Dynasty, 1700–1550 Hyksos expelled; rise of New Kingdom; Period of Disfavor begins, 1567	Semitic pre-Israelite tribes migrating from Mesopotamia to Palestine, 2000–1700 Abraham journeys from Ur to Canaan, c. 1750 Joseph tribes move into Egypt, c. 1700	Epic of Gilgamesh, c. 2000 Hammurabi's Code, c. 1750 Hittites invade Mesopotamia from Asia Minor, 1590
1500 to 1200 B.C.	Egyptian control of Palestine begins, 1482 Pharaoh Seti I, 1309–1290	[400 years of silence ending with Hebrews' bondage in Goshen] Moses leads exodus from Egypt, 1290 Conquest of Canaan, 1250–1200	
1200 to 1000 B.C.	Pharaoh Ramses II, 1290–1224 Egyptian power begins to decline, 1200	Invasion of the Sea Peoples; Philistines settle in Canaan, c. 1200 Period of the Judges, 1200–1050 Fall of Shiloh to Philistines, 1050 Samuel and Saul, 1020–1000	Assyrian power grows; Tiglath-Pileser I, c. 1100
1000 to 922 B.C.		David, the United Monarchy, and the "golden age" of Israel, 1000–961 Solomon, 961–922 Solomon dedicates the temple, c. 950 End of the United Kingdom, 922	

Timeline
The Divided Kingdom to the Exile*

*Names of prophets and the dates of their prophetic careers are in bold type.

PERIOD	GREECE and ROME	JUDAH	ISRAEL	MESOPOTAMIA
1250 to 1000 B.C.	Greeks destroy Troy, 1250 Dorians invade Greece, 1200			Period of Assyrian dominance, from 1100
1000 to 900 B.C.		Schism of 922 results in Southern Kingdom (Judah) and Northern Kingdom (Israel) Rehoboam, 922–915	Jeroboam, 922–901	
900 to 800 B.C.	Etruscans settle in Italy, c. 800		Ahab, 874–850 **Elijah, c. 850** **Elisha, c. 850–800**	
800 to 700 B.C.	Greeks hold first Olympiad, 776 Rome founded, 753	**First Isaiah, 740–687** Judah submits to Assyria, 721 **Micah, c. 722–701** King Hezekiah refuses to pay tribute to Assyria, 705 Assyria invades Judah but leaves Jerusalem intact, 701	"Golden age" under Jeroboam II, 768–746 **Amos, c. 750** **Hosea, 740–700** Israelite alliance with Syria, 735 Fall of Israel to Assyria, 721	Fall of Syria to Assyria, 732 Assyrian King Sargon II destroys Northern Kingdom of Israel, 721 Assyrian King Sennacherib punishes Judah for failure to pay tribute, 701
700 to 600 B.C.	Draco codifies Athenian law, 621	King Josiah asserts Judean independence, 629 **Jeremiah, 626–580** Josiah's Deuteronomic reforms, 621 Pharaoh Necho defeats Judah at Megiddo, 609		Assyrian King Ashburnapal sacks Thebes, 663 Rise of Babylonian Empire; Nineveh (Assyrian capital) falls to Babylonians, 612 Babylonian defeat of Assyrians and Egyptians at Haran, 609 Nebuchadnezzar, King of Babylon, 605–562
		Nebuchadnezzar's first invasion of Judah, 597 Nebuchadnezzar destroys Jerusalem; Babylonian captivity begins, 586 **Second Isaiah, c. 540** **Ezekiel, 593–573**		

Dominant Foreign Powers in the Ancient Near East

EGYPT c. 1500-1200 B.C.	ASSYRIA c. 1100-600 B.C.	BABYLONIA 625-539 B.C.	PERSIA 550-331 B.C.	HELLENISTIC PERIOD Ptolemies in Egypt and Seleucids in Syria 331-167 B.C.	ROME 63 B.C.-324 A.D.

Timeline
The Restoration, the Hellenistic Era, and Roman Occupation*

*Names of prophets and the dates of their prophetic careers are in bold type.

PERIOD	GREECE and ROME	JUDEA	MESOPOTAMIA
550 to 500 B.C.	Romans establish Republic, 509	Restoration: Jews return to Judea from the Exile beginning in 538 Second temple built, 520–515 **Haggai, c. 520** **Zechariah, c. 520**	Cyrus the Great, founds Persian Empire, 550–530 Persians defeat Medes, 550 Persians invade Lydia, 546 Persians enter Babylon, 539 Cyrus' Edict of Toleration, 538: Hebrew Exile ends Darius I, 522–486
500 to 400 B.C.	Athenians resist Persian invasions, 490–479 Athen's golden age under Pericles, c. 445 Peloponnesian Wars, 431–404	**Malachi, 500–450** Nehemiah, governor, rebuilds walls of Jerusalem, c. **444** Ezra, priest and scribe, reads the law in Jerusalem, c. **400**	First Persian invasion of Greece: Battle of Marathon, 490 Xerxes I (Ahasuerus), 486–465 Second Persian invasion of Greece: battles of Salamis, Thermopylae, and Plataea, 479
400 to 300 B.C.	Alexander the Great invades Persia, 334 Alexander defeats Darius III at Arbela, 331 Death of Alexander, 323	Alexander captures Jerusalem, 332	Persian Empire destroyed by Alexander the Great, 331
300 to 200 B.C.	Punic Wars begin, 264 Hannibal invades Italy, 218	Ptolemies in Egypt are overlords of Judea, 323–198: toleration of the Jews Jews in Alexandria translate the OT into Greek (LXX), 275	
200 to 100 B.C.	Romans destroy Carthage, 146	Seleucids in Syria are overlords of Judea 198–167; persecution of the Jews Judas Maccabeus, 166–160, leads revolt against Seleucids, occupies Jerusalem, cleanses temple; independence won	Seleucid King Antiochus Epiphanes, 175–163
100 to 63 B.C.	Birth of Julius Caesar, 100 Pompey annexes Syria and Palestine, including Jerusalem, for Rome, 63	Roman occupation of Judea, 63	

LITERARY GENRES IN THE OLD TESTAMENT

Study Guide

A literary genre is a category of written composition characterized by a particular style, form, or content. Being able to recognize a genre is crucial to understanding the meaning of a literary unit. For example, if you opened your mail and received a business letter, you would immediately recognize this genre by the form and style of writing, and you would correctly expect this type of letter to have a certain content that would not be found in a thank-you note or a postcard from a friend.

The Old Testament is the record of Israel's encounter with God. We would be amiss, however, if we read every word as "history." History is but one of the many genres found in the Old Testament. Not only is the Bible a collection of many different books with many different purposes, but within each book we find a variety of genres which must be defined and recognized. Once we know the "rules" of the genre, we are better prepared to hear what the text actually has to say.

In preparing this study guide, use a good dictionary or English textbook to define each genre. Next, decide whether you think the genre will be written in poetic form or in prose. Then turn to the example(s) cited for the genre and show how the biblical text meets the requirements of the genre you have just defined.

1. allegory:

_____

_____

examples: Proverbs 9:1–6; Isaiah 5:1–7

_____

2. aphorism:

_____

_____

examples: skim the book of Proverbs

_____

3. ancient songs:

_____

_____

examples: Exodus 15:21; Judges 5

_____

4. autobiography:

_____

_____

example: skim Nehemiah 1–7

_____

5. biography:

_____

_____

example: Jeremiah 26

_____

6. creed:

_____

_____

example: Deuteronomy 26:5–10

_____

7. elegy:

_____

_____

example: 2 Samuel 1:19–27

_____

8. epic:

_____

_____

example: Job (skim the first two chapters and the last chapter)

_____

9. etiology:

_____

_____

example: Genesis 32:22–32

_____

10. didactic narrative:

_____

_____

example: skim the book of Jonah

_____

_____

11. fable:

_____

_____

example: Judges 9:7–15

_____

_____

12. history:

_____

_____

example: skim 1 Kings 1–2

_____

_____

13. hymn:

_____

_____

examples: Psalms 100; 149; 150

_____

_____

14. lament:

_____

_____

examples: Psalms 22; 51

_____

_____

15. law:

_____

_____

examples: Exodus 20:1–17; Leviticus 19

_____

_____

16. liturgy:

_____

_____

example: Leviticus 16

_____

_____

17. prophecy:

_____

_____

example: Amos 1–2

_____

_____

18. parable:

_____

_____

example: 2 Samuel 12:1–4

_____

_____

19. short story:

_____

_____

example: skim the book of Ruth

_____

_____

THE OLD TESTAMENT CANON

The word *canon* comes from the Greek for "rule" or "measure." The Hebrew canon is the authoritative list of sacred books (or Holy Scriptures) that have "measured up" to the standards set by the Jewish community. There are four characteristics of canonicity:

1. The books are accepted as having divine authority.
2. The number of books is fixed.
3. The period of time within which the books originated is limited.
4. The text is regarded as fixed and unalterable.

How did the Old Testament canon come to be defined? What steps were taken historically in deciding which texts would be regarded as canon, or Holy Scriptures?

While it is impossible to trace the exact development of canonization, a few stages can be identified. In 621 B.C., the first mention of an authoritative text is made in Israelite history (see 2 Kings 22–23). King Josiah of Judah found a "book of the law" in the temple and used this text as the basis for a sweeping religious reform. Scholars believe this "book" constituted much of the text of Deuteronomy as we have it today. Over two hundred years later, a scribe and priest named Ezra read "the book of the law of Moses" to those Jews who had returned to Jerusalem from exile (see Neh. 8). While we are not sure from what book or books Ezra read, the reforms he instigated indicate that the Torah, or the first five books of the Old Testament, was in existence at this time (c. 400 B.C.).

The key date in the crystallization of the Hebrew canon is A.D. 90, when a group of rabbis met at Jamnia (near Joppa on the coastal plain of Israel). While some books continued to be debated after A.D. 90, for the sake of convenience we can say that the matter of what constituted the Hebrew canon was settled at the Council of Jamnia.

What principles did the rabbis use at the Council of Jamnia? They fixed the number of books at twenty-four, which corresponds to the number of letters in the Hebrew alphabet. Twenty-four was the number symbolizing completeness: "Whoever brings into his house more than the twenty-four books introduces confusion" (Midrash Qoholeth 12:12). The total was arrived at in various ways, depending on how many texts could all be written on a single scroll twenty-five to thirty feet long. Today, the books of the Hebrew canon are numbered in the following manner:

I. The Law (*Torah*) is composed of five books: Genesis, Exodus, Leviticus, Numbers, Deuteronomy.

II. The Prophets (*Nebi'im*) comprises eight books:

A. the four books of the "Former Prophets": Joshua, Judges, First and Second Samuel (count as one book), First and Second Kings (one book)

B. The four books of the "Latter Prophets":

1. "Major" [denoting length]: Isaiah, Jeremiah, Ezekiel (each counts as one book)

2. "Minor" (or shorter), also called "The Twelve": Hosea, Joel, Amos, Obadiah, Jonah, Micah, Nahum, Habakkuk, Zephaniah, Haggai, Zechariah, and Malachi. "The Twelve" are counted as one book or scroll.

III. The Writings (*Kethubim*) comprises eleven books: Psalms, Proverbs, Job, Song of Songs, Ruth, Lamentations, Ecclesiastes, Esther, Daniel, Ezra-Nehemiah (one book), First and Second Chronicles (one book).

Of these three divisions of the Bible, the Torah was probably given its final form by 400 B.C. and had already existed as an authoritative collection of books for centuries before Jamnia. Much of the prophetic collection (*Nebi'im*) was fixed by 200 B.C. So at Jamnia, the rabbinical debates concerned the division of texts known as the Writings (*Kethubim*). The rabbis used the principle of harmony with the written Torah in evaluating problem texts. Furthermore, no books were included that were known to have been written after Malachi (or after 400 B.C.), because the rabbis believed that with the death of the Restoration prophets, "the Holy Spirit departed from Israel." Finally, the rabbis rejected books written first in Greek, because Hebrew was the language of the Torah and the prophets.

The record of debates at Jamnia is interesting because we see that the rabbis recognized a list of books which had *already* been agreed upon as authoritative for the Jewish community. These texts were already central in the life and worship of Israel. The rabbis did not so much create the canon as give their stamp of approval to texts accepted *through practical use*. To use a contemporary analogy, what happened at Jamnia was not an election of candidates for office, but an inauguration ceremony for current officeholders.

What the rabbis did do was set the limits on what books could be considered authoritative in the future; after Jamnia the canon was "closed." One reason for the closure of the canon was the rise of Christianity in the first century A.D. It was important for the rabbis to define which books were sacred, so Jews would not be misled by Christian writings. Another reason for canonization was that, with the destruction of the temple in A.D. 70, the historic sanctuary of the Jews was gone. Sacred writings became more urgent with the removal of the temple—the cultic center and heart of Judaism.

The canon as it was defined at Jamnia in A.D. 90 is the Holy Scripture for Jews and for Protestants (Protestant Bibles number the books differently, arriving at a total of thirty-nine instead of twenty-four). This Bible is called the Hebrew or Palestinian canon. But another list of authoritative books crystallized in Alexandria, Egypt, in the third century B.C. This list includes all the books in the Hebrew canon plus some extra books.* These extra books are set aside and bound separately by Jews and Protestants, and called "apocryphal" (meaning "hidden" or "secret"). They are included in the canon of Roman Catholic and Eastern Orthodox churches and called "deuterocanonical" (or "later added to the canon"). The Alexandrian canon became the authoritative list of books for the Catholic and Orthodox churches.

The legends vary, but one account says that the Alexandrian canon came into existence in the following way. Around 275 B.C., seventy rabbis in Alexandria sat down in seventy different rooms with the Hebrew Scriptures. Their task was to translate these texts into Greek, the language of the Jews in Alexandria. Miraculously, their translations were identical—the seventy rabbis arrived at Greek translations that were exactly the same. This Alexandrian or Greek Old Testament is known as the Septuagint (Greek for "seventy"), abbreviated by the Roman numerals LXX.

Why were many books in the LXX not accepted as canon by the Council of Jamnia? Most of these books date from two centuries before Christ, too late for divine inspiration according to the rabbis. Almost all the apocryphal books were first written in Greek rather than the language of the prophets, Hebrew. Take the case of the apocryphal Wisdom of Solomon. While the author claims to be Solomon, which puts the book in the correct time frame between Moses and Ezra, the book was first written in Greek. It was therefore struck from the Palestinian canon.

Ultimately, the reason these books were not recognized in Palestine was because they simply were not used by the Jewish community there. Remember that practical usage was the real reason for canonization—and the center of Judaism in Palestine did not use these texts.

The LXX became the Old Testament of the early church, however, which was Greek-speaking. While Jesus

* The books of the Apocrypha are First and Second Esdras, Tobit, Judith, Wisdom of Solomon, Ecclesiasticus, Prayer of Azariah and the Song of the Three Young Men, Susanna, Bel and the Dragon, First and Second Maccabees, The Prayer of Manasseh, the Letter of Jeremiah, Baruch, and additions to Esther.

never quoted from the apocryphal books in the LXX, the early Christian fathers quoted extensively from this "additional" literature. When Jerome made the official translation of the Scriptures into Latin in the fourth century A.D., he used the LXX and naturally included the apocryphal books. This Latin translation, called the Vulgate, became the Bible of the Catholic church. When Martin Luther translated the Hebrew canon into German in 1534, he noticed the absence of these extra books, called them "secret" or apocryphal, and put them in a group by themselves. Thus with the Reformation the Apocrypha was born, and the existence of two different canons was officially recognized.

One final note on the Hebrew canon. While the text is regarded as fixed and unalterable, the history of biblical transmission in fact shows that many, many versions of the text existed up until the Middle Ages. This fact is due to the peculiar character of Hebrew writing. In the earliest manuscripts, no punctuation was used and no separation was made between words. For example, the line GODISNOWHERE may have been read "God is now here" or "God is nowhere." To make matters even trickier, no vowels exist in Hebrew. Thus our example should actually read GDSNWHR. Obviously many possibilities existed for confusion by scribes and copyists. We also find examples of scribal explanations and additions to the text. Glosses, comments, and interpretations added by scribes were construed by later copyists as part of the text itself. In comparing manuscripts, then, translators have noted variant readings and corruptions. It is important to refer to footnotes and annotations in your English Bibles, which give several possible translations where the text is corrupt.

Around A.D. 600, a group of Jewish scholars known as Massoretes began to standardize the written text of the Hebrew canon. They devised a method for indicating the missing vowel sounds in Hebrew. They placed dots and dashes above or below the Hebrew letters to indicate the correct vowel sounds. This system is called "pointing," and the Massoretes pointed every word in the Hebrew Bible. They also applied the conventions of punctuation and paragraphing to the text. The Massoretes finished their task by the tenth century A.D. The Massoretic Text (MT) is the standard text of the Hebrew Bible used today, and the basis (along with the LXX) for our English translations of the Old Testament.

INDIVIDUAL PROJECTS ON THE OLD TESTAMENT

Items on this list of suggested projects are designed to take you "one step further" in your study of the Old Testament. Some require research using the library or specialized texts; others call for creative and imaginative reflection on portions of the biblical text. You need not limit yourself to this list.

1. Collages. Create a composite picture using two or more media (photographs, printed matter, paints, fabric, three-dimensional objects) to portray a character or an event in the Old Testament.

2. Murals. Create a large wall decoration, including many pictures that center on one theme in the Old Testament.

3. Models. Create a three-dimensional model of the tabernacle, a battle scene, or a tableau depicting a dramatic moment in Old Testament history.

4. Games. Design a card, board, or quiz game based on a certain historical period of the Old Testament or on the Old Testament in general.

5. Newspapers. Create news stories, headlines, ads, and editorials that might have come from a period in Old Testament history.

6. Interviews. Tape-record or write up an interview with an authority in your community (rabbi, cantor, professor, teacher). Topics for discussion might include that person's view of certain Old Testament passages, observances, and worship, or what it means to be a Jew today.

7. Visuals. Use slides or art prints from books and magazines to illustrate a topic. Suggested topics: Palestinian geography and places; Israel today; Old Testament customs and practices; archaeological methods.

8. Art history. Use slides or art prints from books and magazines to show how painters, sculptors, and illustrators have portrayed Old Testament themes and scenes.

9. Hymns. Present a report on hymns that interpret Old Testament lessons.

10. Music history. Use oratorios based on Old Testament passages, such as "The Creation," by Haydn; "Elijah," by Mendelssohn; or "The Messiah," by Handel. Listen to recordings of selections and show how Scripture is used in the music.

11. Musical composition. Write a hymn, ballad, or song based on a biblical event. Set your piece to music using a guitar, piano, or other instrument.

12. Research. Use the library to find sources, then prepare a report on a specific topic. Some possible topics are:

Archaeology and the Old Testament
Jewish Festivals and Holy Days
Home and Family Life in Biblical Times
Work and Society in Biblical Times
Warfare and Weaponry

CHAPTER 2

Primeval History

GENESIS 1—11: AN INTRODUCTION

The German language has two words that are both translated as "history" in English. *Historie* refers to the simple facts of the past: who did what to whom, where, and when. *Geschichte* refers to the meaning of past events: their causes and effects, the interpretations and explanations of these events. If you were to write your autobiography as *Historie* you would give the names of your parents, your place of birth, the places you had lived, and the ways in which you spent your time. You might include a description of yourself in terms of height, weight, hair and eye color, education, hobbies, and interests. Such an autobiography would be "true" insofar as you had used data that was verifiable. But it would not tell readers who you really are, what made you the kind of person you are, or the way you understand yourself and life. An autobiography told in terms of *Geschichte,* on the other hand, would include your interpretation of your past: the impact of your parents or the influence of your place of birth on the way you look at the world. You might focus on an event and show the way that event shaped you and how you reacted to it. You would be telling your story from a personal point of view in an effort to describe the meaning that events in your past have for you.

Genesis 1—11 contains five stories:

1. Creation (Gen. 1:2—2:4a)
2. Creation and the fall (2:4b—3:24)
3. Cain and Abel (chap. 4)
4. The flood (chaps. 6—9)
5. The tower of Babel (chap. 11)

These stories are not *Historie* in the German sense of the word; instead they are *Geschichte.* They do not give us data in the way a historical timeline or a scientific treatise gives us "the facts." Instead the stories are the vehicles by which the Hebrews explained life. By telling the story of events set in the past, the Hebrews expressed their understanding of the world, themselves, and God.

Genesis 1—11 is called "primeval history." "Primeval" or "original" history is concerned with the origins of things and with explaining how things got to be the way they are. While we must first read these stories on the level of *Historie* (asking, Who is involved? What happened?), we must next explore them on the level of *Geschichte.* In doing so we will ask a different set of questions: Why did these things happen? What do these stories tell us about

the people who told them? How did they understand their relationships to each other and to God? In doing this we move from the level of *what is said* to *what is meant*.

If we look for *Historie* in terms of when and where these events occurred, we see that time and place are irrelevant, or at best shrouded in mystery. If we look for proofs of the existence of God, we will notice once again that such is not a concern of primeval history; the existence of God is simply a given. The concerns of Genesis 1—11 are not philosophical, scientific, or even purely historical. The stories are concerned instead with theology (the nature of God) and anthropology (the nature of humans). The major themes are creation, sin, and judgment. These themes are expressed in terms of relationships—between Adam and Eve, between the humans in the Garden of Eden and God, between Cain and Abel, between Noah and God, and so forth. By using the narrative form to describe what happens to these relationships, the Hebrews expressed their understandings of life and of God.

How did these stories come to be? The written text was probably in final form by 400 B.C., but the stories themselves originated long before the invention of writing. We might look at the document of Genesis 1—11 as a patchwork quilt. The various patches identified as the five episodes in the primeval history originated in oral form. The scraps of material were woven together over hundreds of years. These patches of oral tradition circulated independently. Gradually many different people at different times and in different places wrote down what they knew. Each patch then took on a unique shape, its form serving to express certain truths about life and God. By 400 B.C., the process was completed. The final steps in preparing this quilt are the works of editors who laid the patches out in order, sewed them together (often using genealogies, or family trees, to connect the stories), and completed the quilt known to us as the large document of Genesis 1—11.

Within this document, the attentive reader will notice some discrepancies and some repetitions (called doublets or parallel passages). This is because the editors, working with the pieces of tradition, sometimes laid two similar patches side-by-side or incorporated patches from different traditions, or sources, together in the finished quilt.

Do not be bothered by these discrepancies or repetitions. While the pieces of the quilt may not seem to "fit" in places, we shall see that the overall effect is a mature statement of the Hebrew faith.

THE CREATION EPICS

Study Guide

Draw a line in your Bible to separate Genesis 2:4a (the first half of verse 4) from Genesis 2:4b (the second half). Answer the questions for Genesis 1:1—2:4a in the middle column, making sure that you use *only* the information in the portion of the text above the line you have drawn. Then answer the same questions in the right-hand column using Genesis 2:4b–25, again limiting yourself to the material found below the line you have drawn.

	GENESIS 1:1—2:4a	GENESIS 2:4b-25
1. What is the name of the Creator in this account?	(Hebrew = *Elohim*)	(Hebrew = *Yahweh*)
2. How long did it take for the Creator to complete the task of creation (in days)?	See 2:2.	See 2.4b.
3. From what original "stuff" did the Creator make the world?	See 1:2.	See 2:5; 2:7.
4. In what order or sequence did creation take place? Number and list the order.		
5. How is the creation of humans described?	See 1:27.	See 2:7; 2:21–22.
6. What is the task of the human creatures?	See 1:26, 28–30.	See 2:15–17, 19–20.
7. The Hebrew word *ruah* means "breath," "wind," or "spirit."	How is *ruah* used in 1:2?	How is *ruah* used in 2:7?
8. The Hebrew word *'adam* means "man-kind" or "hu-manity."	How is *'adam* used in 1:27?	How is *'adam* used in 2:7–8?
9. By what means does the Creator cause things to come into being?		

COSMOLOGIES OF THE CREATION EPICS

The purpose of the creation epics in Genesis 1 and Genesis 2 is theological and anthropological; that is, the epics are interested in *who* God is and *what* God's creatures are meant to be. Genesis does not give us a scientific treatise on *how* the world came to be. Nevertheless, it is possible to discern the cosmologies, or pictures of the universe, that underlie the two epics. In Genesis 1:1—2:4a, God brings order out of chaos by driving back the primordial "deep," or waters, to form dry earth. In Gen. 2:4b–25, God works with dry, barren desert and out of it creates the watered, fertile earth.

Genesis 1 Cosmology: From Watery Chaos to Dry Land

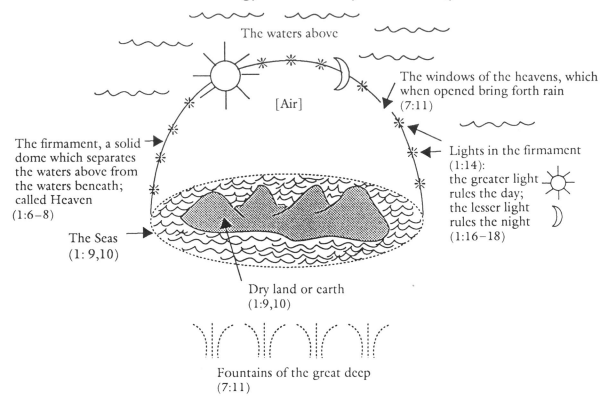

The waters above

[Air]

The windows of the heavens, which when opened bring forth rain (7:11)

The firmament, a solid dome which separates the waters above from the waters beneath; called Heaven (1:6–8)

Lights in the firmament (1:14): the greater light rules the day; the lesser light rules the night (1:16–18)

The Seas (1: 9,10)

Dry land or earth (1:9,10)

Fountains of the great deep (7:11)

Genesis 2 Cosmology: From Parched Earth to Fertile Land

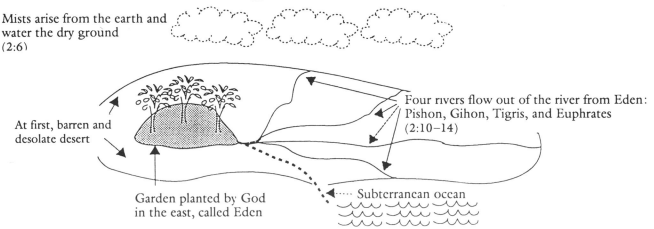

Mists arise from the earth and water the dry ground (2:6)

Four rivers flow out of the river from Eden: Pishon, Gihon, Tigris, and Euphrates (2:10–14)

At first, barren and desolate desert

Subterranean ocean

Garden planted by God in the east, called Eden

THE CREATION EPICS

Questions for Discussion

By completing the Study Guide on the Creation Epics, you have found nine different points of comparison between the account in Genesis 1:1—2:4a and the account in Genesis 2:4b–25. You have also seen that the cosmologies, or conceptions of the universe, underlying these two accounts are radically different. The explanation for this is that two different traditions once circulated independently. They were passed down by word of mouth in different parts of the Hebrew community for centuries before they were finally written down. Both were included in the book of Genesis because each expresses truths about the Creator and creation. By examining their literary characteristics, we find two rich understandings of the ways of God and God's purposes for creation that complement each other.

The style of Genesis 1 is one of grandeur and force. The language is ceremonious and stately. Phrases are echoed in the hymnic refrain after each day of creation: "and God saw that it was good." Each day represents a higher level in the order of creation, with humankind at the top of the hierarchy.

The account in Genesis 2 is not an elaborate, formal design, but a plot with characters. The picture of God is very "human," as God forms the creatures by hand and experiments with different companions for the man creature, finally arriving at the creation of woman. As the narrative unfolds, we are held in suspense by clues that a potential problem exists in Eden. There is a tree there that bears forbidden fruit: the tree of the knowledge of good and evil (i.e., "knowledge of *all* things"). Will the creatures eat of it? What will happen if they do?

1. The Theology of Genesis 1

What view of God do you find here?
Define "omnipotence." Then list the ways in which God's omnipotence is expressed in Genesis 1.

2. The Anthropology of Genesis 1

What view of humankind do you find here?
Define "dominion." With this word in mind, explain how the account shows the truth of the following analogy:

God : humans :: humans : the creatures of the earth

3. The Theology of Genesis 2

What view of the Lord do you find here?
Define "anthropomorphic." What anthropomorphic qualities are attributed to the Lord in this account?

4. The Anthropology of Genesis 2

What view of man do you find here? of woman?
When the man gives names to the creatures, this signifies his ownership of the creatures. How does the naming of the animals in 2:20 complement what God says about humans in 1:28?

5. Taken together, what do the creation epics tell us about the Creator? What do they tell us about the Creator's intention for the human race?

GENESIS 3: THE FALL

Study Guide

The creation epic of Genesis 2 continues in Genesis 3 with the account of the expulsion of man and woman from the Garden of Eden. As you read, resist the temptation to allegorize, or to treat the elements in the account as symbols for something else. Instead, concentrate on the relationships between the characters and the ways in which these relationships undergo change.

1. How is the serpent characterized in 3:1?

2. How did the woman's statement in 3:3 compare with God's statement in 2:17?

3. How does the serpent convince the woman that she should eat the forbidden fruit? To which of her desires did the serpent appeal?

4. What is it about the fruit that tempted the woman?

5. Why do you think the man ate the fruit?

6. What anthropomorphic touch do you find in 3:8?

7. When faced with God's questions, how did the man and the woman respond?

_____

_____

8. How did the man and the woman behave after they had eaten the fruit? What "knowledge" do you think they gained?

_____

_____

9. God does not ask the serpent why it did this thing. Why not?

_____

_____

10. How does the punishment of Adam and Eve differ? In what ways is it the same?

_____

_____

11. What things are cursed by God in the poetic passage 3:14–19? Why are they cursed?

_____

_____

_____

12. Why were Adam and Eve banished from the Garden? What does God fear will happen if they remain in the Garden?

_____

_____

13. By what act of tenderness does God show Adam and Eve that they are still under God's care and protection? What happened to God's decree in 2:17?

_____

_____

GENESIS 3

Questions for Discussion

1. Hamartiology is a part of theology that is concerned with the nature of sin—its causes and results. What is the hamartiology found in Genesis 3? How does the story show us what sin is? The actions of Adam and Eve are open to many interpretations. Thus over the centuries, thinkers and writers have come up with a variety of ways to explain the cause of the fall. Curiosity, pride, disobedience, the desire for power, the desire for knowledge, rebellion, ignorance, egocentricity, unbelief: any one or a combination of these factors has been named as the root or origin of sin. Some theologians describe sin as "concupiscence," meaning an excessive love of some lesser good that upsets the God-given pattern for human life. Thus the poet John Milton, in *Paradise Lost,* writes that Adam ate the fruit because he loved Eve too much.

What do you think is the cause of the fall?

What do you think is the nature of sin?

What is the relationship between sin and human freedom?

2. As a result of the fall, we see the consequences of sin. Instead of communion and companionship, we see that estrangement or alienation now exists in the world, and this estrangement manifests itself in three ways:

    1. in the relationship between God and humans

    2. in the relationship between man and woman

    3. in the relationship between humans and the created order

In what ways does Genesis 3 show the disruption of relationships on these three levels after the fall?

3. Some interpreters have described what happened in Genesis 3 as an "upward fall." By this they mean that the fall from innocence was not such a disastrous thing after all. They say instead that the fall was fortunate (in Latin, *felix culpa*).

Thinking in terms of an "upward fall," what possibilities exist now for Adam and Eve that did not exist in the garden?

What kinds of choices will they now face?

How might their experience of life be broadened by the fall?

4. A story that explains the origins of a phenomenon (a practice, a custom, a place, or anything else) is called an etiology. An etiology answers the question, "How did this thing come to be?" Genesis 3 contains many etiological elements.

What etiologies do you find in Genesis 3?

What questions are addressed in this account?

Some etiologies in this chapter explain practical, mundane matters, while others address very weighty human concerns. List as many as you can.

GENESIS 4: CAIN AND ABEL

Study Guide

1. Who were Cain and Abel?

2. What picture of sin do you get from Genesis 4:7?

3. Why did Cain kill Abel?

Would you describe this killing as an impulsive manslaughter, or as a premeditated ("first degree") murder? Why?

4. Why did Cain ask God, "Am I my brother's keeper?"

5. What was Cain's punishment? Why did Cain say that his punishment was greater than he could bear?

6. In reading about the fall we noted that estrangement or alienation now exists in the world. How is estrangement manifested in this story?
A. Describe the rupture in the relationships between humans in 4:8, 14b.

B. Describe the rupture in the relationship between humans and the created order in 4:10–12.

C. Describe the rupture in the relationship between a human and God in 4:9, 14a, 16.

7. How did the Lord show mercy on Cain before sending him away?

It is tempting to ask questions of the text that are purely factual in nature. Why did the Lord prefer Abel's sacrifice? What was the purpose of sacrifices at this time? If Adam, Eve, and Cain were the only people in the world, why was Cain concerned that someone might kill him? Where did Cain's wife (in 4:17) come from? Indeed, the story of Cain and Abel is problematic if we simply wish to know "who did what to whom and when."

Remember that you are looking for theological understanding rather than historical data as you read the primeval stories. The stories are like the pieces of cloth in a patchwork quilt, pieces that have been passed down through generations before they were finally woven into the form we have today. Each story or "patch" in the quilt of Genesis 1—11 is part of a larger picture, and that picture is a theological one. The point that the primeval history makes is this: that sin has come into the world, and its effects grow more disturbing with each generation. The estrangement or alienation that we first saw in the garden is intensified in the story of Cain and Abel. Indeed, the estrangement we see here is ultimate: the taking of life. The horror of fratricide is the focus of the story.

GENESIS 6–9: THE FLOOD

Study Guide

Accounts of a great flood, or deluge, were common in the ancient Near East. After reading the Genesis story, you will read another account about a flood from the Babylonian *Epic of Gilgamesh*. The Sumerians also told a story about a deluge sent by their gods. But even within the Genesis account itself, we see two traditions woven together that agree in essentials but differ in details. For instance, the number of animals taken aboard the ark is given in Genesis 6:19–21, while a different number is given in 7:1–3. The number of days for the flood given in 7:4 and again in 7:12 differs from its duration in 7:24. We have already noted that the name used for the Creator is *Elohim* in Genesis 1 (translated "God") and *Yahweh* in Genesis 2 (translated "Lord"). In the Noah story, these two names are attached to different blocks of material. While we find some discrepancies between the sources and some confusion as they are put together, the theme of the story as it now stands is nevertheless clear: the righteous God of all the earth acts both to judge and to redeem the earth.

1. The Causes of the Flood (Gen. 6:5–18)

In what ways is the spread of sin throughout the earth described in 6:5 and in 6:11, 12?

_____

_____

Why does the Lord decide to destroy the earth?

_____

Why does the Lord decide to save Noah?

_____

2. The Deluge as a Return to Primeval Chaos

How is the flood described in 7:11 and 7:18–23?

_____

How does the chaos of the deluge compare with the creation account of Genesis 1:6–10?

_____

How is the end of the flood described in 8:1–3?

_____

How does the work of the wind (*ruah*) in 8:1 compare with the Spirit (*ruah*) in Genesis 1:2?

_____

_____

3. After the Flood

Read Genesis 8:6–12. How did Noah know that the deluge was over?

_____

_____

Read 8:20–22. What was Noah's first act after he disembarked? What was the Lord's response to this act?

_____

How does the Lord's vow in 8:21 compare with the Lord's reason for sending the flood in 6:5? How does the vow compare with the curse in Gen. 3:17?

_____

_____

_____

4. The Noachian Covenant

Give a dictionary definition of "covenant":

_____

Read 9:1–7. How does God renew the blessing first given in Gen. 1:28?

_____

Read 9:8–11. What does God promise Noah, his descendants, and the whole earth?

_____

Read 9:12–17. What is the sign of God's covenant with Noah and all humanity?

_____

Is this covenant conditional (that is, does it depend on the humans' response), or is it unconditional (a promise made by God with no strings attached)?

_____

5. The New Age Begins; the Problem of Sin Persists

How does the author show that Noah is the father of all peoples in 9:18–19?

_____

_____

What are Noah's first actions in this new age? (See 9:20–21.)

_____

_____

Discussion Question

"The imagination of [a person's] heart is evil from . . . youth." Such was the state of the human race before the flood (6:5) and *after* God executed judgment on the whole earth (8:21). But with the Noachian covenant, God has promised never again to judge the earth with destruction. The flood has *not* removed the evil thoughts of the heart. If you were God, how would you solve this problem? By what means might God redeem humanity in the future?

THE EPIC OF GILGAMESH

The *Epic of Gilgamesh* is the most important myth of the ancient Near East. It was written on clay tablets in the Akkadian language as early as 1750 B.C. (the time of Hammurabi in Babylon and the Patriarchs in Canaan). Copies of the epic have been found throughout the Fertile Crescent, from ancient Sumer (modern Iraq) to the Hittite capital in modern Turkey. Portions of the epic are included here because they refer to a flood ("deluge"). Because of its close proximity in time and place to the Hebrew culture, we will look at what the Gilgamesh Epic has to say about the flood—its causes and results—and compare the Genesis account with its pagan counterpart.

This translation and notes are from James B. Pritchard, *Ancient Near Eastern Texts: Relating to the Old Testament*. Square brackets indicate restorations; explanatory notes and paraphrased sections are in parentheses.

Tablet II in the epic opens with Gilgamesh's visit to Utnapishtim. Gilgamesh, the hero, is on a search for immortality. Utnapishtim is himself immortal, but Gilgamesh notices that he looks like a mere mortal man. This prompts a question: How did Utnapishtim become one of the gods? What follows is Utnapishtim's account of the deluge. Excerpts from this account are given here.

Tablet II

(1) Gilgamesh said to him, to Utnapishtim the Faraway:
"As I look upon thee, Utnapishtim,
Thy features are not strange; even as I art thou.
Thou are not strange at all; even as I art thou.
. . . .
[Tell me,] how joinedst thou the Assembly of
the gods,
In thy quest of life?"
Utnapishtim said to him, to Gilgamesh:
"I will reveal to thee, Gilgamesh, a hidden matter

(10) And a secret of the gods will I tell thee:
Shurippak—a city which thou knowest,
(And) which on Euphrates' [banks] is situate—
That city was ancient, (as were) the gods within it,
When their heart led the great gods to produce the flood.
[There] were Anu, their father,
(sky god and father of Ea)
Valiant Enlil, their counselor,
(chief god of the Sumerians)
Ninurta, their assistant,
Ennuge, their irrigator.
Ninigiku-Ea was also present with them;
(Ea is god of earth and water)

(20) Their words he repeats to the reed-hut:
'Reed-hut, reed-hut! Wall, wall!
(Ea addresses Utnapishtim through the barrier of a wall)
. . . .

Man of Shuruppak, son of Ubar-Tutu,
Tear down (this) house, build a ship!
Give up possessions, seek thou life.
Forswear (worldly) goods and keep the soul alive!
Aboard the ship take thou the seed of all living things.'
. . . .

(32) I understood, and I said to Ea, my lord:
'[Behold], my lord, what thou hast thus ordered,
I will be honored to carry out.
[But what] shall I answer the city, the people and elders?'
Ea opened his mouth to speak,
Saying to me, his servant:
"Thou shalt then thus speak to them:
"I have learned that Enlil is hostile to me,

(40) So that I cannot reside in your city,
Nor set my f[oo]t in Enlil's territory.
To the Deep I will therefore go down,
To dwell with my lord Ea.
[But upon] you he will shower down abundance . . .""
(In this last line, wily Ea plays on an ambiguity: to the populace, the statement would be a promise of prosperity; to Utnapishtim, it signals the impending flood.)
(What follows is a description of the ship Utnapishtim built. He completed the ship, with the help of many workers, in seven days.)

(80) [Whatever I had] I laded upon her;
Whatever I had of silver I laded upon her;

Whatever I [had] of gold I laded upon her;
Whatever I had of all the living beings I [laded]
   upon her.
All my family and kin I made go aboard the
   ship.
The beasts of the field, the wild creatures of the
   field,
   All the craftsmen I made go aboard.
Shamash had set for me a stated time:
                      (the sun god)
'When he who orders unease at night,
   Will shower down a rain of blight,
Board thou the ship and batten up the entrance!'
That stated time had arrived.
   ....

(91)   I watched the appearance of the weather.
The weather was awesome to behold.
I boarded the ship and battened up the entrance.
   ....

With the first glow of dawn,
A black cloud rose up from the horizon.
Inside it Adad thunders.
          (god of thunder and lightning)
(103) The Anunnaki lift up the torches,
                  (the lesser gods)
Setting the land ablaze with their glare.
Consternation over Adad reaches to the heavens,
Who turned to blackness all that had been light.
[The wide] land was shattered like [a pot]!
For one day the south-storm blew,
Gathering speed as it blew, [submerging the
   mountains],
(110) Overtaking the [people] like a battle.
No one can see his fellow,
Nor can the people be recognized from heaven.
The gods were frightened by the deluge,
And, shrinking back, they ascended to the
   heaven of Anu.
             (the highest of several
       heavens in the Mesopotamian cosmos)
The gods cowered like dogs,
   Crouched against the outer wall.
Ishtar cried out like a woman in travail,
         (goddess of love and war)
The sweet-voiced mistress of the [gods] moans
   aloud:
'The olden days are alas turned to clay,
Because I bespoke evil in the Assembly of the
   gods.
(120) How could I bespeak evil in the Assembly of the
   gods,
Ordering battle for the destruction of my
   people,
When it is I myself who give birth to my people!
Like the spawn of the fishes they fill the sea!'

   ....
(The deluge lasts six days and six nights; on the sev-
   enth day the storm subsides.)
(131) The sea grew quiet, the tempest was still, the
   flood ceased.
I looked at the weather: stillness had set in,
And all of mankind had returned to clay.
The landscape was as level as a flat roof.
I opened a hatch, and light fell upon my face.
Bowing low, I sat and wept,
Tears running down my face.
   ....
(Utnapishtim's ship comes to a halt on Mount Nisir
   and rests there for six days.)
(145) When the seventh day arrived,
I sent forth and set free a dove.
The dove went forth, but came back;
Since no resting-place for it was visible, she
   turned round.
Then I sent forth and set free a swallow.
(150) The swallow went forth, but came back;
Since no resting-place for it was visible, she
   turned round.
Then I sent forth and set free a raven.
The raven went forth and, seeing that the waters
   had diminished,
He eats, circles, caws, and turns not round.
Then I let out (all) to the four winds
   And offered a sacrifice.
I poured out a libation on the top of the moun-
   tain.
Seven and seven cult-vessels I set up,
Upon their pot-stands I heaped cane, cedar-
   wood, and myrtle.
The gods smelled the savor,
(160) The gods smelled the sweet savor,
The gods crowded like flies about the sacrificer.
When at length the great goddess arrived,
                      (Ishtar)
She lifted up the great jewels which Anu had
   fashioned to her liking:
'Ye gods here, as surely as this lapis
   Upon my neck I shall not forget,
        (Ishtar's lapis lazuli necklace is
        bright blue, like a clear sky)
I shall be mindful of these days, forgetting
   (them) never.
Let the gods come to the offering;
(But) let not Enlil come to the offering,
For he, unreasoning, brought on the deluge
And my people consigned to destruction.'
(170) When at length Enlil arrived,
And saw the ship, Enlil was wroth,
He was filled with wrath over the Igigi gods:
                  (the heavenly gods)

'Has some living soul escaped?
   No man was to survive the destruction!'
....
*(Ea admits that he intervened to save Utnapishtim.
Then Ea chastises Enlil for his rash act in bring-
ing about the destruction. Apparently Enlil real-
izes the folly of his ways.)*
Thereupon Enlil went aboard the ship.
(190)   Holding me by the hand, he took me aboard.
   He took my wife aboard and made (her) kneel
      by my side.

Standing between us, he touched our foreheads
   to bless us:
'Hitherto Utnapishtim has been but human.
Henceforth Utnapishtim and his wife shall be
   like unto us gods.
Utnapishtim shall reside far away, at the mouth
   of the rivers!'
Thus they took me and made me reside far away,
   At the mouth of the rivers."
(And so Enlil made Utnapishtim immortal.)

TWO FLOOD EPICS: COMPARISON AND CONTRAST

Study Guide

After completing the study guide on Genesis 6—9 and reading the excerpt from the *Epic of Gilgamesh,* answer the following questions:

1. List all the similarities you can find between the Noah story and the *Epic of Gilgamesh.*

_____

_____

_____

_____

_____

_____

_____

2. How do you account for the similarities?

_____

_____

3. If you are not sure why the gods caused the flood in the *Epic,* this is because no particular reason is given in the text at all. The deluge was simply a result of a capricious decision to wipe out the human race. Ea's reason for intervening and saving Utnapishtim is likewise a mystery. With this point in mind, list all the differences you can find between the Noah story and the *Epic.*

_____

_____

_____

_____

_____

_____

4. Utnapishtim tells his story in the first person. What insights do you, the reader, gain from a first-person narration? If the Genesis story were told from Noah's point of view (rather than an omniscient, third-person point of view), what facts and feelings do you think Noah might have included?

_____

_____

_____

_____

5. How do you account for the differences between the two flood stories?

_____

_____

_____

_____

GENESIS II:I—9: THE TOWER OF BABEL

Study Guide

Immediately preceding the story of the Tower of Babel in Genesis 11 is the table of nations (chap. 10). The table accounts for the genealogies of Noah's three sons: Japheth, Ham, and Shem. The sons of Japheth had their geographical center in Asia Minor. They spread from there to the "coastlands," probably Greece and Europe. The sons of Ham are connected with Egypt and northern Africa, as well as with Canaan. The sons of Shem are the Semitic peoples, including the Hebrews, who first dwelt in Mesopotamia and later invaded Canaan. The Semitic peoples eventually established states such as Syria, Moab, Edom, and Israel.

The table of nations attempts to account for the varieties of lands, languages, and nations in the ancient Near East (see 10:5, 20, 31). The table concludes, "These are the families of the sons of Noah, according to their genealogies, in their nations; and from these the nations spread abroad on the earth after the flood" (10:32). Both the table of nations in Genesis 10 and the tower of Babel story in 11:1—9 deal with the geographical diversity of humankind. They do so in different ways; again, the editors put together two sources which explain the same phenomenon. We will examine the tower of Babel story closely, not as an explanation for geographical diversity, but because of what it says about the desires of humans and the judgment of the Lord.

Ziggurats were religious temples found in ancient Shinar, or Babylonia. They looked like terraced towers. The ziggurat was an artificial mountain with a stairway up to the heavens. This peculiar architecture reflected the Babylonian belief that the worshipers could ascend the stairway and meet the gods at the top—the gateway to heaven.

The tower of Babel story has an etiological element (remember, an etiology is a story that attempts to explain the existence of something), but the etiological element is overshadowed by the theological impact of the story. What was once an explanation for a ruined city with an uncompleted ziggurat on the Mesopotamian plains now stands as the conclusion to the primeval history, and the final note on the spread of sin throughout the earth.

1. As the story opens, how is the "whole earth" described?

_____

_____

2. What motivates the people to build a tower? If urged by the ambition to achieve unity, as some interpreters suggest, what might the results of this unity be?

_____

_____

_____

_____

3. How is the Lord characterized in this story? What is the Lord's judgment, and *why* does the Lord propose to carry out this judgment?

_____

_____

_____

_____

4. *Babel* is similar to the Hebrew word for confusion, *balal* (compare the English *babble*). How does the story end?

_____

_____

_____

_____

PRIMEVAL HISTORY

Questions for Discussion

1. As the conclusion to the primeval history, the tower of Babel story shows the spread of peoples, their languages, and the problem of sin. What common themes tie this story to the stories of (1) Adam and Eve, (2) Cain and Abel, and (3) Noah?

2. The tower of Babel story is concerned with the ambition of the people and the results of their deeds. From Adam and Eve to the tower, we are confronted with the tragic reality of sin. But the primeval history does not explain *how* sin came to be as much as it shows the *effects* of sin. What particular verses in Genesis 1—11 describe these effects?

3. Two motifs are presented in Genesis 1—11:
   A. the righteousness of God, and God's intention that the created order be "good"
   B. the arrogance of humans, and the reality of sin and judgment

The second motif does not stand alone. If it did, we would have a very pessimistic picture. How does God's intention that creation be good persist in spite of human wrongdoing? What evidence do you find in the text for this first motif?

CHAPTER 3

Patriarchal History

INTRODUCTION TO PATRIARCHAL HISTORY: GENESIS 12—50

The purpose of this introduction is twofold: to acquaint the reader with the historical background of chapters 12—50 in Genesis and to point out some characteristics of this literary unit.

As we begin our reading of the stories of the patriarchs, or "fathers of the Hebrew faith," we notice a new historical setting and a new theological purpose. Beginning with chapter 12 in Genesis, we move from the sweeping panorama of primeval history to a pinpoint: an individual named Abram. We were concerned with the "whole earth" in Genesis 1—11. God flooded the whole earth (Gen. 6:17) and later scattered peoples all over the face of the earth in confusion (Gen. 11:8). Now the focus is on Abram in Ur. Why?

Picture the spread of sin, beginning in the Garden of Eden, moving out from it with Cain, being washed away with the flood only to return, moving out from the tower of Babel to the four corners of the earth. Estrangement from God, from nature, and between persons is the story of the primeval history.

"I will solve the problem of sin," God seems to say, "not by destroying it, but by working through an individual, and eventually, through his offspring, to all the families of the earth." Who was this Abram? Where did he come from? How was his God different from the other gods in his world?

Around 4000 B.C., a swarthy, dark-haired, Semitic people who called themselves Sumerians began settling in Mesopotamia near the mouth of the Tigris and Euphrates rivers (modern Iraq). These amazing people were the prime movers in the development of ancient Near Eastern civilization. By 3300 B.C. they had developed a system of writing on clay tablets using letters based on sounds rather than pictures or hieroglyphs. They enjoyed running water, irrigated fields, tiled baths, and walled cities. They built fantastic ziggurats, or temples, which looked like stacks of building blocks. Each level or block was smaller than the one below, with the effect being a huge set of steppingstones to the heavens. The Sumerian culture existed as a collection of city-states rather than as a unified nation. Each little republic was often hostile toward its neighbors. The land was eventually divided into two great empires: Babylonia and Persia. By 1700 B.C. Hammurabi, the brilliant Babylonian king, had gained ascendancy over Mesopotamia, and Babylon was capital of all the land.

Each Sumerian city-state was considered the personal estate of one of the major gods in the Sumerian pantheon. Each god would help the city-state to the extent that those people pleased him through sacrifice and ritual. Each major god was the personification of one of the forces of nature (sun, moon, storms), and by serving its god, each city-state believed it enabled a particular natural phenomenon to continue to function. These ancient peoples looked to their pantheon of deities to give order and stability to a universe that was often capricious and baffling.

Abram (later renamed Abraham, or "father of a multitude") originally came from Ur, the Sumerian city of the moon god Sin. He was an Amorite; that is, his clan was part of a large migratory movement into the Fertile Crescent that occurred sometime before 2000 B.C. His call by God cannot be dated with certainty, but it probably occurred sometime in the eighteenth century B.C. You will trace his journey out of the comparative ease and comforts of life in Ur to a place called Canaan (modern Israel and Jordan).

The Canaanites had been in this region for a thousand years before Abraham came. They settled in large, fortified city-states in the fertile valleys of the Jordan River. Abraham and his clan avoided these cities and maintained a nomadic existence, living the pastoral life of the herdsman (Abraham did not buy a plot of land until his wife Sarah died). These Amorites were called 'abiru or "Hebrews" by the native Canaanites. The word means "wanderer" or "outsider," and indeed the Hebrews lived on the margins of Canaanite agrarian culture. Hebrew social structure remained based on the family, clan, and tribe rather than upon identification with a particular city.

Patriarchal history is concerned with Abraham and his descendants. Abraham's son Isaac, his grandson Jacob, and Jacob's twelve sons are the heirs to God's promises and the beginning of the genealogy for those people who were specifically chosen by God.

As you read the patriarchal history, be alert for certain characteristics of this literature. Look for humor: Abraham's intercession on behalf of Lot's family in Sodom is Near Eastern marketplace bargaining at its best. Notice how Abraham haggles with God over the number of righteous people needed to spare the entire city. Years later, the birth of Isaac is shrouded in the mystery that is comedy. The fact that Abraham and Sarah conceived a son when they were well past their childbearing years is a wry twist of the miraculous; God points this out by naming the son Isaac, or "laughter."

The view of persons found in this literature is highly realistic. We see strength and weakness, evil and nobility, saint and sinner intertwined in these very human actors in God's drama. Abraham is more interested in protecting himself than keeping his wife (twice this happens, once with the pharaoh in Egypt and once with a king named Abimelech). His grandson Jacob becomes a man of integrity, but he was first chosen by God when he was a thief. Jacob's son Joseph cannot resist making his brothers miserable in order to prove his point—that God has turned their evil actions into good. Patriarchal literature is not concerned with heroes, but with very real persons who were chosen despite who they were.

This brings us to the understanding of the deity, or the view of God, found in these chapters. The German term for this type of history is *Heilsgeschichte:* the story of salvation. We see God choosing a people and leading them throughout the ancient Near East. They are constantly on the move—led through time and space in a dynamic relationship known as the covenant. God is not "out there," but close at hand. God makes himself known to his people in the most personal way. Appearances of God (theophanies) take the forms of fire or dreams. Dreams were channels of divine communication when properly interpreted; two dreams with the same meaning indicated that the event was "fixed" or doubly sure to happen. Often God appeared simply as a man.

Abraham's religion differed from that of his Mesopotamian and Canaanite neighbors. He did not worship a host of gods; instead he is constantly portrayed as one guided and protected by one God—a personal God who entered into a covenant relationship with him and his descendants. While his neighbors were trying to placate their diverse and capricious deities through numerous rituals, the faith of Abraham allowed its followers to face life's uncertainties with a sense of purpose, of destiny. Life was moving, not in a vicious cycle, but toward a definite end that God had promised. This sense of history is new: it is linear, rather than cyclical. With it we find a notion of development, or of progressive revelation in Scripture. We shall see how the tribal god of Abraham comes to be understood later as the God of the nation Israel, and finally as Lord God of the universe.

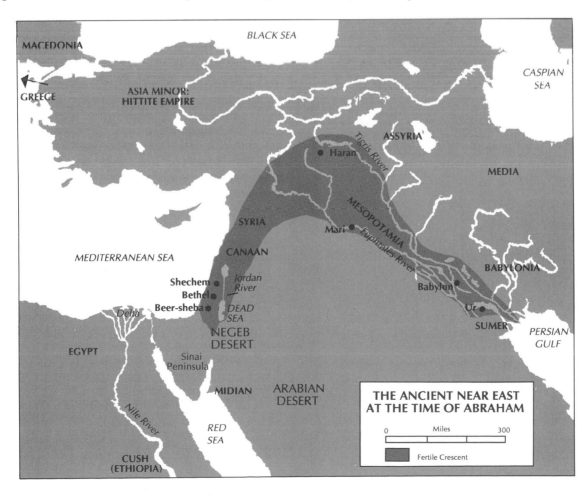

THE ANCIENT NEAR EAST AT THE TIME OF ABRAHAM

PATRIARCHAL HISTORY: GENESIS 11:27—22:19

Study Guide

1. Read Genesis 11:27-29; then fill in the family tree:

```
 _____ _____ _____ (father)
         ↙              ↓              ↘

(spouse) _____  _____  _____  _____  _____ (spouse)
                                     ↓

                              _____
```

2. God makes a covenant with Abram, which consists of a threefold promise. See 12:1–3 and 13:14–17. What did the Lord promise Abram concerning the following?

A. Abram's descendants

_____

_____

B. land

_____

_____

C. the other nations of the earth

_____

_____

3. Fill in the geographic sites as you trace Abram's migration:

(11:31) from _____

    to _____;

(12:5) from _____

    to _____;

(12:10) from _____

    to _____;

(13:1) from _____

    to _____;

(13:11–12) from _____

    to _____.

4. What happened to Abram and Sarai while they were in Egypt? (See 12:10–20.)

_____

_____

_____

How was God's promise to Abram almost jeopardized there?

_____

_____

5. Why did Abram and Lot separate? (See 13:2–11.)

_____

_____

_____

6. See 13:16; 15:1–6; and note item A. in question 2 above. What problem does Abram mention concerning God's promise to him?

_____

_____

7. Read and note the key features of the covenant ceremony described in 15:7–20.

_____

_____

_____

8. Read Gen. 16:1–6. Who is Hagar?

_____

What is wrong with her attitude, according to Sarai?

_____

_____

_____

9. Read 16:7–12. Who is Ishmael?

_____

What does God promise him?

_____

_____

Ishmael is also the "patriarch" or forefather of the Arab peoples. How then are the Arabs characterized in the Old Testament?

_____

_____

10. Read 17:1–8. Again, note the features of the covenant. How long will it last?

_____

Is the covenant conditional or unconditional?

_____

11. What is the *sign* of the covenant? (See 17:9–14.)

_____

12. Read 17:15–21. What caused Abraham to fall down laughing?

_____

13. Read 18:1–15. Isaac means "he laughs." Why did the three men feel this was an appropriate name for Sarah's son?

_____

14. Read 18:16–20. What reason does the Lord give for revealing his plan to Abraham?

_____

15. Look up "intercession" in a dictionary and give a short definition.

_____

16. Describe Abraham's intercession on behalf of Lot and his family in 18:22–33.

_____

_____

17. Read 19:1–11. What was the sin of the men of Sodom?

_____

Who are Lot's guests, and how do they show their power?

_____

_____

18. Read 19:12–16. Do Lot and his family realize the danger?

_____

How do you know?

_____

_____

19. Read 19:17–29. What happened to Lot's wife, and why?

_____

_____

20. Read all of chapter 20. How does this story compare with the episode of Genesis 12:10–20?

_____

How would you characterize King Abimelech and his attitude toward Abraham?

_____

_____

Who do you think acted rightly in this account?

_____

21. How did the Lord fulfill part of the threefold promise in 21:1–3?

_____

22. Read 22:1–10 closely. What is God's test of Abraham?

_____

How does Abraham respond to God's command?

_____

What do you imagine is going on in Abraham's mind during this episode? Write out a few thoughts and feelings.

_____

_____

_____

What do you think is going on in Isaac's mind?

_____

23. Read 22:12–18. What is the significance of Abraham's obedience?

_____

_____

PATRIARCHAL LITERATURE

Customs and Practices

We find many customs faithfully transmitted in the biblical record of the patriarchs which have long since lost their original meaning or been abandoned as practices within Judaism.

• Circumcision was at one time a practice unique to the Hebrews. While Abraham was not circumcised, God told him to circumcise his son Isaac as a sign of the covenant. This practice became a distinctive way to identify God's chosen people.

• Readers will find it strange that polygamy was accepted in patriarchal times. While Abraham was monogamous and it appears that his son Isaac was as well, Jacob had two wives (the sisters Leah and Rachel). Eventually, we will see that Hebrew men took on as many wives as they were able to support.

• Surrogate mothers were used as well. If a wife could not bear children (and sterility was a sign of disgrace in patriarchal times), her maidservant would bear children for her. The child was delivered "on the knees" of the wife, thereby becoming her own. (This practice is also mentioned in Hammurabi's Code, a Babylonian set of laws dating from c. 1700 B.C.) If later the wife conceived and bore a son, the maidservant's offspring had to be compensated in some way. As with Ishmael, Abraham's first son by the surrogate mother Hagar, the maid's son lost the inheritance but gained some other reward.

• The "birthright" mentioned in patriarchal literature refers to the rights of the eldest son to a double share of the inheritance. When Jacob swindled Esau out of his birthright, he took claim to quite a fortune in return for lentil pottage (soup)!

• While the patriarchs were seminomadic, their settled neighbors held land and property, which was protected by *teraphim*, or household gods. These gods were fashioned of clay, fired as pottery, and placed in a niche in the wall of the home. The *teraphim* signified ownership of property, like a deed to an estate. Thus when Jacob's wife Rachel stole the household gods from her father Laban, she took no less than his claim to his property.

• Children grew up in a hurry in patriarchal times. We find that Joseph deviated from ancient Near Eastern custom by living at home at the ripe of old age of seventeen, when most young men had already married. Marriages were arranged for girls as young as twelve and for boys as young as thirteen.

• When Abraham was told to sacrifice his son Isaac, it must have called to mind the Canaanite practice of sacrificing the eldest son to appease the gods (called *baals*) of that culture. Such a thing was done only in the direst of circumstances in Canaan; nevertheless, it is fortunate for Abraham that his God scorned this local custom.

PATRIARCHAL HISTORY: GENESIS 24—36

Study Guide

1. Read 24:1–10. Where did Abraham send his servant to find a wife for Isaac?

_____

Why do you think Abraham sent his servant there?

_____

_____

2. Read 24:11–27. How did Abraham's servant know that Rebekah was the right choice?

_____

_____

3. See 24:28–33, 50–58; then identify Laban. What evidence of his greedy nature can you find?

_____

_____

4. Read 25:19–28. While Isaac was living in Beersheba, twins were born to him and Rebekah. How were the two boys different from each other?

_____

_____

_____

5. Read 25:29–34. How did Jacob "steal" the birthright from Esau?

_____

_____

6. Does 26:1–11 sound familiar? Why?

_____

7. Read 27:1–33. How did Jacob acquire the blessing from his father Isaac?

_____

_____

_____

_____

_____

8. What was Esau's reaction to this trickery in 27:34–41?

_____

_____

9. Read 27:42—28:5. Rebekah had a plan for her favorite son. What was this plan?

_____

_____

10. Read 28:10–22. On the way to Haran, Jacob had a dream. What was the content and meaning of the dream?

_____

_____

_____

Where did the dream take place?

_____

11. Describe Jacob's first meeting with Rachel in 29:1–12. Then compare this account with his father Isaac's first meeting with Rebekah in 24:62–67.

_____

_____

_____

_____

12. Read 29:13–20. What deal did Jacob make with Rachel's father Laban?

_____

_____

13. Read 29:21–30. How did Laban trick Jacob? What is ironic about this trickery?

_____

_____

_____

_____

14. Give the names of Jacob's first four sons (29:31–35):

_____   _____

_____   _____

Give the names of Jacob's fifth and sixth sons, and their mother (see 30:1–8):

_____   _____

mother: _____

Give the names of his seventh and eighth sons, and their mother (see 30:9–13):

_____   _____

mother: _____

Give the names of Jacob's next two sons in 30:14–20:

_____   _____.

Rachel's first son was named _____ (30:22–24).

Now read 35:23–26 and double-check your answers.

15. How did Jacob trick Laban? Read 30:25–43.

_____

_____

_____

16. Jacob and his wives finally made their escape from Laban. Read about this escape in chapter 31. Then describe Laban's behavior and Rachel's behavior.

_____

_____

_____

_____

17. How many years did Jacob work for Laban (31:41)?

_____

18. On his way back home to Canaan, Jacob decided to make reconciliation with his brother Esau. Read 32:3–21. What was his plan?

_____

_____

_____

19. A famous wrestling match is described in 32:22–30. Read it, and give the new name which Jacob received at the end of the match: _____.

Jacob means "the deceiver" or "the trickster." What is the meaning of his new name?

_____

_____

20. Describe the reunion of the twin brothers in 33:1–11.

_____

_____

_____

21. Jacob and his huge family settled in _____ (33:18).

A Note About Language in the Old Testament

The power of the word for the Hebrews was immense. Words were not to be taken lightly. A blessing or a curse, once spoken, could not be taken back. Like an arrow shot into the air, both blessings and curses continued on their courses until they reached the target and were fulfilled. Thus when Isaac mistakenly blessed Jacob, this blessing could not be retracted. Names, too, were bearers of power and meaning. They tell us something about character: Isaac means "laughter," Jacob means "swindler." Ancient names also tell us something about the character of their descendants. Ishmael, the father of the Arabs, is a "wild ass of a man," and Israel denotes those people who will always "struggle with God."

ABRAHAM*

If a *schlemiel* is a person who goes through life spilling soup on people and a *schlemozzle* is the one it keeps getting spilled on, then Abraham was a *schlemozzle*. It all began when God told him to go to the land of Canaan where he promised to make him the father of a great nation and he went.

The first thing that happened was that his [nephew] Lot took over the rich bottom-land and Abraham was left with the scrub country around Dead Man's Gulch. The second thing was that the prospective father of a great nation found out his wife couldn't have babies. The third thing was that when, as a special present on his hundredth birthday, God arranged for his wife Sarah to have a son anyway, it wasn't long before he told Abraham to go up into the hills and sacrifice him. It's true that at the last minute God stepped in and said he'd only wanted to see if the old man's money was where his mouth was, but from that day forward Abraham had a habit of breaking into tears at odd moments, and his relationship with his son Isaac was never close.

In spite of everything, however, he never stopped having faith that God was going to keep his promise about making him the father of a great nation. Night after night, it was the dream he rode to sleep on—the glittering cities, the up-to-date armies, the curly-bearded kings. There was a group photograph he had taken not long before he died. It was a bar mitzvah, and they were all there down to the last poor relation. They weren't a great nation yet by a long shot, but you'd never know it from the way Abraham sits enthroned there in his velvet yarmulke with several great-grandchildren on his lap and soup on his tie.

Even through his thick lenses, you can read the look of faith in his eye, and more than all the kosher meals, the Ethical Culture Societies, the shaved heads of the women, the achievement of Maimonides, Einstein, Kissinger, it was that look that God loved him for and had chosen him for in the first place.

"They will all be winners, God willing. Even the losers will be winners. They'll all get their names up in lights," say the old schlemozzle's eyes.

"Someday—who knows when?—I'll be talking about my son, the Light of the world."

(Gen. 12—18; 22)

* Excerpted from Frederick Buechner, *Peculiar Treasures: A Biblical Who's Who*, Harper & Row, 1979.

THE JOSEPH "SHORT STORY": GENESIS 37–50

Study Guide

1. Read chapter 37. How did his brothers feel toward Joseph?

_____

_____

Why did they feel this way?

_____

_____

What scheme did they devise?

_____

_____

_____

2. Skip to chapter 39. Who was Potiphar?

_____

How would you characterize his wife, and why?

_____

_____

_____

3. Read chapter 40. What happened to Joseph while he was in prison?

_____

_____

_____

4. Read chapter 41. How did Joseph get out of prison?

_____

_____

How did he become second in command to the pharaoh of Egypt?

_____

_____

_____

5. Read chapter 42. What happened the first time Joseph's brothers came to Egypt?

_____

_____

_____

Why didn't they recognize him?

_____

_____

6. Read chapter 43. What happened the second time the brothers came to Egypt?

_____

_____

_____

7. Read chapter 44. What happened to the youngest brother, Benjamin?

_____

_____

_____

8. See 44:18–34. Describe the tone and substance of Judah's speech.

_____

_____

_____

What plan does Judah propose?

_____

_____

9. Read chapter 45. According to Joseph, what was God's plan for Joseph and his family?

_____

_____

10. Skip to chapter 50 and read. Jacob has died and his sons have settled in Egypt. What do his sons do after their father's death?

_____

_____

_____   In what sense are his words the climax of the story?

_____   _____

11. What is Joseph's reaction in 50:19–21?   _____

_____   _____

_____   _____

_____

WRITING CREATIVELY ABOUT THE STORY OF JOSEPH

Essay Topic

Use your Bible (Gen. 37, 39—50) and notes to write an essay on Joseph. The title of your essay will be "Joseph: A Contemporary Account." Take a section of the Joseph short story and rewrite it in a modern setting of your choice. You will need to decide:

(1) Exactly where and when the story takes place.

(2) Who is telling the story:

A. The narration is told in the first person (e.g., you are Joseph, or Josephine, or one of the brothers, or the pharaoh, etc.).
   OR
B. The narration is told in the third person (and you are an omniscient viewer).

(3) What particular section of the narrative you will use. Do NOT rewrite the entire Joseph story. Instead, choose an episode of the story and focus on it. Some possible subsections of the narrative are:

• Joseph's boyhood in Canaan
• Joseph as a slave and prisoner in Egypt
• Joseph's interpretation of dreams and elevation to power
• Joseph's meeting(s) with his brothers
• Joseph's reunion with his family in Egypt

(4) What kind of person you think Joseph is in this section. How will you characterize him (or her)? What might his thoughts and feelings be? Do this same thing for the other characters you choose to include. Feel free to use plenty of dialogue. Remember: this is a creative endeavor. Use your imagination, but do not invent a totally different character for Joseph than that which you find in the Old Testament.

CHAPTER 4

Exodus

HISTORICAL BACKGROUND OF EXODUS: BONDAGE IN EGYPT

As you turn the page in your Bible from the last chapter of Genesis to the first chapter of Exodus, you turn the clock forward some four hundred years. Times have changed dramatically. The Hebrews have grown from "seventy people of the house of Jacob" (Gen. 46:26–27) to a nation undergoing a population explosion. The hospitable treatment the Hebrews enjoyed under the Egyptian pharaoh at the time of Joseph has been superseded by enslavement and plans to exterminate Hebrew children. Joseph had sent for his brothers and Jacob during a famine and set them up in the land of Goshen. This prime real estate has now become a Hebrew ghetto. What happened in the interval to account for such a drastic change in Egypt?

Joseph's remarkable rise to power was due to the tolerant regime of the Hyksos rulers (the fifteenth to seventeenth dynasties, or the Middle Kingdom, in Egypt). The Hyksos were themselves Semitic peoples who had migrated from the region east of the Black Sea. Through the use of horse-drawn chariots, the Hyksos (whose name means "foreign chiefs") overthrew the native Egyptian rulers around 1700 B.C. They ruled for over a century. Under the Hyksos Dynasty, Egypt served as a haven from famine for less fortunate neighbors to the east. Since Egypt had the Nile River, she could prosper independently of the rains which were vital to Canaan. The Hyksos maintained an open-door policy toward foreigners. Toleration of alien peoples and immigration were encouraged. Foreigners found employment in Egypt at various levels, from slaves to high stewards. During this "Period of Favor," conditions were right for Joseph's rise to a position of leadership in the royal court.

"Now there arose a new king over Egypt, who did not know Joseph" (Exod. 1:8). This "Period of Oppression" actually began when the native Egyptians overthrew their foreign, Hyksos rulers around 1500 B.C. With the return to Egyptian control under Ahmose I (the eighteenth dynasty), Semitic peoples were either expelled from the country or enslaved. Slave labor over the next few centuries was used for an ambitious building program. Ramses II, one of the greatest of the pharaohs, and his father, Seti I, were responsible for two building projects: the cities of Pithom and Ramses. The latter had been the capital from which the Hyksos ruled Egypt and is specifically mentioned in Exodus 1:11. We know that these pharaohs used 'abiru—a word meaning "wanderers" or "outsiders"—in their building projects. This term probably included the particular Hebrews with whom we are concerned. Another of Ramses' projects was the temple at Abu Simbel, which was recently moved, brick by brick and at a fabulous cost, to higher ground because of the rising lake formed by Aswan Dam.

Read Exodus 1 closely. Describe what life was like for the Hebrews at this time.

_____

_____

_____

Seti I (ruled 1309–1290 B.C.) was probably the pharaoh of Exodus 1. He had a problem on his hands concerning a large alien group in Goshen. What was the problem and how did he attempt to solve it?

_____

_____

_____

EXODUS 2–14

Study Guide

1. What do you learn about Moses' birth, character, and personality in chapter 2?

_____

_____

_____

2. The Egyptian name *Moses* is similar to the Hebrew word *mashah,* which means "to draw out." What symbolic references might Moses' name carry?

_____

3. Using a dictionary, write brief definitions for the following:

A. theophany

_____

_____

B. miracle

_____

_____

4. What do you think are the differences between "miracles" and "magic"?

_____

5. Read chapters 3 and 4. List four objections Moses made when the Lord told him to go to Egypt and rescue the Hebrews. Next to each objection, write the Lord's response.

_____

_____

_____

6. Read chapter 5. How did the pharaoh react when Moses confronted him?

_____

_____

How did the Hebrews react?

_____

_____

7. Write out and memorize Exodus 6:7.

_____

_____

_____

8. Read chapters 7–10. List the first nine plagues, giving the chapter and verse numbers for each. In what sense are the plagues miraculous?

_____

_____

_____

_____

_____

_____

_____

_____

_____

9. Read chapter 11. What is the tenth and final plague?

_____

10. Read chapter 12. How is the Passover night celebrated?

_____

_____

_____

11. See Exodus 12:12–13, 23. What was the purpose of the blood of the lamb?

_____

What do you think the blood symbolizes in this account?

_____

12. The word *know* appears a number of times in Exodus 7–12. Go through these chapters and underline every place the word occurs. What is it the Lord wants both the Egyptians and the Hebrews to "know"? Use chapter and verse citations for each point you make.

_____

_____

_____

_____

13. Read chapter 13. Why didn't the Hebrews take the direct coastal route out of Egypt?

_____

_____

14. The Hebrew *Yam suph* means "sea of reeds," or marshy lake. The Septuagint, which is the Greek translation of the Hebrew Bible, mistranslates *Yam suph* as "Red Sea." Read chapter 14. What does the Lord do when the Egyptians catch up with the Hebrews at the Sea of Reeds? Why did the Lord do it?

_____

_____

_____

_____

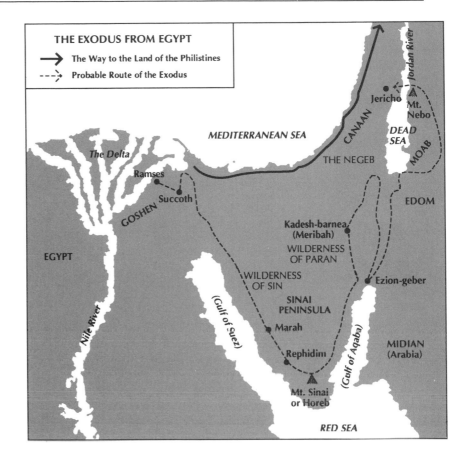

THE EXODUS FROM EGYPT
→ The Way to the Land of the Philistines
- - -> Probable Route of the Exodus

MODERN DAY PRACTICES OF PASSOVER

Passover celebrates a great theme of human existence: freedom. The Hebrew word for Passover is *Pesach,* the Feast of Freedom, which commemorates the Hebrews' deliverance from slavery in Egypt. In celebrating *Pesach,* Jewish families all over the world relive the "creation story" of God's chosen people.

Celebrated during Nisan, the first month of spring in the Jewish calendar (March-April), Passover is an eight-day holiday (seven days for Reform Jews). During this time leavened breads are forbidden; only unleavened bread may be eaten. The celebration on the first night of Passover is the highlight of the holiday. It is called the seder, a banquet full of elaborate ritual and symbols, which is carried out by family members at home. The seder illustrates and dramatizes the story of the Exodus from Egypt. The idea is not only to keep the memory of these events alive, but actually to *relive* the deliverance of Yahweh's people. The *Haggadah,* a guide for conducting the service, declares that "in each generation, the Jew must [feel] as though [she or] he personally had been delivered from the hands of the Egyptians." For those who ask why, the answer is that they would still be slaves in Egypt if their ancestors had not been set free.

In order to make the event contemporary, the youngest child at the seder table asks the father four questions:

1. Why is this night different from all other nights? *Because on this night we eat not leavened bread, but* matzah.

2. Why on other nights do we eat various herbs, but on this night only bitter herbs? *We do this to recall the bitter lives of our ancestors, who were slaves in Egypt.*

3. Why on other nights do we not dip our food even once, and twice on this night? *The ancient custom was to dip on other nights. The second time is to remind us that our ancestors dipped a leafy branch to smear lamb's blood on their doorposts.*

4. Why on other nights do we sit up to eat, but recline on this night? *Because free people reclined in ancient times, and our ancestors became free on this night.*

The *Haggadah* as a handbook for the ritual was already in use by 200 B.C. New material has been added over the centuries, and some sections have been dropped. In the first century B.C., the rabbis said that the door of the home should be opened and the father should call out into the street, "Let all who are hungry come and eat." During the Middle Ages, persecution of Jews in Europe made it unsafe to begin the evening celebration by throwing open the door, so practical considerations modified the ritual: the family could check first to see if all was clear. The act was kept as a symbol of faith: the door is opened briefly today.

After the Middle Ages, another custom was added. An empty cup is now placed on the table and filled with wine for Elijah. Elijah was the prophet who did not die, but was "translated" into the heavens, and it was said that he would come again before the Messianic Age. Elijah's cup is the symbol of both the humble wayfarer and the anticipation of the coming of the Messiah.

In the sixteenth century A.D., the ritual of spilling wine was added to the seder. It developed from a story ancient rabbis used to tell. When the Jews crossed over the sea into safety and the Egyptians were drowned, the angels wanted to sing. But God silenced them, saying, "What, human beings of my creation have drowned, and you want to sing?" Now, as the ten plagues are recited, each person at the table deliberately spills wine into a saucer or bowl (children spill grape juice). They say, "The Egyp-

tians are children of God, as are we all, and we do not rejoice over their defeat." Wine, a symbol of joy, is spilled to lessen their joy over the death of their enemies.

On the table in front of the seder leader is a Passover tray with six symbolic foods:

1. *matzah* (pl. *matzot*)—the unleavened bread the Hebrews ate on the night they left Egypt
2. *haroset*—a fruit sauce made of baked apples or dates with nuts, cinnamon, and wine; a symbol of the mortar used to build cities for the pharaoh
3. *marov*—bitter herbs; a symbol of the bitterness of the Hebrew slaves' lives in Egypt
4. *zeroah*—either a roasted shank bone or a chicken wing; it stands for the Passover lamb
5. *karpas*—a green vegetable (celery, parsley, or watercress); a symbol of spring harvest. It is dipped in salt water, symbolizing the tears of the Hebrews.
6. *beitzah*—a roasted egg; symbolizes new life

The Fourteen Steps listed in the *Haggadah* for performing the seder include recital of blessings, washing of hands, eating the symbolic foods and a banquet that follows, reciting psalms, and singing. The leader ends the seder by saying "Next year in Jerusalem!" In Israel, the leader says instead, "Next year in rebuilt Jerusalem!" Since the creation of the Jewish homeland in 1947, a new custom has been added in Israel. The rabbis have decreed that an extra chair be placed at the seder table: a symbolic seat for those who are not free to celebrate and for those who wish to come to Israel but are prevented by their governments from doing so.

EXODUS 15–19; 32–34

Study Guide

1. Describe in a sentence or two the important experience that occurred at each of the following places during the trip in the wilderness:

A. Marah (15:23–26)

_____

B. the Wilderness of Sin (chap. 16)

_____

C. Rephidim (17:1–16)

_____

_____

D. Mount Sinai (or Mount Horeb) (chap. 19)

_____

_____

Note that in the sequence of the narrative, the Hebrews arrive at Mount Sinai in Exodus 19:1. They do not break camp again until Numbers 10:11!

2. Read Exodus 24. This is the account of Moses' meeting with Yahweh on Mount Sinai. Who was Moses' companion?

_____

How long were they gone from the camp?

_____

Who was left in charge of the people back at the camp?

3. Read chapters 32—34. This account includes the "sin of the golden calf." What was the sin?

What was fundamentally wrong in the episode of the golden calf?

Who do you think was to blame for the sin?

How did Yahweh respond?

Did Aaron consider the golden calf a *substitute* for Yahweh or a *means* of worshiping Yahweh? Cite references to prove your point.

What did Moses do when he came down from the mountain?

COVENANT TREATIES

Study Guide

Look up the word *covenant* in a dictionary and write out its definition:

The Hittites, a Semitic people, controlled most of modern-day Turkey and expanded into Canaan at the expense of Egyptian power in the fourteenth century B.C. The Hittite manner of incorporating territories into their empire was unique. They did not simply subjugate peoples after a battle; instead they extended offers of peace and mutual benefits to these peoples. Their offer was simply, "Join with us and we will protect you." Investigation of Hittite treaties from the fourteenth century shows us that a clearly established form for civil covenants between the Hittite king, or suzerain, and a subject state, or vassal, existed in the ancient Near East. The covenant that lays out these terms is called a suzerainty covenant.

Old Testament covenants respect this form used by the Hittites, adapting it to the understanding that Yahweh is the suzerain and the Hebrews are vassals. Yahweh freely enters into the covenant relationship with his people and sets forth the terms of the covenant.

Using the form outlined here, compare the Abrahamic covenant with the Mosaic covenant. Read the citations in the Old Testament that relate to each of the treaty elements, and then fill in the chart.

ELEMENTS IN THE SUZERAINTY COVENANT	ABRAHAMIC COVENANT	MOSAIC COVENANT
1. Preamble: in which the author of the covenant is identified	Genesis 17:1	Exodus 3:13–15; 6:2–3
2. Historical prologue: describing the suzerain's past deeds on behalf of the vassal	—	Exodus 19:4

ELEMENTS IN THE SUZERAINTY COVENANT	ABRAHAMIC COVENANT	MOSAIC COVENANT
3. Obligations binding the vassal to the suzerain	Genesis 12:1; 15:6; 17:9	Exodus 19:5a, 7, 8
4. Lists of blessings and curses: what the suzerain will do to or for the vassal in the future	Genesis 12:2–3; 15:5, 12–21; 17:2–8	Exodus 6:7–8; 19:5b, 6
5. Witnesses (in Hittite treaties, these were usually gods) and the sign of the covenant	Genesis 15:17; 17:11–14	Exodus 24:3–8

Questions

1. Define the terms "conditional" and "unconditional."

_____

_____

Which term applies to the Abrahamic covenant?

_____

Which term applies to the Mosaic covenant?

_____

2. Define the terms "unilateral" and "bilateral."

_____

_____

Which term applies to the Abrahamic covenant?

_____

Which term applies to the Mosaic covenant?

_____

3. In what ways does the Mosaic covenant represent a *continuation* of the Abrahamic covenant?

_____

_____

_____

4. In what ways are the covenants different?

_____

_____

_____

5. What response(s) does Yahweh desire in each covenant?

_____

_____

6. If a covenant defines a relationship between two parties, what metaphor do you think best expresses that relationship in the Abrahamic covenant? in the Mosaic covenant?

_____

_____

_____

_____

THE TABERNACLE

The book of Exodus actually contains three "subbooks": (1) the story of the deliverance from Egypt and the beginning of the journey toward Canaan; (2) a body of law, including the Ten Commandments; and (3) the description of the Tent of Meeting and its furnishings.

This last item, which includes the tabernacle, is found in the last few chapters of the book of Exodus.

The floor plan of the Tent of Meeting might have looked something like this. Identify the numbered items and tell how they were used after looking up the Scripture references.

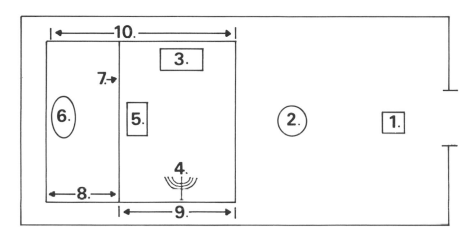

Scripture reference	Item name	Function or use
Exod. 27:1–8; 29:38–42	1. _____	_____
Exod. 30:17–21	2. _____	_____
Exod. 25:23–30	3. _____	_____
Exod. 25:31–40; 27:20–21	4. _____	_____
Exod. 30:1–8	5. _____	_____
Exod. 25:10–22	6. _____	_____
Exod. 26:31–33	7. _____	_____
Exod. 26:33–34	8. _____	_____
Exod. 26:33–34	9. _____	_____
Exod. 29:43–46; 25:8–9; 40:34–38	10. _____	_____

Possible choices for the item names are:

tabernacle, holy of holies, holy place, brazen altar, candlestick, altar of incense, veil, table of showbread, mercy seat and ark of the covenant, laver

Discussion Question

When God said, "I will take you for my people, and I will be your God" (Exod. 6:7), God literally took up residence among the Hebrews. How did the Tent of Meeting represent the completion and climax of God's redemption of the Hebrew people?

CHAPTER 5

Law and Sacrifice

INTRODUCTION

If we are to understand the theology of the Old Testament, we must shed whatever notions we have of law as restrictive, burdensome, or oppressive. Such thinking is simply foreign to the Scriptures. The law, or torah, is instead a precious gift and an expression of God's love.

Imagine the capricious deities of the ancient Near East. These gods were held to control nature, but they had nothing to do with the morality or the history of the peoples who sought desperately to appease them. Then imagine a God who chooses a people, the Hebrews, and makes this choice known to them through both history (God's "mighty acts") and through laws. Torah is the basis for the Mosaic covenant. It is the sign of the Hebrews' unique status before God. It is therefore a delight to follow! It is little wonder that the most often-read section of Hebrew Scripture, the Pentateuch, consists primarily of history and of laws. Of the first five books of the Bible we find only one (Genesis) that does not contain large bodies of law. Torah is placed in the center of the Pentateuch and in the context of the Sinai experience.

What then are the unique features of Israelite law? All laws are first and foremost God's laws. Yahweh is the author. No leader or king can claim this authorship, and no persons are exempt from the law. And because all laws are God's there is no distinction between various types of law: civil, ethical, religious, sacrificial. There is simply no arena of human activity that does not fall under God's instruction or teaching. Even the most practical, mundane matters are God's concern. Put up a guardrail around your roof (Deut. 22:8)! Keep your livestock tied up (Exod. 21:29)! The intention of the law is to protect the community. Torah may be pictured as a "hedge" around Israel.

As familiar as the Ten Commandments are to us today, the form these laws take—called "apodictic"—was unique in the ancient Near East. The Hebrews were the first to receive and attempt to live by absolute laws, the "thou shalt nots" of the Decalogue. Apodictic laws are stated in the imperative. They are brief, straightforward, and unconditional. Apodictic laws are statements of general policy. In the Old Testament, they form the basis for all ethical and religious teaching. These short, pithy statements reflect the conditions in a simple, nomadic society.

As the Hebrews later became settled in Canaan there arose a body of case laws dealing with specific circumstances. The form these laws take is called procedural, or "casuistic," law. Casuistic laws are conditional: *if* a certain crime is committed, *then* this punishment will follow. Casuistic laws in the Old Testament interpret and apply the principles of apodictic laws. For example, the sixth commandment states in apodictic form, "You shall not kill" (Exod. 20:13). Questions arose later about specific types of killing; thus casuistic laws such as Exodus 21:12–13 were applied: "Whoever strikes [someone] so that [that person] dies shall be put to death. But if [the attacker] did not lie in wait for [the person], but God let [the person] fall into [the attacker's] hand, then I will appoint for you a place to which [the attacker] may flee."

Torah distinguished the Hebrews from other nations. Marriage between brother and sister, common in Egypt, was forbidden. Laws prohibited the prostitution, transvestism, and child sacrifices associated with the Canaanite religious cultus. Pure food laws (kosher) and restrictions on the slaughter of animals prevented the Israelites from conforming to certain Egyptian rituals and Phoenician practices.

Laws regarding sacrificial rites were common in the ancient Near East. Sacrifice was understood as a means of appeasing the wrath of the gods or of controlling their capricious behavior. Pagan sacrifices were grim reminders that the worshiper must direct the gods to do their jobs properly. Unlike these polytheistic practices, Hebrew sacrifices served two functions: (1) they were joyful gifts of gratitude to God, or (2) they were a means of atonement, or reconciliation with God. The sin offering was a ritual ordained by God so the believer might participate in and realize God's forgiveness. A large body of law is concerned with sacrificial regulations. This concern reflects the Hebrews' keen awareness of the power of sin and of the need for reconciliation with the holy God of Israel.

While laws tended to preserve social inequality in the ancient Near East, Hebrew law destroys social inequality. It is egalitarian. Torah seeks to conserve human rights. We see great concern for the poor, the widowed, the orphaned. Over and over again we read commands to provide for the helpless, welcome the sojourner, and honor the aged. Consideration is due the weak and disenfranchised because "you were once slaves in Egypt." If any members of society are to be awarded special treatment, they are not the most powerful, but the least.

EXODUS LAW CODES

Study Guide

There are three major bodies of law in the book of Exodus: the Ten Commandments (20:1–17), the Book of the Covenant (20:18—23:33), and the Ritual Decalogue (34:11–26). While legal material in the Old Testament actually arose over a long period—from the Exodus, around 1290 B.C., to the return from exile, around 538 B.C.—all laws are attributed ultimately to Moses. The central tone and character of torah was initiated by God through Moses; Moses began the practice of understanding Israel's relationship to God as one of obedience to that torah. Thus later codifications of the law were not thought of as new, but simply as developments of the law given through Moses and adapted to new circumstances.

I. *The Ten Commandments* (in Greek, *Decalogue;* in Hebrew, *Debarim;* both meaning "ten words")

Read Exodus 20:1–17 and fill in the chart. Begin numbering with verse 3.

COMMAND (COPY FROM EXODUS)	REWRITE THE COMMAND IN YOUR OWN WORDS, EXPRESSED POSITIVELY ("YOU SHALL . . ."), EXCEPT 4 AND 5 ("YOU SHALL NOT . . .").	EXPLAIN HOW THIS COMMAND PRESERVES SOCIETY OR PROTECTS THE COMMUNITY.
1.		
2.		
3.		
4.		

5.		
6.		
7.		
8.		
9.		
10.		

Note that the first four commandments concern the community as a whole: they give Israel's obligations toward God. The next six concern individuals, and the relationship of individuals to each other. Put differently, the first four laws set forth a people's relationship to their God, while the last six show the way in which people ought to behave toward other people.

II. *The Book of the Covenant*. First skim Exodus 20:18–23:33, noting in your Bible any laws you find interesting or that you wish to discuss in class. Then write brief summaries for the following citations:

A. What crimes are punishable by death?

21:12–14 (note the conditions set forth here)

_____

21:15 and 21:17

_____

21:16

_____

22:18

_____

22:19

_____

22:20

_____

21:28–29 (What would be the modern equivalent of this law?)

_____

B. Slavery was an accepted practice in the ancient Near East. Read Exodus 21:1–11, and note the laws concerning slaves. Then indicate with verse numbers the points at which the idea of "slavery for life" is abolished.

_____

_____

C. What provisions are made for the needy in the following verses, and *why*?

22:21–22

_____

23:9

_____

23:10–11

_____

D. What provisions for worship are required in the following verses?

22:29–30

_____

23:12

_____

23:14–17 and the "Ritual Decalogue" of 34:11–26. What are the three great feasts of the liturgical calendar?

_____

_____

E. Read Exodus 21:23–25 and paraphrase these verses in your own words:

_____

This teaching constitutes the *lex talionis,* the law that calls for the punishment to fit the crime. It restricted the legal brutality that was common in the ancient Near Eastern cultures surrounding Israel. In these societies, a whole tribe could be killed for an offense against another tribe, and powerful folk received lighter punishments than the less privileged. The *lex talionis,* in contrast to these cultural practices, was progressive for its time.

Discussion Question

What is the relationship between religious law and ethical law in Hebrew society?

INTRODUCTION TO LEVITICUS

The name Leviticus means "of the priesthood." Aaron, the first high priest of the Hebrews and also Moses' brother, was from the tribe of Levi. His descendants, the Levites, formed the family of priests in Israel. The book of Leviticus is actually a continuation of the legal material found at the end of the book of Exodus, but it is directed toward these Levitical priests who were responsible for carrying out public worship.

Such words as "holy," "hallow," and "sanctify" are used over one hundred times in Leviticus. The injunction to "be holy" is often repeated, but it does not mean "be morally perfect." Holiness is the state of being set apart from the rest of the world by God, for the service and glory of God. Holiness in Israel called for sacrifices (the Latin *sacrificium* means "to make holy"). Leviticus gives regulations for three broad categories of sacrifices:

1. the burnt offering: a sacrifice of praise and thanksgiving to God
2. the peace offering: a covenantal meal between the worshiper, fellow Israelites, and God
3. the sin offering: a sacrifice that makes atonement for sins committed inadvertently (deliberate or willful sins were not covered by the sacrificial system). It is preceded by confession (Lev. 5:5).

It is this last category, and the concept of atonement, that is unique to Hebrew worship. Atonement is the reconciliation of two parties; when atonement occurs these two parties become "at one" again. Atonement restores the covenant relationship when it has been broken by sin. Picture sin as any obstacle that separates God from God's people. When the obstacle is removed, atonement has taken place. The estrangement between God and persons, brought about by sin, is erased.

What then is the relationship between sacrifice and atonement? We have seen in the *lex talionis* of Exodus 21:23–25 that any sin against one's neighbor is to be paid for "eye for eye, tooth for tooth." But what is the proper payment for sin against God? Not an eye, not a tooth, but one's very life is at stake. The Hebrews solved the problem of sin not by offering (and thereby ending) their own lives, but by offering the life of something that was dear to them. All sacrifices are therefore vicarious, meaning "substitutionary." The animal offering becomes a substitute for the worshiper, and the sin is atoned for, "life for life." That is why the worshiper laid hands on the head of the animal before the kill, in symbolic identification with the sacrifice.

This brings us to the symbolic power of blood in the Old Testament. If all the bloodletting in Leviticus strikes you as messy and gory, you have the right idea. In Exodus 24:5–8, Moses collected oxen for the offerings, killed them, and then took the blood and threw it on the people! In this case, blood established a community between God and his people; this sacrifice was part of the covenant ceremony. But in the sin offering, blood has a slightly different symbolic power. It literally "puts a cover" over the sin and makes atonement possible. The obstacle we pictured above as sin is covered up, nullified. Sin no longer has the power to put a rift in the covenant relationship. It is blotted out by the blood of the sacrificed animal.

Sacrifices ended with the destruction of the temple in Jerusalem by the Romans in A.D. 70. Prayer thenceforth took the place of sacrifices in Judaism. But we must imagine how important the book of Leviticus, and the priesthood it addressed, was for Israelite worship. The priests administered all public sacrifices. The law makes it clear that the proper approach to God is through sacrifice. Therefore the priests served as the means by which the Israelites approached God.

LEVITICUS

Study Guide

1. Read all of Leviticus 1. Give the verse numbers for the following steps in the sacrificial rites:

A. Presentation of the sacrifice at the door of the sanctuary by the worshiper: verses _____.

B. Laying on of hands: verses _____.
C. Slaying of the animal by the worshiper, who thus symbolically accepts the punishment due for sin: verses _____.

D. Symbolic application of the blood of the animal: verses _____.

E. Burning the sacrifice on the altar of burnt offering: verses _____.

2. What kinds of animals were used in the sacrificial rites?

1:3 _____

1:10 _____

1:14 _____
The offering in 1:14 was to be made by the poor. Read Leviticus 5:7 and explain why.

3. Read Leviticus 16, especially verses 6–10, 20–22, and 29–34. This is the account of the most important holiday in the Jewish calendar, the Day of Atonement or Yom Kippur.

Two goats were involved in the sacrifice. What happened to each?

_____

At the part of the ceremony described in 16:21–22, the congregation would let out a great shout of thanksgiving. Why do you think this was done?

_____

What was the point of Yom Kippur? Note especially verses 30, 34.

_____

4. Read Leviticus 19 (all) and note the laws and verse numbers that interest you.

_____

Write out Leviticus 19:18b (the last half of the verse). What do you think is the meaning of this great law?

_____

_____

What Canaanite practices are forbidden in 19:26–31? Jot down at least four.

_____

_____

_____

5. Turn to Leviticus 23. Note the key features of the great feasts of the Hebrew calendar.

A. Passover and Unleavened Bread (23:5–8).

_____

B. The Feast of Harvest or Weeks (23:15–21). This festival is also called Pentecost. Jewish tradition held that the law or torah was given to Moses on this day, seven weeks after Passover.

_____

C. The Feast of Booths or Tabernacles (23:33–36, 39–43).

_____

What is the meaning of this festival? See 23:42–43.

_____

6. Turn to Leviticus 25. What is the sabbatical year? See verses 1–7.

_____

What is the year of jubilees? See verses 8–12.

_____

After the seventh sabbatical year, the next year (that is, seven times seven plus one, or the fiftieth year) was called Jubilee. This name comes from the Hebrew *yobhel,* or the sound of the horn. The year was heralded by the sound of a loud trumpet.

Write out Leviticus 25:23.

_____

While we have no record of the Jubilee program being carried out, the spirit of the program was this: property should not be amassed in ancestral holdings, as it was in foreign nations. Do you think the year of Jubilees is too advanced an ideal? Why or why not?

_____

_____

INTRODUCTION TO DEUTERONOMY

First, read 2 Kings 22—23. These chapters are set in 621 B.C., when the king Josiah found a scroll while having the temple repaired in Jerusalem. This scroll prompted a sweeping reform in Judah, and it almost certainly contained the oldest form of our present book of Deuteronomy.

Deuteronomy is a Greek word meaning "second law." It takes the form of three sermons delivered by Moses to the Hebrews forty years after they left Egypt. The congregation is pictured standing on the plains of Moab to the east of the Dead Sea. They are about to enter Canaan, the promised land. At this point Moses preaches to this "second generation" of Hebrews, folk who have neither lived in Egypt nor experienced the Exodus. The material is actually not a "second law" but rather a repetition of the law for this new generation. Many of the law codes in Deuteronomy are duplicated in Exodus and Leviticus (Deut. 5:6–21 is a restatement of the Decalogue, or Ten Commandments, found in Exod. 20).

The sermons also contain much history in the frequent references to the mighty acts of God on behalf of God's people. Probably the oldest credal statement of Israel's past is found in Deuteronomy 26:5–11, a capsule summary of what God has done for the Hebrews. It begins, "A wandering Aramean was my father," a reference to the patriarch Abraham. God makes himself known through the law and through history. Unlike the Canaanite gods of the land they are about to enter, God moves the Hebrews through time and space. In doing so God shows *hesed,* the Hebrew word for steadfast love, and this is one of Deuteronomy's greatest teachings. Lest anyone suppose that the Hebrews deserved credit for being God's chosen people, the teaching makes it clear that God's *hesed* is at work, not their fine qualities! Moses tells them, you were chosen not because you were great in number (7:7); in fact you were the fewest of peoples. You were not chosen for your righteousness (9:5); in fact you are a stiff-necked and stubborn people. Israel was chosen simply because "the LORD loves you" (7:8). In other words, God chose them in spite of, not because of, who they were.

In the last chapter of the book, we read of Moses breathing his last in Moab and being buried there (34:5–8). While still alive, he laid hands on Joshua and desig-nated him as successor, the one who would actually bring the Hebrews into the Promised Land. The editors of the book conclude that the man credited with these sermons was the greatest leader ever: "There has not arisen a prophet since in Israel like Moses, whom the LORD knew face to face" (34:10).

DEUTERONOMY

Study Guide

1. The laws in Deuteronomy anticipate or reflect a move from a nomadic society to a settled society. When they get to Canaan, what guidelines should the Hebrews follow?

Briefly summarize the laws found in the following verses:

    A. Economic guidelines
       23:19–20

_____

       25:13–15

_____

    B. Justice and judges
       16:18–20

_____

    C. Slaves in Israel
       15:12–18

_____

    D. Pagan practices to be shunned
       14:1–2

_____

       14:21

_____

       22:5

_____

       23:17–18

_____

    E. Dietary laws (kosher)
       14:3–20

    F. Care for sojourners and the helpless
       24:17–22

_____

Why are the Hebrews told to care for them?

_____

2. Write out and memorize the great commandment of 6:4–5. This is known as the *shema,* Hebrew for the first word of this command, "hear." The "heart" denotes the mind or will, the "soul" is the self or vital being, and "might" means one's power or ability.

_____

In what sense is this commandment a summary of all torah?

_____

Deuteronomy 6:9 calls for the *mezuzah,* a small con-tainer, to be put on the front doorpost of all Hebrew homes. This container houses tiny scrolls of Deuteron-omy 6:4–9 and 11:13–21. Why do you think these verses are put in the *mezuzah?*

_____

3. The "Deuteronomic Formula" is central to Old Tes-tament teaching. The formula outlines a system of re-wards and punishments for the nation. Read 8:1–20; 11:8–17; 11:26–28; and all of chapter 28. Fill in the chart as you read:

What is OBEDIENCE?
What BLESSINGS accompany obedience?

What is DISOBEDIENCE?

What CURSES accompany disobedience?

4. Turn to chapter 30. What point is made in 30:11—14 about our ability to follow the law?

The congregation is asked to make a choice in 30:19—20. What is the choice?

In what sense do these verses constitute a summary of the entire book of Deuteronomy?

5. Finally, skim Deuteronomy 21:18—22:30. Jot down laws and verse numbers which interest you.

HAMMURABI'S CODE: INTRODUCTION AND QUESTIONS*

Hammurabi's Code was discovered in 1902 at Susa in Elam (modern Iran) by Jacques de Morgan. The Code is inscribed on a black diorite stone standing seven feet tall. It consists of three sections: a prologue describing Hammurabi's greatness, a body of over three hundred laws, and an epilogue, which gives more information on Hammurabi's greatness and curses on those who do not obey his laws. Hammurabi became king of Babylon around 1800 B.C.; the law code dates from late in his reign, around 1750 B.C.

Read the questions on the following page through once before you look at the code; this will give you an idea of the types of information you will need to find.

Do skim the entire code. *Do not* try to use all the laws! A handful of well-chosen laws will suffice to give you a feel for Babylonian culture. The point of the exercise is not to make you an expert in ancient Near Eastern law, but to help you understand the cultural context out of which Old Testament law grew and to see the unique features of Old Testament law.

As you answer the questions, use the numbers of the laws to which you are referring along with your written responses. For instance, Law 108 tells about a Babylonian occupation (beer shop mistress) and a crime punishable by death (taking too much payment in return for too little beer). This law then might be used in your responses to questions 2 and 5.

1. What can you learn about the society's religion from the code? (Use the Prologue and Epilogue as well as the body of laws.)

2. What occupations and professions do you find mentioned in the code?

3. What evidence of class structure do you find? Diagram the structure if you can. (Hint: pay attention to footnotes!)

* Excerpts from Hammurabi's Code are taken from William O. Kellogg's *Out of the Past,* Independent School Press (Wellesley Hills, Massachusetts), 1969.

4. What evidence do you find that class status (or lack of status) determined the degree of punishment?

_____

_____

5. What crimes were punishable by death?

_____

_____

6. What was the position of women in this society?

_____

_____

7. What picture do you get of marriage and family life?

_____

_____

8. What laws do you recognize as similar to practices found in the Old Testament? (Again, see footnotes.)

_____

_____

9. What is (are) the major source(s) of authority in this code?

_____

_____

_____

10. What seem to be the major concerns of this society?

_____

_____

EXCERPTS FROM THE LAW CODE OF HAMMURABI

Prologue

When Enlil, the decider of the destiny of the land enthroned Marduk as great in the assembly of the gods and director of the future of Babylon, when Enlil made Babylon supreme among nations, then Enlil chose me, Hammurabi, the god-fearing prince, to cause justice to prevail in Babylon, to destroy wicked and evil, to stop the strong from oppressing the weak, to rule like the sun over the black-headed people. Hammurabi, the shepherd, called by Enlil, to make wealth abound, to make Babylon great. Supreme through the four quarters of the world, to make Marduk, his lord, rejoice, the pious, wise king.

The monarch of kings who made riches abound; the terror of the enemy, chief of kings, the wise one. The rescuer of the people from trouble, who prescribed the sacrifices for all time; the subduer of villages along the Euphrates; the savior of his people; the shepherd of his people whose acts are pleasing to Ishtar; who brings security to Babylon; who makes law to reign; the devout one, from royalty sprung, the great king, who spreads light over Sumer and Akkad, who makes the four quarters of the world tremble.

When Marduk chose me to bring order, to lead the land, I established law and justice in the common tongue, I brought welfare to the people, I decreed:

The Laws

1. If a free man[1] has accused another of laying a death spell upon him, but has not proved it, he shall be put to death.

2. If a free man has accused another of laying a spell upon him, but has not proved it, the accused shall go to the sacred river, he shall plunge into the sacred river, and if the sacred river shall conquer him, he that accused him shall take possession of his house. If the sacred river shall show his innocence and he is saved, his accuser shall be put to death. He that plunged into the sacred river shall appropriate the house of him that accused him.

3. If a free man has born false witness in a trial, or has not established the statement that he has made, if that case be a capital trial, that man shall be put to death.

[1] The term *free man* or *man* is used to designate all those who are not slaves, regardless of position.

5. If a judge had judged a judgment, or decided a decision, and granted a legal document, and afterwards his judgment is changed, for the alteration of the judgment he shall be held responsible. As regards the punishment which was dependent upon the said judgment, twelve times the amount he shall pay. The assembly shall cast him from the judgment seat, and he shall not return; with the judges, in a judgment, he shall not take his seat.

6. If a free man the property of god, temple, or palace has stolen, that man shall be put to death, and he who received the stolen property from his hand shall be put to death.

8. If a man has stolen either from a god (temple) or a palace, an ox, sheep, or ass, or pig, or boat, he shall pay thirty-fold. If from a common man, he shall pay tenfold. If the thief has nothing to pay with, he shall be put to death.

14. If a free man has stolen a child, he shall be put to death.

15. If a free man had induced either a male or a female slave from the state, or from the house of a patrician, or from the house of a pleb[e]ian, to leave the city, he shall be put to death.

21. If a free man has broken into a house he shall be killed before the breach and buried there.

22. If a free man has committed highway robbery and has been caught, that man shall be put to death.

25. If a fire has broken out in a free man's house and one who has come to put it out has coveted the property of the householder and appropriated any of it, that man shall be cast into the self-same fire.

26. If an officer or soldier has been sent on a military campaign by the king, and he goes not, but a hireling he hires, and as his substitute sends him, that officer or soldier shall be put to death, and his hireling take his house.

33. If either a governor or a magistrate on the king's business a hired substitute has taken or sent, that governor or magistrate shall be put to death.

45. If a free man has rented his field to a farmer, and has received the rent, and afterward a thunderstorm has inundated the field or carried away the produce of the field, the loss is the farmer's.

53. If a free man has neglected to strengthen his dike and has not kept his dike strong, and a breach has broken out in his dike, and the waters have flooded the meadow, the man whose dike broke shall restore the corn he has caused to be lost.

108. If the mistress of a beer-shop has not received corn as the price of beer or has demanded silver on an excessive scale, and has made the measure of beer less than the measure of corn, that beer-seller shall be prosecuted and drowned.

109. If the mistress of a beer-shop has allowed outlaws or riotous characters to assemble in her house, and if those riotous characters have not been arrested and haled to the palace, that beer-seller shall be put to death.

117. If a free man has been seized for debt, and has given his wife, or his son, or his daughter to work off the debt, the hostage shall labor for three years in the house of the creditor, but in the fourth year he shall set him free.

127. If a free man has caused the finger to be pointed to another free man's wife, and has not proved his charge, the accuser shall be thrown down before the judges and shall be branded on the forehead.

128. If a patrician has taken a wife and has not executed a marriage-contract, that woman is not a wife.

129. If a patrician's wife be taken in adultery with another, they shall be strangled and cast into the water. If the wife's husband would save his wife, the king can spare his subject.

130. If a patrician shall force and lie upon the (betrothed) wife of another man who has not known a male, and who abides in her father's house, if the patrician be taken, he shall die, and that woman she shall go free.

132. If the wife of a free man has had a finger pointed at her in regard to another male, and in lying she has not been taken, for her husband into the holy river she shall plunge.

138. If a patrician has divorced his wife, who has not borne him children, he shall pay over to her as much money as was given for her bride-price and the marriage portion which she brought from her father's house, and so shall divorce her.

139. If there was no bride-price, he shall give her one mina of silver, as a price of divorce.

140. If he be a plebeian, he shall give her one-third of a mina of silver.

141. If a patrician's wife, living in her husband's house, has gone out to engage in business thus neglecting her house and humiliating her husband, he shall prosecute her. If her husband has said "I divorce her," she shall go her way; he shall give her nothing as her price of divorce. If her husband has said "I will not divorce her," he may take another woman to wife; the first wife shall live as a slave in her husband's house.

142. If a woman hates her husband, and says, "Thou shalt not possess me" they shall inquire what is her failing. If she has been careful, and was not at fault and her husband has gone forth and greatly depreciated her, that woman has no blame; she shall take her marriage portion and go to her father's house.

146. If a man marries a wife, and she gives a female slave to her husband, and she bears children, and afterwards that woman with her mistress assumes equality, on account of the children she bore her master, he may not sell her for money; a mark shall he put upon her, and with the female slaves count her.[2]

---

[2] See Gen. 16:1–6.

153. If a man's wife, for the sake of another, has caused her husband to be killed, that woman shall be impaled.

154. If a man know his own daughter, from the city they shall expel that man.

157. If a free man after his father, in the bosom of his mother has slept, they shall burn them both together.[3]

170. If to a man his wife has borne children, and his maidservant also has borne him children, and the father in his lifetime to the children has said "My sons," and with his sons of his wife has counted them, after the father has gone to his fate, in the property of the paternal house the sons of the wife and the sons of the maidservant shall share equally, but the sons of the wife shall take the first choice.[4]

190. If a man does not treat an adopted son the same as he treats his own children, then that adopted child may return to his father's house.

195. If a son has struck his father, his hands shall be cut off.[5]

196. If a patrician has knocked out the eye of a patrician, his own eye shall be knocked out.

197. If he has broken the limb of a patrician, his limb shall be broken.

198. If he has knocked out the eye of a plebeian or has broken the limb of a plebeian, he shall pay one mina of silver.

199. If he has knocked out the eye of a patrician's servant, or broken the limb of a patrician's servant, he shall pay half his value.

202. If a man strike the head of a man who is his superior, he shall receive sixty blows of an ox-hide whip in public.

203. If a plebeian strike the head of another plebeian equal to himself, he shall pay one mina of silver.

205. If the slave of a plebeian strike a plebeian, his ear shall be cut off.

209. If a free man strike a freeborn woman and she drop that which is in her womb, he shall pay ten shekels for that which was in her womb.

210. But if the woman die, his daughter shall be put to death.

211. If a woman of the freed class (former slave) lose that which is in her womb by a blow, he shall pay five shekels of silver.

212. If the woman die, he shall pay half a mina of silver.

215. If a doctor has made a large incision with a bronze lance and cured a free man, or has opened the abscess (in the eye) with the lance, and saved the eye of the man, ten shekels of silver shall he take.

216. If it was a freed man [former slave], five shekels of silver he takes.

217. If it was the slave of a free man, the master of the slave shall give two shekels of silver to the doctor.

218. If a doctor has made a large incision with a bronze lance, and has caused the free man to die, or opened an abscess with the lance, and has put out the eye, his hands shall be cut off.

229. If a builder build a house for a free man, and has not made his work strong, and the house has fallen in and killed the owner of the house, then that builder shall be put to death.

230. If it kill the son of the owner of the house, the son of that builder they shall kill.

235. If a shipbuilder a ship for a free man has built, and has not perfected his work, and in that year that ship is sent on a voyage, and it has shown faults, the boatbuilder that vessel shall take to pieces, and at his own expense make strong, and the strong ship he shall give to the owner.

250. If a bull walking the street has gored a free man, and caused him to die, there is no crime in that case.

251. If the ox has pushed a free man, and by pushing has made known his vice, and his horn has not been blunted, or the ox has not been chained up, and the ox gore a freeborn man, and kill him, half a shekel of silver he shall pay.

274. If any one hire an artisan he shall pay . . .
For a brick-maker he shall pay 5 SE of silver.
For a weaver he shall pay 5 SE of silver . . .
For a carpenter, 4 SE of silver he shall pay.
For a ropemaker, 4 SE of silver he shall pay . . .
For a builder . . . [6]

Epilogue

The laws of righteousness which Hammurabi the mighty king had established, and whereby he caused the land to learn a pious law and have good government.

Hammurabi, the benefactor king, I am he. . . .

I am he whom the great gods proclaimed. I am the salvation-giving shepherd, the beneficent shadow which over-spreads my city; on my heart I fold the people of Sumer and Akkad; in my spirit let them repose in peace. By my deep wisdom I directed them, so that the strong should not injure the weak, and to protect the widows and orphans.

In Babylon, the city where Marduk and Enlil raise their heads, the temple of which its foundation is firm as heaven or earth, to guide judgment in the land, and to enact edicts in the land, and to make straight wrong, my precious words upon my stele I wrote, and before my statute as King of Righteousness, I placed it. The king who rules among the kings of cities, I am he. My words

[3] See Deut. 27:20, 22–23; Lev. 20:11.
[4] See Gen. 30.
[5] See Exod. 21 for parallels to Laws 195–212.

[6] Unfortunately, this law is badly damaged on the stele [stone slab].

are precious; my power has no equal. By command of Shamesh, the great judge of heaven and earth, let righteousness be glorified in the land. . . .

[There follows a number of appeals to the various gods asking them to punish any man who disregards Hammurabi's laws. The epilogue then concludes:]

With potent curses may Enlil, whose command changes not, curse him and quickly may they seize him.

LAW IN THE ANCIENT NEAR EAST

Essay Question

Now it is time to use what you have learned about law in the ancient Near East to write a well-organized, sufficiently detailed essay.

Compare and contrast Hammurabi's Code with the various Old Testament law codes you have studied. You will want to consider the following questions as you prepare your response:

1. Based upon your reading of the laws, what were the major concerns of each society?

2. How did the Israelite and Babylonian societies differ in regard to:

A. types of government
B. use of capital punishment
C. treatment of slaves
D. social classes
E. occupations and professions

And in what ways were these societies similar?

3. What was the purpose of law in each society? Whose authority stood behind the law codes?

4. What do the types of punishments suggest about the value each society placed on human life? How would you describe the spirit or general outlook of Babylonian and Israelite law?

CHAPTER 6

From the Wilderness to the Conquest

INTRODUCTION

That motley band of 'abiru who left Egypt under Moses' leadership had a long way to go, and grow, before they would be forged into the nation Israel. We might picture them as children who were taught to walk out of Egypt in the Exodus. They spent their turbulent and troubled adolescent years in the Sinai Peninsula. After forty years of wandering, they were entering young adulthood. They still had much to learn about what it means to be a covenant people. Their growth was often painful; that they matured as God's people at all is debatable. The Old Testament record seems to say: learn from the Israelites' mistakes!

The journey from the wilderness to the conquest is told in the historical narrative found in the books of Numbers, Joshua, and Judges. The archaeological era is the end of the Bronze Age and the beginning of the Iron Age. Seafaring peoples who settled the coast of Canaan, the Philistines (from whose name we get the world *Palestinians*), were using iron weapons against the Israelites as early as 1200 B.C. We might conveniently date the conquest of Canaan under Joshua around 1250 B.C., the death of Joshua around 1200, and the period of the Judges from 1200 to 1050 B.C.

The book of Numbers gets its name from its frequent use of lists: lists of tribes, leaders, offerings, march formations, and a census of the numbers in the march from Mount Sinai to Moab. The Hebrew name for the book is *Bamidbar,* meaning "in the wilderness," the setting for the entire book. Two major themes are played out in this narrative. On one hand we see the leadership and greatness of Moses, who is obedient to Yahweh (with one possible exception) and intercedes constantly on behalf of his people. On the other hand we see the contentiousness of the Hebrews, who constantly "murmur," if not rebel, against Moses and God. The wilderness account is one long, sad story of complaining and discontent on the part of this young nation.

Their forty years of wandering is in one sense literal. Physically and geographically they move about the Sinai Peninsula, readying themselves for the attack on Canaan. But it is also a spiritual wandering as the story unfolds of their constant grumbling, disbelief, and disobedience. Throughout the narrative, however, God's covenant with Moses stands. God is faithful even when the community

is not. Like a parent, God disciplines them and guides them to the land God promised their ancestors.

"Forty years" of wandering is the time it takes for the older generation, a people born into slavery in Egypt, to die off and for a new generation to take its place. Moses appoints his successor in the book of Numbers, and Aaron dies, his son taking his place as chief priest of the people. It is truly a new generation, one that has not been disheartened by slavery, which inherits the promised land.

The Old Testament gives us two very different accounts of the conquest of Canaan. Under Joshua, the Israelites staged a series of "holy wars" that amounted to a blitzkrieg—a sweeping conquest of all the land. The book of Judges, on the other hand, is the story of a series of bitter struggles against foreign oppressors in Canaan over a period of almost two hundred years. Aside from the constant strife with the Canaanites, some Hebrew tribes had to contend with the Philistines on the southern coastal plain, others with the Midianites to the southwest of Canaan, still others with the Moabites and Ammonites dwelling east and north of the Dead Sea.

Politically, the Hebrew tribes who settled in Canaan were an amphictyony—a confederacy—loosely held together by religious bonds that were tenuous at best. After the death of Joshua the old patriarchal system broke down with no new form of centralized authority to take its place. The book of Judges fills in the gap between Joshua, the hero of the conquest, and Saul, the first king of Israel.

The judges were probably tribal heroes rather than national figures. A judge was a deliverer (*not* a lawyer) who was given the *ruah,* the breath or spirit of God, at a time of tribal emergencies. When the spirit of the Lord came upon the judge, this person was able to deliver his or her people from suffering at the hands of foreign oppressors. This spirit (or the Greek word *charisma*) was like a mantle that rested on an otherwise inconspicuous character, making that person capable of mighty acts. It was not passed on from parent to child.

The judges, then, were actually chieftains of various tribes who distinguished themselves through military accomplishments. As in any confederacy, the tribes were politically autonomous; however, they would unite in some military actions, and the twelve tribes gathered yearly at Shiloh for a "feast of the LORD" (see Judg. 21:19). Major tribes began to emerge: Judah in the south, Ephraim in the north. Times were turbulent. The era was one of loosely organized tribal systems with local leadership that was confined to emergency situations.

The Canaanites were actually no better organized than the Hebrews. The "kings" of Canaan mentioned in the Old Testament were no more than chieftains of little city-states. They were not easy to conquer, however, because they lived in walled cities and were well armed. The major valleys to the west of the Jordan River bristled with their fortresses. The Philistines on the coast likewise had well-trained armies and a major advantage—iron weapons. The Philistines were part of the sea peoples' invasion of the eastern Mediterranean that occurred around 1200 B.C.

Not numerous, they were confined to five cities along the coast of Canaan. Despite the successes of the judge Samson, their power expanded during the next century until they were finally checked by King David around 1000 B.C.

In contrast to Moses and Joshua, some of the judges were anything but true people of God. Hideous slaughter, revenge, and irresponsible behavior are key features of this era. It is a time of religious primitivism, and the "heroes" of Judges were people of their age. The conquest of Canaan is a power struggle told on two levels: between the Hebrew tribes and the natives for control of the land, and between the Yahwist faith and the pagan religions of their neighbors and adversaries. Once again we see God using these people, not because they were righteous, but in spite of their shortcomings.

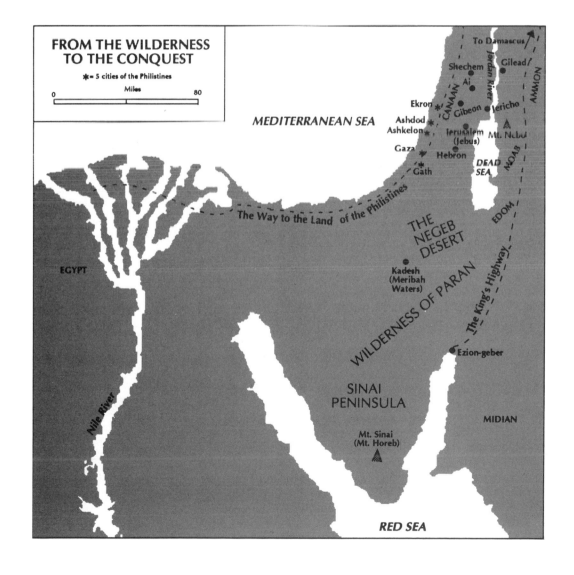

NUMBERS

Study Guide

1. Skim Numbers 1. Where did the book get its name?

_____

2. Chapters 2—9 give the arrangement of the tribes for the march into Canaan, lists of sacrifices made in preparation for the journey, and more laws. The narrative of the trip toward the promised land resumes in chapter 10. A year after they arrived at Mount Sinai, the tribes set out toward Canaan through the Wilderness of Paran. See 10:33—36; then describe what guided them in their march.

_____

3. *In the Wilderness of Paran: Chapter 11*
What do the Hebrews complain about in 11:4—9?

_____

How does Moses intercede with the Lord on behalf of the Hebrews in 11:10—15?

_____
_____

What is the function of the seventy elders in 11:16—17, 24—30?

_____
_____

Read 11:18—23, 31—35. The Lord answered their prayers literally. How was this answered prayer disastrous for the Hebrews?

_____
_____

4. *The Rebellion of Miriam and Aaron: Chapter 12*
Why were Moses' brother and sister moved to jealousy?

_____

What was God's defense of Moses?

_____

What was Miriam's punishment?

_____

How did Aaron intercede in Miriam's behalf?

_____

5. *Reconnaissance Mission into Canaan: Chapter 13*
How many spies were sent out? (13:1—16.)

_____

The spy representing the tribe of Ephraim was _____

(13:8); he was renamed _____ by Moses (13:16).
Where did the spies go? (13:17—23.)

_____

Where were the people encamped?_____ (13:26.)

_____

What sort of information were the spies to obtain? See 13:17—20.

_____

Read 13:27—33. When the spies returned, they had "some good news, and some bad news." What was their report?

_____
_____

6. *Rebellion and Its Consequences: Chapter 14*
What wish do the people express in 14:1—4?

_____

Read 14:6—10. What advice did Joshua and Caleb give, and how did the Hebrews respond to their advice?

_____
_____

Read 14:20—38. How is Yahweh's punishment a fulfillment of the older generations' wish?

_____

See 14:30. Who of the older generation would be allowed to enter the promised land, and why?

_____

Why were the Hebrew armies defeated (14:39—45)?

_____

7. *More Rebellions: Chapter 16*
Read 16:1—11. What was the basis of Korah's revolt?

_____

Read 16:12–14. What was the complaint of Dathan and Abiram?

_____

_____

What happens to these three men in 16:25–35?

_____

_____

See 16:36–40. Henceforth, who will constitute the legitimate priesthood?

_____

_____

How does Aaron act as priest in 16:41–48?

_____

_____

8. *The Priesthood: Chapter 17*
Read 17:1–11. In Hebrew, the root word for "rod" and "household" is the same, as is the Hebrew root for "almond" and "chosen." How does this story re-establish the priestly role for Aaron's family?

_____

_____

_____

Read 17:12–13, then 18:6–7. What is the role of the Levitical priests?

_____

_____

Go back to Numbers 3:5–13. What role will Aaron's descendants play in Hebrew worship? How will God use the Levites?

_____

_____

_____

Write out and memorize Aaron's benediction, or blessing, found in Numbers 6:24–26.

_____

_____

_____

_____

9. *The Waters of Meribah: Chapter 20*
At Kadesh-barnea, the congregation once again complained. Read 20:1–13. What was the problem, and how did Moses deal with it?

_____

_____

_____

Look closely at 20:10–12. What was Moses' sin?

_____

Are you satisfied with this account of why Moses did not enter the promised land? That such a great leader as Moses did not set foot in the promised land was a problem for the Jews and the Old Testament editors. Does this story solve the problem or not?

_____

_____

Read the account of Aaron's death in 20:22–29. His son, _____, was the father of the Zadokite priesthood.
Read 20:14–22. Why was it necessary for the Hebrews to detour around Edom and the King's Highway?

_____

_____

Like the Hebrews, the Edomites were a Semitic people, descendants of Esau. How is the conflict between Jacob (Israel) and Esau (Edom) seen in this story about their descendants?

_____

_____

10. *The Bronze Serpent: Chapter 21*
Read 21:4–9. What was the problem this time?

_____

How did Yahweh punish the people?

_____

_____

What did the bronze serpent symbolize?

_____

11. *Balak and Balaam: Chapters 22–24*
The Moabites were descendants of Moab, a son of Lot by an incestuous relationship with his daughter (see Gen. 19:30–38). Lying immediately east of the Dead Sea, the nation of Moab had a population of roughly 100,000 at this time. Read all of chapters 22—24. Who is Balak?

_____

Who is Balaam?

_____

What does Balak want Balaam to do?

_____

_____

What do you think is the point of the talking donkey in 22:22–35?

_____

_____

_____

What evidence can you find of Balaam's faith in Yahweh? Give citations, e.g., 23:8.

_____

What do you think is the meaning of this long account in chapters 22–24?

_____

_____

_____

12. *Trouble in Moab: Chapter 25:1–9*
Why did God unleash a plague against the Hebrews?

_____

Why did it stop?

_____

13. *Moses' Successor: Chapter 27*
Read 27:12–23. Why do you think the Lord allows Moses to see the promised land?

_____

_____

Who is made Moses' successor?

_____

What are the signs of this man's authority?

_____

_____

14. *Holy War: Chapter 31*
Read all of chapter 31, which describes a "holy war" against the Midianites. What "rules" appear to govern the practice of holy war?

_____

_____

_____

15. *The Cities of Refuge: Chapter 35*
Six "cities of refuge" are named in 35:6–34. Look back at Exodus 21:12–13; then give the reasons these cities are to be established in the promised land.

_____

_____

Discussion Question

Review your work on the book of Numbers. Is God more severe in his treatment of the people in this narrative than he was in the book of Exodus? Why or why not?

WRITING CREATIVELY ABOUT THE OLD TESTAMENT

Essay Topic

(Do this exercise after completing the study guide on Numbers.)

In writing creatively about the Old Testament, you should keep some rules in mind. You want your writing to be fresh and imaginative; however, your creation must be rooted in the "facts": the historical narrative found in the Old Testament. Your descriptions and dialogue must be consistent with the text. You are focusing in on some places, amplifying in others, what you know to be true about your subject matter. While either one of the topics below requires lots of original thinking on your part, do not create a new Moses who bears no resemblance to the OT personality! Instead, use your imagination to make this character come alive to your reader. Choose one of the following topics:

A. You have been asked to direct a film entitled *Moses: Chosen for Leadership*. The script uses scenes from the books of Exodus and Numbers; it concludes with Moses' death as recorded in Deuteronomy 34. As director you have hired an excellent actor to play the part of Moses. Unfortunately, this actor has no idea what Moses was like: what kind of person he was and how he reacted in various situations. Instruct your actor as to the kind of man he is to portray. Use plenty of description and various scenes from your movie.

B. Moses, dead and gone to heaven, stumbles on Abraham. The two of them have much to say to each other. Record their dialogue as they are comparing their experience on earth, and their views on such things as:

• their earthly conceptions of who God is—what they thought of God

• their earthly conceptions of themselves and the roles they were chosen to carry out

• their most difficult situations and their greatest successes on earth

JOSHUA

Study Guide

1. Read chapter 1. Who was Joshua, and how did he continue the tradition established by Moses?

_____

_____

_____

2. Read chapter 2. Who was Rahab?

_____

What did she do on behalf of the Israelite spies? What was the significance of the scarlet cord?

_____

_____

3. Read chapter 3 on the crossing of the Jordan River into Canaan. Then compare this account with the crossing of the Red Sea in Exodus 14:10–31. How are the two events similar?

_____

_____

_____

How do they differ?

_____

_____

_____

4. Read chapter 4. What was the significance of the twelve stones?

_____

What will these stones mean to future generations?

_____

5. Read chapter 5 closely, then indicate what happened to the Hebrews on the eve of their entry into the promised land with regard to each of the following:

A. circumcision

_____

B. Passover

_____

C. manna

_____

D. a theophany

_____

What follows, in chapters 6—11, is the account of the military conquest of Canaan. The Hebrews were engaged in what is called "holy war." Certain rules and features govern holy war: (1) The ark of the covenant and the priests (blowing trumpets!) lead the army into battle. (2) The battle is actually God's battle ("the LORD fought for Israel") and is often accompanied by miracles, uneven odds, or clever strategies that establish this fact. (3) The victory is God's victory, lest the Israelites should boast. (4) The foreign peoples, and often their property, are devoted to God as a great offering and destroyed.

This last feature of holy war is called *herem,* or the ban. *Herem* strikes us today as a repugnant practice. Why were the defeated peoples wiped out? Property was destroyed to keep the soldiers from greedily amassing it as booty. If booty was taken, it was to be given to the priests or divided among the people. But all foreign influences, including people, were to be destroyed. This was because of the real concern that pagan practices would influence the young nation of Israel. Idolatry was a threat to Israel and a real concern; we shall see it was a valid one.

6. Read chapter 6. What was extraordinary about the siege of Jericho?

_____

Who in that city was spared, and why?

_____

7. Read chapter 7. What was Achan's sin?

_____

What was the consequences of this sin for the Israelites? for Achan?

_____

_____

8. Read chapter 8 on the second attack of Ai. What clever strategy enabled the Israelites to take the city of Ai?

_____

_____

Draw the battle plan.

9. Read chapter 9. How did the crafty Gibeonites manage to have themselves spared from certain death?

_____

_____

_____

10. Read chapter 10 on the War of the Five Kings. Why did the kings of five Canaanite cities attack the Gibeonites?

_____

_____

What miraculous events gave the Israelites victory over the five kings?

_____

_____

11. The conquest of Canaan is summarized in 10:40–43 and 11:16–23. What are the key features in this summary?

_____

_____

12. Caleb reappears in 14:6–12. How is he both boastful and faithful at eighty-five years old?

_____

_____

_____

JOSHUA'S FAREWELL ADDRESSES

Study Guide

1. As an old man, Joshua summoned the elders of the congregation and gave them a farewell address. Read Joshua 23. What warnings did Joshua give the leaders?

_____

_____

What promises did he give them and future generations?

_____

_____

How did Joshua explain their successes up to that point?

_____

2. Next, Joshua summoned all the people to Shechem for a covenant renewal ceremony. Read chapter 24. What important individuals are named in the history of the Hebrew people?

_____

_____

What miracles and mighty acts are recounted in this history?

_____

_____

What choice did Joshua give the people?

_____

How many times did Joshua make the people pledge allegiance to the Lord?

_____

What was the visible witness of this pledge?

_____

Now go back and read Exodus 24:3–8. In what ways is the covenant renewal ceremony at Shechem similar to an earlier generation's covenant ceremony with Moses?

_____

_____

_____

3. Read Joshua 24:29–33 on the end of a faithful generation. Who dies in 24:29?_____Who dies in 24:33?_____What point is made about this generation under Joshua's leadership in 24:31?

_____

_____

Discussion Question

Do you think Joshua's leadership is overshadowed by the figure of Moses? Why or why not?

PAGAN RELIGION IN CANAAN

Study Guide

Read the following article on pagan religion in Canaan to get an idea of the religious and cultural milieu in Canaan at the time of the conquest. Remember that Canaanite influences persisted even after Joshua's spectacular successes. This influence was seductive. It is thus important to know what is meant when we read that "Israel went after pagan gods," as they often did. Answer these questions as you read:

1. What is a "baal"?

_____

2. What was the reason for sacred prostitution?

_____

_____

_____

3. What is "imitative magic"?

_____

_____

4. In the Ras Shamra epic, who is Baal? What is his story?

_____

_____

_____

5. What was the reason for a nature religion in Canaan?

_____

_____

6. What is syncretism? How does it differ from apostasy? (Use a dictionary to define these terms.)

_____

_____

_____

7. In what ways did the Israelites tend toward syncretism in Canaan? What was wrong with this tendency?

_____

_____

_____

8. What was the role of sex in Canaanite religion?

_____

_____

9. Read the last page carefully. What are the basic differences between the Baal religion and Israelite faith? Fill in the chart:

BAAL RELIGION	ISRAELITE FAITH

PAGAN RELIGION IN CANAAN *

Religion and Culture

To appreciate the nature of the struggle of the period of the judges, we must know something about the religion of Canaan, which in the Old Testament is described as the worship of the Baals and Ashtarts [Ashtaroth] (Judg. 2:13; 10:6; 1 Sam. 7:4; 12:10). The title "Baal" means "lord" or "owner," and designates the male deity who owns the land and controls its fertility. His female partner is known as "Baalath," "lady," although in the cases cited above her personal name is Ashtart. It was believed that these fertility powers were connected with particular localities or towns, in which case one could speak of many Baals and Ashtarts, as numerous as the cities of the land (see Jer. 2:28). But it was also possible to regard these local powers as manifestations of the great "Lord" and "Lady" who dwell in the heavens, in which case worshipers could address Baal and Ashtart in the singular as cosmic deities.

. . . The land, it was believed, is the sphere of divine powers. The Baal of a region is the "lord" or "owner" of the land; its fertility is dependent upon sexual relations between him and his consort. When the rains came and the earth and water mingled, the mysterious powers of fertility stirred again. New life was resurrected after the barrenness of winter. This astonishing revival of nature, people believed, was due to sexual intercourse between Baal and his partner, Baalath.

Furthermore, farmers were not mere spectators of the sacred marriage. It was believed that by ritually enacting the drama of Baal it was possible to assist—through magical power—the fertility powers to reach their consummation, and thereby to insure the welfare and prosperity of the land. The cooperation with the powers of fertility involved the dramatization in the temples of the story of Baal's loves and wars. Besides the rehearsal of this mythology, a prominent feature of the Canaanite cult was sacred prostitution (see Deut. 23:18). In the act of temple prostitution the man identified himself with Baal, the woman with Ashtart. It was believed that human pairs, by imitating the action of Baal and his partner, could bring the divine pair together in fertilizing union.

. . . Through sexual ceremonies farmers could swing into the rhythms of the agricultural world and even keep those rhythms going through the techniques of religious magic. The kind of magic in question is often called sympathetic or imitative magic. It rests on the assumption that when persons imitate the action of the gods, a power is released to bring that action about (For example: the "rainmaker" who, by pouring water from a tree and thereby imitating rain, induces the gods to end a drought.)

The Ras Shamra Epic

The pattern of Baal religion found in Canaan was of one piece with the myth and ritual which, in varying forms, was spread throughout the whole Fertile Crescent. In Babylonia, for example, the Tammuz cult dramatized the relations between the god Tammuz and the goddess Ishtar. In Egypt the Isis cult was based on the worship of the god Osiris (Horus) and his female counterpart Isis (Hathor). And, as we have seen, in Canaan the Baal cult dramatized the relations between the storm god Baal and his consort, known as Anath or Ashtart (the Canaanite equivalent of Ishtar). . . .

We can get a clear picture of Canaanite religion from the Ras Shamra tablets, first discovered in 1929 at Ras Shamra on the coast of northern Syria, the site of the ancient Canaanite city of Ugarit. These mythological texts date from about 1400 B.C. . . . At the head of the Canaanite pantheon was the high god, El, "the King, Father of Years," whose consort was Asherah. Next in rank was the great storm-god, Baal, the god of rain and fertility. His consort-sister is the warrior goddess Anath, known for violent sexual passion and sadistic brutality. . . . We hear of Baal's preparations to build a temple with the assistance of his sister, the maiden Anath. Evidently these plans are interrupted by the action of Mot ("Death"), the god of summer drought, who kills Baal and carries him down to the underworld. When the gods hear that "the lord of the earth" has perished, they mourn deeply; but Anath is seized by a great passion for Baal and searches for him. When she finally finds him in the possession of Mot, a furious struggle ensues. Mot is killed, Baal is resurrected and put on his throne, and the lovers are reunited. There is great rejoicing in heaven.

. . . The myth of Baal's death and resurrection represents the conflict waged in nature as the seasons come and go. Baal personifies the fertilizing powers of springtime; Mot personifies the destructive powers that bring death to vegetation and life. There is a rhythm in nature: springtime and summer, fertility and drought, life and death. According to the ancient view, the farmer's life is caught up in this alternation. Existence is a precarious dependence upon the powers of nature. It is believed that religion provided a way to control these powers and thereby to insure the fruitfulness of the soil. By reenact-

* From Bernhard W. Anderson, *Understanding the Old Testament*, 4th edition, © 1986, pp. 184–92. Excerpted by permission of Prentice-Hall, Inc., Englewood Cliffs, New Jersey.

ing the mythological drama of Baal's death and resurrection in the temple, so it was believed, a magical power was released that would guarantee fertility and well-being. And through myth and ritual the worshipers were related to what was believed to be divine.

Attempts at Compromise

Here, then, was a practical religion for farmers. In Canaan, Baal was recognized as the lord of the earth: the owner of the land, the giver of rain, the source of grain, wine, and oil. People believed that the agricultural harvest would not be plentiful unless the fertility powers were worshiped according to the ways of Canaan. To have ignored the Baal rites in those days would have seemed as impractical as for a modern farmer to ignore science in the cultivation of the land.

. . . It is not surprising that many Israelites turned to the gods of the land. People did not mean to turn away from Yahweh, the God of the Exodus and the Sinai covenant. They would serve Yahweh and Baal side by side, like modern people who keep religion and science in separate compartments, or they would identify Yahweh [with] Baal, like those today for whom "God" is the symbol for the values of civil religion. In any case, it was not felt that the two religions were contradictory or mutually exclusive. Indeed, there was a tendency for the two faiths to coalesce in popular worship. . . . As late as the eighth century, Israelites—according to the prophet Hosea—actually addressed Yahweh as "Baal," and by worshiping Yahweh according to the rituals of Baal sought the blessings of fertility (Hos. 2). At the popular level this syncretism—that is, the fusion of different religious forms and views—went on to some degree from the time Israel first set foot on Canaanite soil.

As we have noticed, this syncretism was going on constantly in the commingling of cultures of the Fertile Crescent, for the religions of the area had a great deal in common. But Israel's faith was based on the novel belief in a *jealous* God who would tolerate no rivals. According to the terms of the covenant, Israel was to have "no other gods before Yahweh." Yahweh's lordship over the people was absolute, extending into every sphere of life. Therefore, to believe that Yahweh was lord in one sphere (history) and Baal in another (fertilization of the soil) was a fundamental violation of the meaning of the covenant. Later, prophets saw clearly the basic conflict between the two faiths and threw down the challenge: Yahweh versus Baal. Joshua's appeal, voiced at Shechem, echoed through the years. "Choose this day whom you will serve!" There could be no compromise, for Yahweh claimed to be the sovereign of the whole of life and to receive the devotion of the whole heart.

Religion and Sex

In Canaanite religion, sex was elevated to the realm of the divine. The divine powers, it was believed, were disclosed in the sphere of nature—that is, in the mystery of fertility. The gods were sexual in nature and were worshiped in sexual rites. The erotic relations of god and goddess were hidden within the ever-recurring cycle of the death and renewal of fertility, represented mythologically by the annual death and resurrection of Baal. But this cycle of fertility, according to the ancient view, did not take place by itself through natural law. Rather, the purpose of religion was to preserve and enhance the fertility upon which people were dependent for their existence. It sought to control the gods in the interest of human well-being. And since this religion aimed to maintain the harmony and rhythm of the natural order, it was a serviceable tool for the aristocracy who wished to maintain the social *status quo* against disruptive changes. Baalism catered to the desire for security in the precarious environment of the Fertile Crescent.

In the perspective of Israel's faith, on the other hand, the power of the divine was disclosed in nonrecurring historical events, primarily the Exodus, which were perceived to be signs of God's liberation of the people from bondage and God's creation of a covenant community. . . . Unlike Baal, Yahweh has no consort, no female counterpart. As the holy God, who transcends the human world, Yahweh is beyond sexuality. To be sure, in concession to the limitations of grammar and to ancient patriarchal society, Yahweh is spoken of in masculine terms; but this literary convention should not blind us to the fact that God-language includes feminine, as well as masculine, dimensions. Moreover, Yahweh, like Baal, is lord of fertility; but Yahweh is not a fertility god subject to the death and resurrection of the natural world. Yahweh is "the Living God" whose vitality is disclosed in the social arena, where human lives touch one another, where injustices oppress and yearnings for deliverance are felt, where people are called to make decisions that alter the course of the future. Finally, the ethical demands of the covenant preclude worshiping Yahweh in licentious sexual rites (sacred prostitution) or in religious rituals that attempt to guarantee fertility of soil and womb. While Baal religion taught worshipers to *control* the gods, Israel's faith stressed *serving* God in gratitude for benevolent deeds and in fidelity to the demands of the covenant. Yahweh could not be coerced by magic. Yahweh could be trusted or betrayed, obeyed or disobeyed, but in all things the divine will is free and supreme.

JUDGES

Study Guide

1. Read Judges 1:1, 2:23—3:5. What evidence do we have that the conquest of Canaan was not completed under Joshua?

_____

_____

_____

2. See 1:19. The Canaanites, using iron weapons, chariots, and cavalry, had the advantage in what type of terrain?

_____ The Hebrews, using primitive weapons and guerrilla warfare, were successful in what type of terrain?_____

3. According to 1:27–35, what was the social position of the Canaanites during this era of the conquest?

_____

_____

How does this account compare with the status of the pagan peoples in 2:1–3 and 3:5–6?

_____

_____

4. Read chapter 2. The Baals and Ashtaroth (or Asheroth) were the male and female deities of the Canaanites. What major problems concerning the covenant with Yahweh do you foresee?

_____

_____

_____

5. According to 2:16–19, what is the role of the "judge" in Israel? Be specific.

_____

_____

6. The tribes are constantly repeating their mistakes in this period of Israelite history. Look up "apostasy" in a dictionary and write out its definition:

_____

_____

Israelite history in this period takes the form of a "cycle of apostasy," first outlined (and subsequently repeated seven times) in the story of the judge Othniel in 3:7–12.

Read this summary, then give the steps in the cycle of apostasy:

A.

_____

B.

_____

C.

_____

D.

_____

E.

_____

(Then the cycle begins again with "A.")

7. Read about Ehud (3:12–30). Who were the oppressors of Israel?_____

What was Ehud's "left-handed tribute" to King Eglon?

_____

What details in this story show the Israelites' contempt for their oppressors?

_____

_____

8. Read about Deborah (chapters 4 and 5). The cast of characters in this account includes:
   *Deborah—judge and prophetess
   Barak—general of the Israelite forces
   Jabin—king of Canaan and oppressor of the Israelites
   Sisera—general of King Jabin's armies
   *Jael—wife of Heber the Kenite, slayer of Sisera
   *Sisera's unnamed mother

What do the actions of these three women (*) tell you about life and war?

_____

_____

_____

_____

9. Read about Gideon (chapters 6—8). He is also called Jerubbaal. Who were the oppressors of Israel this time? (Notice that these invaders successfully used fleets of camels, which terrified the Israelites!) _____

When Gideon was called by God to be a judge, how did he respond? See 6:11–24.

_____

_____

_____

How is this account of a call similar to the call of Moses in Exodus 3:1—4:17?

_____

_____

_____

What evidence of Israel's apostasy do you find in 6:25–32?

_____

_____

See 6:36–40. How did Gideon use the sign of the fleece to test (once again) God's call?

_____

_____

_____

See 7:1–9. Gideon's force of 32,000 soldiers was cut down to _____ men. What tests were used to reduce the number?

_____

_____

Why do you think God reduced the number so drastically?

_____

See 7:15–23. What caused the Midianites to kill each other?

_____

_____

How does Gideon show good diplomatic skills in 8:1–3?

_____

_____

What is Gideon's response to the offer of kingship in 8:22–23?

_____

Gideon's last act, recorded in 8:24–28, was a huge blunder. An "ephod" was a priestly garment, but it appears to have a different use here. What was his last act, and its consequences?

_____

_____

10. Read about Abimelech (chapter 9). See 8:31. Abimelech was the son of Gideon (which was good) and a Canaanite concubine from Shechem (which was bad).

Read 9:1–6. In what ways did Abimelech depart from the role of "judge"?

_____

_____

Jotham, Abimelech's remaining half brother, told a parable to the Canaanites in Shechem. Look up and define "parable":

_____

_____

The olive tree is the finest tree in Israel; the bramble is a worthless bush. What point does Jotham's "parable of the bramble" make about kingship in 9:7–15?

_____

_____

_____

Abimelech, crowned king of Shechem, reigned three years before a revolt broke out. How did he quench the revolt? (See 9:46–49.)

_____

_____

How does this revolt relate to Jotham's speech in 9:16–20?

_____

_____

How did Abimelech die? See 9:50–56.

_____

11. Read about Jephthah (10:6—12:7). Who were the oppressors of Israel this time?

_____

_____

What were Jephthah's "credentials"? (See 11:1–3.)

_____

_____

See 11:9, 10, 29. Was Jephthah a true judge? How do you know?

_____

See 11:30–31. The word "whoever" in verse 31 is better translated "whatever creature." What was Jephthah's vow?

_____

_____

Why did he make this vow?

_____

What tragedy resulted from the vow in 11:32–40?

_____

_____

Look up and write out a definition for *shibboleth*.

_____

_____

What is the origin of the term *shibboleth* according to 12:1–6?

_____

_____

_____

12. Read about Samson (chapters 13—16). Who was the oppressor of Israel this time? _____

What were the miraculous events that accompanied Samson's birth in 13:2–25?

_____

_____

_____

Samson was to be a Nazirite. Go back to Numbers 6:1–8 and list the vows of Nazirite men. Keep these vows in mind as you read the story.

_____

_____

_____

_____

Read 14:1–20. Why did Samson's brief marriage to a Philistine woman end?

_____

_____

_____

See 14:6, 19. What happened when the Spirit of the Lord came upon Samson?

_____

See chapter 15. Why was Samson angry?

_____

_____

What acts of vengeance did he wreak upon the Philistines?

_____

_____

What feat does Samson perform in 16:1–3? (Gaza was a Philistine stronghold, forty miles from the town of Hebron.)

_____

What was the secret of Samson's strength? (See chap. 16.)

_____

How did Delilah determine this secret?

_____

_____

_____

How did Samson die? (See 16:23–31.)

_____

_____

_____

Discussion Questions

1. In what ways does Samson fit the role of a judge? How is he different from the other judges in the book?

2. Read the concluding verse of the book of Judges (21:25). Based on what you have read about this historical period, is this conclusion criticism or praise? Why?

3. The era of the judges has been called the Dark Ages of Israel. Do you agree or disagree? Give specific proofs to support your argument.

4. How does the book of Judges show us what leaders ought to be like? How does it show us what leaders ought *not* to be like?

CHAPTER 7

The Early Monarchy

INTRODUCTION

The period of the early monarchy in Israelite history is one of high drama told in matchless prose. We will look closely at the books of First and Second Samuel, but first we must examine the historical background, general content, and style of this literary masterpiece.

The Hebrews who settled in Canaan around 1200 B.C. were under the leadership of tribal or clan chieftains. Over the next two centuries, when the need arose, charismatic leaders were raised up by Yahweh. Their job was to rally a tribe or tribes for military enterprises, to deliver their tribe or tribes from foreign oppressors. The authors of the book of Judges systematized this history, making the tribal chieftains national military heroes, or judges. This was the era of the Tribal Confederacy, a loose league wherein the only link holding the people together was their faith in Yahweh. This link was tenuous at best; no political or military organization embraced the twelve tribes.

As the nomadic Hebrews became settled in an agrarian society, the need arose for greater political cohesion. The situation under the Philistines was desperate. Those territories which escaped the Philistine yoke suffered attacks from the Ammonites in the south and the Amalekites east of the Jordan River. It was this pressure from the outside that actually prompted Israel's political unity under a monarch. King David, once he had checked the Philistine threat, found himself in a favorable position for the expansion of the Israelite empire. Babylon, to the east, was weak after the demise of Hammurabi's regime, and it would remain so for another five hundred years. The Assyrians, to the north, had sunk into political obscurity after the reign of Tiglath Pileser I (c. 1100 B.C.), not to become a threat until the ninth century. To the west, Egypt and her control over Canaan waned after 1200 B.C. Egypt was to remain politically impotent for the next three centuries except for a brief revival during Solomon's reign.

Samuel, who marks the transition from the era of the Judges to the monarchy, stands like a giant straddling these two periods. Arising in Israel's dark hour and functioning as judge, priest, prophet, and kingmaker, Samuel was a pivotal figure. He anointed first Saul (c. 1020), then David (who reigned from 1000 to 961 B.C.), as kings over Israel. As you read of Samuel's career, note that two competing perspectives on the monarchy emerge. One historical source sees Israel's desire for a king as apostasy: Yahweh is king (a theocracy) and the monarchy is a rejection of Yahweh's rule. According to this source, an earthly dynasty makes Israel "like the other nations" in the worst possible sense. Another source looks favorably on the monarchy, seeing the king as God's "anointed" or God's chosen steward of Israel's political life. As you read, keep this question in mind: What are the potential *problems* with having a visible, earthly king, and what might the *advantages* be for Israel?

Both sources agree, however, that if Israel is to have a king, they can do no worse than Saul and no better than David. The historical narrative makes it clear that Saul was unfit for kingship. The Spirit of the Lord descended on him briefly; then it departed. Meanwhile David became all that Saul was not. The shepherd boy grew to be the beloved hero of Israel. While Saul was vengeful, David was magnanimous. While Saul wreaked havoc, David won hearts. It was with relief that Israel proclaimed him king after Saul's death. Second Samuel ends with David's empire stretching from Egypt to the Euphrates. Jerusalem, his new capital, was the symbol of centralized government and centralized worship. His was a stunning military and political achievement.

The books of First and Second Samuel, originally one long scroll, are written in a matchless style. Tension is maintained throughout: Who is to sit on the throne? Who will succeed him? Will the empire last? Realism characterizes the narrative. In frank recognition of the humanity of Israel's heroes, even David is not whitewashed. His impulsiveness, his ambition, and his cunning are portrayed with frank honesty. The book of Second Samuel in particular gives us firsthand historical writing and a vivid description of David's intrigues. You might ask as you read: What member of the royal court, who was obviously an eyewitness to the events, is the source for this history? The trustworthiness of the source and the masterful style in which the events are told make this history of the early monarchy some of the most remarkable reading in the Old Testament.

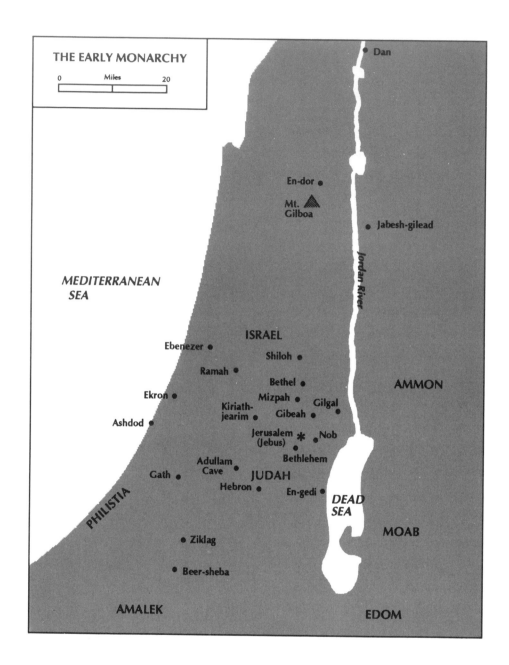

THE JUDGESHIP OF SAMUEL: 1 SAMUEL 1–15

Study Guide

1. Read 1 Samuel 1: the birth of Samuel. Hannah and her husband Elkanah went to worship annually at

_____, where the ark of the covenant was kept.

Eli and his two sons, _____ and _____, were priests there. What does 1:13 tell us about a problem with worshipers at this time?

_____

What was unusual about Samuel's birth to Hannah?

_____

_____

What other miraculous births have you read about in the Old Testament (e.g., in Genesis, Judges)?

_____

_____

In what ways does Hannah give her son to Yahweh?

_____

_____

2.   Read 2:12—36: the corruption of Eli's dynasty. What were the sins of Eli's sons?

_____

_____

_____

As Eli's sons became more corrupt, Samuel became more and more righteous. What verses in chapter 2 make this point?

_____

What prophecy does the "man of God" give to Eli?

_____

_____

3.   Read chapter 3: Samuel's call. Where did Samuel's call take place?

_____

What does this location tell you about young Samuel's responsibilities?

_____

What is Samuel's response to God's call?

_____

_____

_____

Read about one other call in the Old Testament. See either Moses in Exodus 3–4; Gideon in Judges 6:11—24; Jeremiah in Jeremiah 1; or Isaiah in Isaiah 6. Then compare your choice with Samuel's call by God in this account.

_____

_____

_____

How does 3:1 compare with 3:20—21? How do you account for this difference?

_____

_____

_____

4.   Read chapter 4: the capture of the ark and the fall of Eli's dynasty. The Philistines mustered up their forces, and the ark was carried into battle by the Hebrews, almost like a good luck charm and definitely as an afterthought. How does the prophecy of doom to Eli's house move into action in 4:5—11?

_____

_____

_____

What shocking news led to Eli's death?

_____

Eli's daughter-in-law died in childbirth. What was her son's name, and the meaning of this name?

_____

Look back over chapter 3. How would you characterize Eli the priest? Eli the father?

_____

_____

_____

5.   Read chapters 5 and 6: the Philistines play hot potato with the ark. What happened in the Philistine city of Ashdod when the ark was placed beside their idol Dagon?

_____

_____

To what Philistine city was the ark sent next? What happened there?

_____

Where was the ark sent next?

_____

The Philistine priests came up with a way to test the ark by putting it in a cart drawn by two milk cows, which were not accustomed to roads. What was the test, and its results?

_____

_____

The ark stayed in the town of Kiriath-jearim until David had it brought to Jerusalem.

6.   Read chapter 7: Samuel's judgeship. At Mizpah, Samuel conducted a purification ceremony (see 7:1—6).

What did the Israelites there agree to do?

_____

_____

What libation did Samuel use to symbolize their purification?

_____

_____

The Philistines made one last attack before they were finally subdued. See 7:7—11. With what "ammunition" did the judge Samuel wage war?

_____

_____

What did Samuel do at Ebenezer, the place of Israelite defeat in 5:1?

_____

_____

How does the author show us that the crisis has passed and that harmony characterizes Samuel's judgeship?

_____

_____

In the chapters that follow we have two different "sources," or viewpoints, which are intertwined in the text as it now stands. The narrative known as the Early Source favors Saul and the monarchy, while the Late Source sees Israel's request for a king as the greatest of Israel's sins, and Saul as a moral reprobate. This ambivalence toward the Israelite monarchy was never resolved, and the tension persists throughout the Old Testament. We will read from the Early Source first, then return to pick up the Late Source.

7.   Read 9:1—10:16: the Early Source on the Lord's choice of Saul. How is Saul characterized in 9:2? in 9:21?

_____

_____

What events bring Saul and Samuel together in chapter 9?

_____

_____

How did Samuel know that God had chosen Saul?

_____

_____

Samuel privately anoints Saul as prince over Israel in 10:1. Pouring holy oil on Saul's head symbolized the consecration of this man for God's service. Samuel called

him "prince," in Hebrew *nagid* (the Hebrew word for king is *melek*). *Nagid* literally means "the one who had been announced." In what ways was Saul changed after his meeting with Samuel?

_____

_____

8.   Read chapter 11: the Early Source on Saul's coronation. How did Saul rally the Israelite armies?

_____

_____

How did Saul prove himself as a military leader?

_____

_____

What happened at Gilgal?

_____

_____

9.   Read chapter 8: the Late Source on Israel's request for a king. For what reasons did the elders of Israel ask Samuel to appoint a king over Israel?

_____

_____

What was Yahweh's reaction to this request?

_____

_____

Keep in mind Samuel's description of the ways of a king when you read about Solomon, who ruled fifty years after Saul. As Samuel paints the picture of the monarchy, what details do you find most undesirable?

_____

_____

10.   Read 10:17—27: the Late Source on Saul's coronation. What is Samuel's opinion of the monarchy here?

_____

_____

How was Saul chosen to be king (*melek*)?

_____

_____

Where was Saul when the choice was made?

_____

11. Read 13:1—15: the sin of Saul. Some time has lapsed since 9:2, when Saul was described as a "handsome *young* man," for now we read of his son Jonathan, old enough to lead some Israelite forces against the Philistines. With the Israelites hiding in terror, Saul waited seven days as Samuel instructed him in 10:8; then he gave up. What was Saul's ritual sin, and Samuel's response when he finally arrived?

_____

_____

_____

_____

12. Read chapter 15: another account of Saul's rejection as king. Samuel instructed Saul to commit all the Amalekites to the *herem,* or to utter destruction. Why do you think Saul spared the Amalekite king Agag and the best of his livestock? Give verse citations to support your opinion.

_____

_____

What was Saul's problem, according to Samuel?

_____

_____

What action symbolized the rejection of Saul as king over Israel?

_____

We read in 15:35 that Samuel, the kingmaker, and Saul, the rejected king, never met again. Henceforth the narrative shifts our attention to a new star on the horizon: David.

Discussion Question

In what ways does the figure of Samuel mark a turning point in Israelite history?

DAVID BECOMES A HERO: I SAMUEL 16—20

Study Guide

1. Read 1 Samuel 16:1–13: the anointing of David. In what ways is this account similar to the anointing of Saul in 1 Samuel 9–10?

_____

_____

On what basis does Yahweh make the choice of David?

_____

List all the facts that describe David in this passage (place of birth, family, appearance, occupation).

_____

_____

2. Read 16:14–23: David meets King Saul. What happened to Saul when the Spirit of the Lord left him?

_____

How is David described in this passage?

_____

_____

What brought David to Saul's court?

_____

_____

3. Read 17:1–11 and 17:32–54: David and Goliath. Why did Goliath strike fear in the hearts of Saul and all Israel?

_____

_____

_____

How was Saul persuaded to let David go and fight Goliath?

_____

_____

_____

What was the substance of David's speech to Goliath?

_____

_____

What caused the Philistines to flee in terror?

_____

_____

4. Read 17:12–31 and 17:55–58: a second account of David's introduction to Saul. What brought David to the Israelite camp?

_____

_____

How does David meet Saul in this account?

_____

_____

5. Read 18:1–4: David and Jonathan. What marks the beginning of a deep friendship between David, the future king, and Jonathan, Saul's son and heir?

_____

_____

6. Read 18:5–9: the rivalry begins. How did the Israelite women show their support for David?

_____

_____

Did Saul suspect that David had been anointed? How do you know?

_____

_____

7. Read 18:10—19:17: the rivalry grows. What attempts did Saul make on David's life?

_____

_____

_____

Why did Saul offer his daughter Michal as David's bride?

_____

_____

How did Jonathan side with his friend David against Saul?

_____

_____

How did Michal side with her husband David against Saul?

_____

_____

Note that Saul's anger is now aimed not only at David, but at his own son and daughter.

8. Read chapter 20: the friendship between Jonathan and David grows. What test did the friends devise to determine whether Saul was angry with David?

_____

_____

What were the results of their experiment?

_____

_____

What is the irony of Saul's behavior in 20:30–33?

_____

_____

When the two friends met in the field face to face, what evidence do you find that a strong covenant existed between them?

_____

_____

Discussion Question

As David's destiny grew brighter, Saul's situation grew dimmer. How does the biblical text show that David's rise parallels Saul's decline?

DAVID, THE OUTLAW LEADER: I SAMUEL 21—31

Study Guide

1. Read 1 Samuel 21: David on the run. After the Philistines destroyed Shiloh, the Israelite priesthood moved to Nob, outside Jerusalem. How did David deceive the priest at Nob? (Note in verse 7 the presence of Doeg the Edomite, an unsavory character.)

How did David deceive the king of the Philistine city-state Gath?

2. Read chapter 22: David's band of merry men; Saul's atrocity at Nob. What folk joined David at the cave of Adullam?

Where did David send his parents for safekeeping?

How is Saul's paranoia evident in 22:6—9?

What bit of information did Doeg the Edomite give to Saul?

Who carried out Saul's orders at Nob? Why was Saul unable to command his Israelite soldiers to do his bidding?

Note that the high priest's son, Abiathar, escaped the massacre and joined up with David. The only remaining priest in Israel was thereafter under David's care, and Saul had destroyed this crucial link with Yahweh.

3. Read 23:19—24:22: David spares Saul's life. Saul pursued David from the wilderness of Ziph to En-gedi. In what sense did David have the advantage over Saul in the cave at En-gedi?

What did David's words to his soldiers, and later to Saul, say about his understanding of God's activity? Note especially 24:6 and 24:12.

How did Saul react to David's speech?

Note that Samuel's death is recorded in 25:1.

4. Read chapter 26: David spares Saul's life. In what ways did David have the advantage over Saul in this account?

How did David taunt Abner, Saul's general?

What was Saul's reaction when he learned that David had spared his life?

5. Read 27:1—28:2: David in the land of the Philistines. Why did David escape to the Philistine city of Gath?

How did he deceive the Philistine king, Achish? Note that the places mentioned in verse 8 were hostile to Israel; the places mentioned in verse 10 were friendly to Israel. See also 28:1—2.

6. Read chapter 28: Saul and the witch of Endor. Why did Saul consult the witch (or medium) at Endor?

Why did Saul disguise himself at their meeting?

The witch called up the "god" (Hebrew *elohim* or "spirit") of Samuel from the dead. The Hebrew word for the place of the departed is *Sheol*. *Sheol* is neither a heaven nor a hell; like the Greek concept of Hades it is simply a place of deep sleep for the dead. Like a person who is suddenly awakened, Samuel is angry at being "brought up" from *Sheol*. What tragedy did Samuel foretell?

_____

_____

_____

Why and how did the witch show great kindness to Saul after his meeting with Samuel?

_____

_____

7. Read chapter 29: David leaves the Philistines. Why was David rejected by the Philistine commanders?

_____

_____

How do his words to Achish, the Philistine king, compare with his words during his last visit with Saul (compare 26:18 and 29:8)?

_____

_____

This time David was unable to pass himself off as an ally to Achish. He and his men were not to take part in the Philistine attack on Saul's armies.

8. Read chapter 31: the death of Saul. In what ways was the Philistine attack an immense success for the enemy?

_____

_____

How did Saul die?

_____

In what ways did the armor bearer show his loyalty and love for Saul?

_____

_____

What is your reaction to Saul's death? Does it make you sorrowful or relieved? Was it a noble, kingly end? Or was it a just punishment?

_____

_____

_____

Skip to 2 Samuel 1:17–27 and read David's lament when he hears the news. How would you describe David's reaction to Saul's death?

_____

_____

DEBATE: WAS SAUL A TRAGIC HERO?

Class Project

The tragic hero, according to Aristotle, is the protagonist in a drama whose misfortune is brought about not by vice or depravity, but by some error or frailty in the protagonist's character. This tragic flaw (in Greek, *hamartia*) in the hero expresses itself either through a definite action, or through failure to perform a definite action. The tragic drama emphasizes the significance of a choice, or choices, made by the hero but dictated by his tragic flaw. The tragic hero faces his destiny, however unmerited, with courage and dignity.

1. The class as a group should decide what is meant by the term *tragic hero,* using the description above as a starting point and adding to it as the class sees fit.

2. The class should decide:

A. How much time is allowed for the preparation of the arguments.

B. How much time is allowed for the affirmative case(s), the negative case(s), and rebuttals. A suggested schedule for the debate is as follows:

Affirmative Speaker A	5 minutes
Negative Speaker A	5 minutes
Affirmative Speaker B	3 minutes
Negative Speaker B	3 minutes
Affirmative Rebuttal	2 minutes
Negative Rebuttal	2 minutes
(total time 20 minutes)	

C. Who will act as timekeeper.

D. Who will judge the debate, and the criteria this person should use in judging.

3. The class should be divided in half arbitrarily, with "Group A" taking the affirmative argument ("Saul *was* a tragic hero"), and "Group N" taking the negative argument ("Saul *was not* a tragic hero").

4. Preparation:

A. Each group should amass evidence for its case, using the book of First Samuel to prove all points.

B. Each group should decide on the speaker(s) they wish to present the arguments.

5. Conduct the debate.

DAVID CONSOLIDATES HIS KINGDOM: 2 SAMUEL 1–8

Study Guide

The characters in this section of the narrative are:

DAVID. King of Israel's Golden Age

ISHBOSHETH. Saul's remaining son

ABNER. Saul's cousin and commander-in-chief of his armies (both before and after Saul's death)

JOAB. David's nephew and commander-in-chief of his armies

MICHAL. Saul's daughter, married to David, taken from her by Saul and married to Paltiel, then given to David again

NATHAN. The prophet

1. Read 2 Samuel 1: David learns of Saul's death. An Amalekite came to David's camp with a story by which he hoped to gain favor with David. What was his story?

_____

_____

_____

How does his version compare with the record in 1 Samuel 31:1–6?

_____

_____

What was David's "reward," and why did he have it carried out?

_____

_____

Does 1:19–27 deserve to be called an "elegy," defined as a poem expressing sorrow or lamentation for the dead? Why or why not?

_____

_____

_____

2. Read 2:1—3:1: War breaks out between the house of Saul and the house of David. How does David secure his position in Hebron, the center for the tribe of Judah, in 2:1–7?

_____

_____

_____

How did Abner secure the position for Saul's son Ishbosheth (also known as Ishbaal) in the north? See 2:8–10.

_____

_____

What event brought about a blood feud between Abner and Joab?

_____

_____

_____

_____

3. Read chapter 3: the power struggle continues. Why did Abner become angry at his king Ishbosheth? (It was customary for ancient Near Eastern kings to keep concubines, or mistresses, in their courts. These concubines were regarded as royal property belonging *only* to the monarch. Now that Israel had a king, they fell heir to this practice.)

_____

_____

_____

What deal did Abner make with David? Who actually fulfilled David's request? See 3:12–21.

_____

_____

_____

What motives did Joab have for murdering Abner?

_____

_____

How did David make it known that it was not his will for Abner to die?

_____

_____

4. Read chapter 4: the murder of King Ishbosheth. How was Ishbosheth killed?

_____

_____

How do you explain David's reaction to Ishbosheth's death? In what ways does his reaction to the news remind you of David's behavior in 2 Samuel 1?

_____

_____

5. Read chapter 5: David's united kingdom. In this account, "Israel" refers to the northern tribes, once loyal to Saul, while "Judah" refers to the southern tribe of David. The center for Judah was Hebron. After David's capture of the Jebusite stronghold in Judah, he moved the royal household to Jebus and renamed it Zion or Jerusalem—"the city of David." In what ways does David consolidate his kingdom in chapter 5?

_____

_____

_____

6. Read chapter 6: the return of the ark. How did David show his enthusiasm when the ark of the covenant was brought into Jerusalem?

_____

_____

_____

Why did his wife Michal despise him? Note that not everyone loves King David!

_____

_____

7. Read chapter 7: the Davidic covenant. This chapter became central to the Jews' understanding of their subsequent history. The theologically important verses 4–17 are called "The Prophecy of Nathan." Therein we find the substance of the Davidic covenant, one of the four major covenants found in the Old Testament (the others are made with Abraham and with Moses, and are foretold by

the prophet Jeremiah). The entire passage depends on the use of the word "house."

To what does "house" refer in verses 1 and 2?

_____

What does "house" mean in verses 5, 6, 7, and 13?

_____

What does "house" mean in verses 11, 16, 25, and 26?

_____

Is the "kingdom" spoken of in 7:16 an earthly kingdom or an eternal one?

_____

Summarize your understanding of the Davidic covenant. To whom is it addressed? Is it conditional or unconditional? What are the terms or promises of the covenant? How long will it last?

_____

_____

_____

_____

8. Read chapter 8: David's military successes. What foreign nations did David subdue?

_____

How did David accumulate great wealth for his Israelite empire?

_____

_____

Discussion Question

In what ways was David's reign made secure politically? militarily? theologically?

DAVID'S DOMESTIC AND POLITICAL PREDICAMENTS: 2 SAMUEL 9—20

Study Guide

1. Read 2 Samuel 9: David and Mephibosheth. Who was Mephibosheth? (See also 5:4).

_____

How did David keep his covenant of friendship with Jonathan?

_____

2. Skip to chapter 11 and read the account of David and Bathsheba. While his bravest men—the "royal guard"—were engaged in a battle against the Ammonites, David stayed behind in Jerusalem. A king's bidding was nothing less than a command. In what way did David take advantage of Bathsheba?

_____

_____

In what ways did David try to solve the problem he created with Bathsheba?

_____

_____

_____

What does 11:26 tell you about Bathsheba?

_____

In what ways did Uriah's behavior contrast sharply with David's actions?

_____

_____

_____

Note that the sins of David are not whitewashed here. Realism instead of idealism typifies the narrator's account of David's reign.

3. Read chapter 12: Nathan's rebuke; further consequences of David's sins. Why does Nathan tell the parable of the ewe lamb in 12:1–6?

_____

_____

What punishments would David and his "house" suffer?

_____

Characterize David's reactions to the tragedy in 12:15–23.

_____

_____

Who was born to David and Bathsheba in 12:24?

_____

Chapters 13—18 tell the tragic events surrounding Absalom, David's favorite son. As you read, look for the complexity of motives and the dual nature of the crisis: it is both domestic and political.

4. Read chapter 13: Absalom leaves home. List the events leading up to Absalom's flight from the royal household.

_____

_____

_____

_____

5. Read chapter 14: an uneasy truce. After three long years, how did Joab persuade David to bring Absalom back to Jerusalem?

_____

_____

While he was in Jerusalem, Absalom was not admitted back into the royal household. David refused to see his son for two more years. How did Absalom use Joab to force a meeting with his father?

_____

_____

6. Read chapter 15: revolt! How does Absalom "steal the hearts" of the Israelites in 15:1–6?

_____

How did he initiate the revolt against David at Hebron?

_____

See 15:13–31. What did David do when he heard of the revolt?

_____

_____

Note that in 15:32–37 David planted a spy named Hushai in Absalom's retinue.

7. Read chapter 16: Absalom takes Jerusalem. While David was in flight from Jerusalem, he came across a man

from the house of Saul named Shimei. How did Shimei show his disaffection for David?

_____

_____

What was David's response to Shimei's behavior?

_____

How did Absalom fulfill Nathan's prophecy found in 12:10–11?

_____

_____

8. Read chapter 17: Absalom is deceived. What bad advice did David's spy Hushai give to Absalom?

_____

_____

Why did Absalom follow Hushai's advice?

_____

_____

9. Read chapter 18: the death of Absalom. As David's forces prepared for battle, what specific order did David give his three generals?

_____

How did Absalom die?

_____

_____

Why did the narrator record that a common soldier would not slay Absalom?

_____

_____

The revolt was crushed and two messengers rushed to David with the news. What does the account in 18:19–33 tell you about David's feelings for his son?

_____

_____

_____

10. Read chapter 19: David tries to restore unity and mend fences. Why does Joab rebuke David in 19:1–8?

_____

_____

Why do you think David appointed Amasa, Absalom's general, as commander over his army?

_____

_____

How did David deal with Shimei, the stone thrower in chapter 16?

_____

_____

Jonathan's son Mephibosheth had been accused of treason against David in 16:1–4. How did David deal with Mephibosheth and his accuser, Ziba?

_____

_____

Note that the antagonism between Israel (the northern tribes) and Judah (in the south) continues in 19:40–43.

11. Read chapter 20: yet another revolt. Sheba was a Benjaminite, as was Saul. Note his call to arms in verse 1. Who sided with Sheba in this revolt?

_____

_____

How did Joab regain command of David's army? See 20:4–13.

_____

_____

_____

How did Joab obtain Sheba's head?

_____

_____

_____

Note Adoram's job in verse 24:

_____

This concludes our reading of Second Samuel. Chapters 21–24, which we will skip, consist of historical fragments and hymns. These chapters form an appendix to the book, interrupting rather than concluding the narrative of David's reign.

Discussion Questions

1. What do the rebellions of chapters 15—20 imply about the union of Israel and Judah?

2. What is your opinion of David the husband? the father? the friend?

3. In what ways does the narrator show David's humanness? his faults and weaknesses?

4. Why do you suppose David became the "ideal king" in the minds of later Israelites? What part of the Abrahamic covenant is fulfilled by David?

CHAPTER 8

The Divided Kingdom and the Rise of Prophecy

SOLOMON *

The reign of Solomon is usually thought of as one of unparalleled magnificence. The [Old Testament] makes it clear, however, that there was a seamy side to this magnificence. At the very outset Solomon did away with his eldest brother, Adonijah, who had claimed the throne as his by right of birth. In addition Solomon executed two generals who had supported Adonijah, and banished a third. Thus he served notice on the kingdom that he intended to rule with an iron hand, and would brook no disaffection. Such an attitude was, of course, far from pleasing to the people. . . . But [the Hebrews] were helpless. Solomon, with the aid of the military organization which his father [David] had established, made himself an absolute autocrat. His ambition seems to have been to reveal himself a man of power, a great oriental emperor whose outward splendor was in a class with that of the despots of Egypt and Babylonia.

But outward splendor is expensive, and therefore Solomon's greatest concern had to be the getting of wealth. Now David had acquired wealth by conquering the peoples around him. He had pillaged the lands of the Philistines and Arameans and the like, and had used the spoils to beautify Jerusalem. But Solomon was not a warrior. Indeed, far from seeking to make further conquests, he even lost part of the territory which his father had secured. Edom in the south revolted almost as soon as Solomon ascended the throne. . . . And thereupon Moab, taking courage from Edom's action, likewise rebelled. Next Syria freed itself. A certain sheikh named Rezon, who had escaped the sword of David, now returned from the desert where he had long been hiding and raised the flag of revolt in Damascus. Solomon was powerless to stop him. . . .

Despite these revolts, Solomon still claimed to be suzerain over the whole of the empire his father had conquered. But, of course, he was unable to collect tribute save from the inhabitants of his own small kingdom. And this made the burden on [Israel] almost beyond bearing, for Solomon needed a tremendous amount of tribute to carry out his ambitious schemes.

. . . Solomon's [most] splendid—and expensive—project was the beautifying of Jerusalem in the center of the land. Here he wanted to erect a magnificent palace and temple to show the world how vast was his power and how deep his devotion to Yahweh. But no Israelite was capable of planning and erecting such structures, for none had seen any great palaces or temples. So Solomon had to call on his neighbors, the Phoenicians, for help. Phoenicia . . . was a narrow strip of coastland [on the Mediterranean Sea, to the northwest of Israel]. The Phoenicians had never once tried to invade the Hebrew kingdom, probably because they had never felt the need to spread inland. They had all the seven seas to roam. They were the great traders of the ancient world, and their galleys were to be seen in the ports of the furthest empires. Also they were the most noted industrial people of the time, and their dye-products, jewelry, silk, and glassware were to be found in all the great cities of the world.

It was natural, therefore, that Solomon should call on these neighbors for help. The Phoenicians knew all about architecture [but] more than that, they could also provide fine building material, for the forests of their Lebanon Mountains were thick with tall cedars. And the Phoenicians were delighted to dispose of both their knowledge and timber—for a price. So Solomon struck a bargain with Hiram, who was king of Tyre, one of Phoenicia's chief cities, and forthwith the building operations in Jerusalem began.

. . . Fortunately for Solomon, he was a brilliant organizer, and this alone made it possible for him to draw out of his little kingdom the great wealth he needed. Disregarding the old tribal divisions he substituted twelve federal districts, each with a governor in charge. These governors had to collect the produce for the Phoenician hirelings and also for Solomon and his court. The [Old Testament] tells us that each day the provisions for the royal court alone consisted of 330 bushels of fine flour, 660 bushels of meal, 30 oxen, 100 sheep, and an odd assortment of gazelles, roebucks, harts, and fat fowl. So much provender was needed because Solomon had a large family to feed. Not merely was there his standing army, his corps of servants, his counselors and secretaries to care for, but in addition he had his harem of a thou-

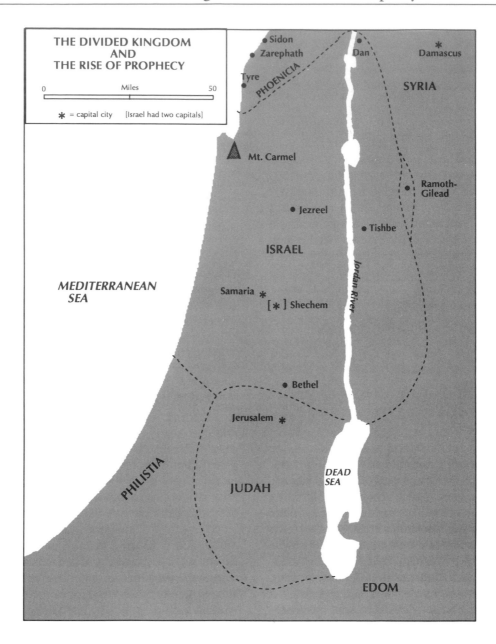

THE DIVIDED KINGDOM
AND
THE RISE OF PROPHECY

0   Miles   50

✳ = capital city   [Israel had two capitals]

sand wives and concubines. This harem, it must be real-ized, was more for show than comfort, for in those days a king's wealth was measured by the number of his wives. But whatever may have been the reason for this extensive harem, it was an expensive luxury.

And for all this immense entourage Solomon had to provide shelter as well as food. For his wives, some of whom were princesses from neighboring lands, he had to provide palaces, and for his army, which could now boast cavalry and chariots, he had to build garrisons and roads. All this required a vast number of workmen. . . . Accordingly Solomon had to resort to slavery. At first he drafted the non-Hebrew inhabitants of Israel into his labor gangs. He took what Canaanites, Amorites, Jebusites, Gibeonites and the like were still surviving in the land, and made them state slaves—precisely as his own ances-tors had been made state slaves by Pharaoh of Egypt two centuries earlier. But since there were not enough of these non-Hebrews for all the work Solomon planned, he ac-tually drafted Hebrews too. He forced his own people to supply 30,000 men to work as his serfs one month out of every three.

But it was impossible for Solomon to finance all his projects with revenues collected from his own realm, and he was forced after a while to take to trading. Situated as he was between two continents, he could very conveniently go in for commerce. He bought horses from the Egyptians in the south, and sold them to the Hittites in the north. And he levied a high tariff on all merchandise transported through his realm by foreign traders. Later he extended his activities and, with a fleet of merchant ships built for him by the Phoenicians, sent agents to distant lands to acquire gold and other precious commodities for him. . . .

And thus the Hebrews suddenly discovered the outside world. Until then they had remained an almost primitive folk, pasturing their flocks and tending their olive groves amid the remote hills alongside the Jordan. But now they became a cosmopolitan people, and the fame of their great king was spread far and wide. People came from all parts of the world to see the monarch. The queen of Sheba traveled with a train of attendants all the way from southwestern Arabia, about 1,500 miles away, to discover whether Solomon was really as wise as he was reputed to be.

But this sudden plunge into the vortex of civilization had dire consequences for Israel. The foreign princesses whom Solomon took into his harem brought with them their foreign gods and priests; and the Israelites ceased to worship [God] with perfect hearts. Moreover, the extravagance of Solomon was a great burden on the people, and some of them began to talk of ending the union of the tribes. Rebellion seethed in the masses, especially in the north, which was still not reconciled to serving a king who belonged to the south. Solomon's last years were not nearly so glorious as the first. He became lax in his religion and powerless among his people. And when at last he died, the whole structure his father had reared, and which he himself had tried to embellish, came tottering to the ground.

THE GLORY OF SOLOMON: I KINGS 1—10

Study Guide

1. Read 1 Kings 1: David on his deathbed; the struggle for succession. Who was Abishag?

_____

_____

David had not made it clear who was to succeed him as king. Primogeniture, wherein the eldest son has exclusive rights to the inheritance, is a system which had not yet been established. Two rival parties formed around David's two remaining sons (Amnon, Absalom, and Chileab were dead). List the supporters of each son.

Adonijah:

_____

_____

Solomon:

_____

_____

How did Nathan and Bathsheba scheme together on Solomon's behalf?

_____

_____

_____

What was the result of their scheme?

_____

_____

Adonijah, who had proclaimed himself king in 1:5–10, grabs hold of the horns of the altar in 1:50. By doing so, he was claiming sanctuary. Why did he fear for his life?

_____

What does Solomon's statement in 1:52 tell you about Adonijah's fate?

_____

2. Read chapter 2: David dies; a purge follows. What three men are eliminated in this chapter, and why?

_____

_____

3. Chapters 3 and 4: the wisdom of King Solomon. Read the famous prayer of Solomon in 3:5–15. What was his request and Yahweh's reply?

_____

_____

How does Solomon show wisdom in 3:16–28?

_____

_____

_____

Skip to 4:29–34 and read. What evidence is given here of Solomon's wisdom?

_____

_____

How does the picture of Solomon in the passages above compare with his conduct in chapters 1 and 2?

_____

_____

_____

4. Chapters 4 and 5: Solomon's administration. Keep this question in mind as you read: How did Solomon achieve the splendor of the Golden Age of Israel?

_____

What is Adoniram's task in 4:6? This is the same Adoram who was mentioned in David's court in 2 Samuel 10:24.

_____

See 4:7, 22–28. What were the tasks of the twelve district governors?

_____

_____

What deal did Solomon make with Hiram, king of the Phoenician city of Tyre? See 5:1–12.

_____

_____

See 5:13–18. Who served in the labor gangs, and what was their task?

_____

_____

5. Read chapter 6: the temple is built. What were the dimensions of the temple? (One cubit = 18 inches.)

_____

How was the temple decorated?

_____

_____

_____

What objects were placed inside the temple?

_____

_____

_____

_____

Draw (on a separate sheet of paper) an architect's plan for the temple based on the information found in chapter 6 and in 7:13–50.

See 6:37–38. How long did it take to build the temple?

_____

6. Chapters 8 and 9: Solomon's dedication of the temple. What sacred object was put in the temple in 8:1–11?

Solomon's prayer of dedication in 8:22–53 gives us much information about Israelite theology (their understanding of God) and Israelite anthropology (their understanding of humanity). What do you consider to be the major *theological* points in this prayer? (Note especially 8:27–30 and 8:41–43.)

_____

_____

_____

What do you consider to be the major *anthropological* points in this prayer? (Note especially 8:46).

_____

_____

_____

Yahweh responds to Solomon's prayer in 9:1–9. What conditions did Yahweh set forth ("If _____,"), and what would be the results if these conditions were not upheld ("then _____.")?

_____

7. Chapter 9: Solomon's methods of achieving his splendor. See 9:10–11. How did Solomon pay Hiram for the expensive building program in Jerusalem?

_____

Who were made state slaves by Solomon according to 9:15–22?

_____

How does 9:22 compare with 5:13?

_____

What was the purpose of Solomon's fleet in 9:26–28?

_____

8. Read chapter 10: the magnificence of Solomon's reign. What points are made by the account in 10:1–13 of Solomon's meeting with the queen of Sheba?

_____

_____

_____

List some indications of prosperity under Solomon in 10:14–29.

_____

_____

_____

_____

Discussion Questions

1. What hints can you find in this reading (1 Kings 1–10) that Solomon's glory might be short-lived?

2. Reread Deuteronomy 8:1–20. What would Moses have to say about the reign of Solomon? What specifically are the dangers of prosperity? Can you think of other dangers besides those mentioned here?

3. Reread 1 Samuel 8:10–18. How does this passage apply to the Golden Age of Israel under Solomon?

THE KINGDOM DIVIDES: 1 KINGS 11–14

Study Guide

1. Read 1 Kings 11:1–10. List the sins of Solomon and the reasons why Yahweh became angry with him.

_____

_____

Who got the blame for Solomon's evil?

_____

2. Read 11:11–13. What was to be the punishment for Solomon's sins?

_____

_____

3. What political adversaries harass Solomon in 11:14–23?

_____

_____

4. Read 11:26–28. Who was Jeroboam? What was his position in Solomon's court?

_____

5. Read 11:29–43. What prophecy did Ahijah give Jeroboam?

_____

_____

How did Solomon react when he heard of it?

_____

_____

6. Read 12:1–15. Solomon's son Rehoboam went to Shechem, the chief city in the north, to be confirmed as king after Solomon's death. Jeroboam returned from exile in Egypt and joined the assembly at Shechem. What was the assembly's request, and how did Rehoboam respond to this request?

_____

_____

_____

7. Read 12:16–24. Why did the northern tribes revolt and make Jeroboam their king?

_____

_____

What tribe was left to be ruled by Rehoboam?

_____

Why was civil war averted for the time being?

_____

8. Read 12:25–33. Jeroboam, ruling from Shechem, wished to keep the Israelites from going down south to Jerusalem, Rehoboam's capital city. Why?

_____

What measures did Jeroboam take to make the Jerusalem temple irrelevant in the north? List three.

_____

_____

What is theologically wrong with Jeroboam's statement in 12:28?

_____

_____

Would you describe Jeroboam's actions as syncretism or as apostasy? Defend your answer.

_____

_____

9. Read 13:1–10. What is the main point in the prophecy given by the "man of God from Judah"?

_____

_____

10. Read 14:1–20. Jeroboam sent his wife to see Ahijah, the same prophet who tore up his cloak in 11:30. Why?

_____

_____

Why did Ahijah turn against Jeroboam?

_____

_____

According to Ahijah, what doom would befall Jeroboam's house?

_____

_____

What doom would befall the Northern Kingdom of Israel?

_____

_____

11. Read 14:21–24. How does the writer make it clear that Rehoboam, the king of Judah, was no better than his rival Jeroboam in the north?

_____

_____

_____

THE KINGS OF ISRAEL AND JUDAH

Class Project

The division of the Hebrew kingdom, recorded in 1 Kings 12, is dated 922 B.C. The rest of the books of First and Second Kings gives us a brief outline of the reigns of the kings in the south (henceforth called Judah) and the kings in the north (henceforth called Israel). It is a tragic story of three and a half centuries of division. Despite repeated warnings from the prophets, the narrative records the fall of Israel to Assyria (in 2 Kings 17) and the fall of Judah to Babylonia (in 2 Kings 25).

In this exercise, you will skim the material found in First and Second Kings, looking for clues as to why the kingdoms crumbled. The historian gives us merely a skeletal outline; we will return to sections of this history and fill in the details later as we look at the books of the great prophets of the divided kingdom. The purpose of this exercise is to acquaint you with the historian's conviction: that Israel and Judah came to their ruin not by chance, but because of the faithlessness of their leaders and in spite of the warnings of their prophets.

As you read, look for the stereotyped summary of each monarch's reign. The formula used by the historian is simple. The kings of Judah are evaluated in comparison to David, the ideal king. The kings of Israel are compared to Jeroboam, the idolatrous leader of the secession who "did evil in the sight of God." Notice how the kings are evaluated by the historian. How many are considered righteous? How many fail miserably? It is little wonder

why the destruction of each kingdom occurred once you tally up the "grades" given their kings!

Of course the writer of Kings did not use our system of dating. Instead, each ruler's accession to the throne is dated in terms of his rival's reign. For example, in the eighteenth year of King Jeroboam (in Israel), Abijam began to reign over Judah (1 Kings 15:1). While the writer skillfully moves back and forth between the two kingdoms, the method is sometimes confusing. To make things more difficult, the Judean king Joash is also called Jehoash, and there are two Jehorams—one in Israel and one in Judah.

As you work through this exercise, do not use any other sources of information besides the Bible. Whether you work individually or as a group, follow the steps listed here.

1. Use these passages from the Bible:

Begin with 1 Kings 14:19 and skim through 16:34.
Omit 1 Kings 17:1–22:36 (the account of the prophet Elijah).
Skim 1 Kings 22:37–53.
Omit 2 Kings 1–7 (the account of the prophet Elisha) *except* 2 Kings 1:17–18 and 3:1–3.
Skim 2 Kings 8—25.

2. Make two parallel columns on a sheet of paper, one for Israel and one for Judah. Begin at the top with Jero-

boam in Israel and Rehoboam in Judah. Mark the date 922 B.C.

3. Now list the kings of Israel and the kings of Judah as you read through the passages given in Step 1. Make sure the columns correspond by lining up the name of the Judean monarch with that of his Israelite contemporary or contemporaries.

4. Next to each king's name, indicate the length of his reign and how he died (briefly, and if known).

THE RISE OF PROPHECY

Study Guide

Before the establishment of the monarchy, the Hebrew word *nabi* denoted two quite different vocations. Aaron was called the *nabi* of Moses, meaning that Aaron served as Moses' mouthpiece or spokesman. A *nabi* was also a member of a group of holy men who displayed ecstatic or trancelike behavior. Saul met up with a band of such folk who played tambourines, flutes, and lyres as a sort of musical accompaniment to their dances and frenzied activity. In the former sense, the *nabi* was one who spoke on behalf of another. In the latter sense, the *nabi* was one who might be called "possessed"—but possessed by the spirit of Yahweh.

Samuel, the last of the judges, was also called a *nabi*, and it is in Samuel that we get a glimpse of what the *nabi* was to become in the ninth and eighth centuries B.C.— the prophet of Yahweh. It was Samuel who "told the words of the LORD to the people." Like Nathan in the next generation (under David), Samuel had close relations with the monarch (Saul). Yet he stood over and against the king. He called the king and the people alike to account. His words to Saul thunder down through the generations: "Behold, to obey is better than to sacrifice" (1 Sam. 15:22). His task was to render the judgment of God in a time of great social and political change.

When the kingdom divided in 922 B.C., Jeroboam became ruler of Israel, or the Northern Kingdom. Turbulence and political chaos ensued for the next two hundred years, when Israel finally fell to the Assyrian Empire. Even when Israel appeared to be at peace, doom was always on the horizon. And it was in the North that prophecy took its shape. Elijah and Elisha were active there in the ninth century, and Amos and Hosea spoke there a century later. There seems to be a strong link between political disaster and prophetic activity. You might want to think of the reasons for this link as you read about the careers of Israel's prophets.

In order to understand the role played by the prophets during the time of the Divided Kingdom, study the account of Micaiah ben ["son of"] Imlah in 1 Kings 22. His story will provide us with a model for prophetic activity. Certain general statements about the prophet's role are

made below. Read through them, then turn to 1 Kings 22:1–40. Find citations from this account to support each point. Keep these points in mind as you read about Elijah and Elisha.

1. The prophet is characterized by a special call or obligation from Yahweh. One meaning of the Hebrew word for prophet, *nabi*, is "mouthpiece." The prophet acts as God's spokesman to Israel. _____

2. The prophet appears in threatening times. He sees trouble ahead and warns his audience. Crisis is the classical context of prophecy. _____

3. The prophet was not concerned with the *distant* future, but with the present and the immediate future, with the decisions made by the rulers and the people in their current crises. _____

4. The prophet is compelled to speak that which he has heard from the Lord. _____

5. The prophet's task is to provoke "the fear of the Lord." The prophet gives words of confrontation rather than consolation. _____

6. Prophetic oracles take a variety of forms:

A. Sometimes the prophetic utterance is straightforward: "Thus says the LORD. . . ."

_____

B. At times the prophecy takes the form of a vision.

_____

C. It was common for prophets to dramatize their messages, often using bizarre actions.

_____

7. It was common for ancient Near Eastern monarchs to have a guild of royal prophets attached to their courts. In contrast to the true *nabi*, these prophets worked for hire. They were often merely "yes men" to the king.

8. The true prophet is a solitary figure: typically unpopular, often alienated from the rest of society.

9. The prophet stands in an adversary relationship to the powers that be. As Samuel confronted Saul and Nathan confronted David, the prophet challenges the king with his words of judgment.

10. Prophets often suffered for the content of their message. Many believed that if the prophet were silenced, the doom he spoke of would not occur. Thus the prophet's very life was at stake.

11. The authenticity of the prophetic message was often difficult to determine. A true prophet is known only "after the fact," that is, after his words are proven true by the course of events.

THE ELIJAH CYCLE: I KINGS 17—19, 21

Study Guide

The story of Elijah begins abruptly in the book of First Kings. There is no introduction or transition to prepare us for his entrance on the stage of Israelite history. We move suddenly from the stereotyped schema of reigns in the Divided Kingdom to the Elijah cycle, which hits (as Elijah himself was wont to do) like a flash of lightning. Appearing without warning, the prophet confronts the Israelite king, Ahab.

1. Read 1 Kings 16:29–34: the introduction to the reign of Ahab in Israel. Ahab succeeded his father, Omri, to the Northern Kingdom throne in 869 B.C. Omri had moved the capital city from Shechem to Samaria. What structure did Ahab build in Samaria, and why?

_____

Ahab married a Sidonian (Phoenician) princess named.

_____

How does the historian evaluate the reign of Ahab?

_____

2. Read chapter 17: the beginning of Elijah's prophetic career. What words of disaster does Elijah give King Ahab in 17:1–7?

_____

What miracles does Elijah perform while living in the widow's house at Zarephath?

_____

_____

_____

See 17:24. What is the moral of these stories about Elijah?

_____

3. Read 18:1–16: the search for Elijah. Ahab sends Obadiah throughout the kingdom, seeking Elijah. What evidence can you find that Elijah's life was in danger?

_____

_____

What points does Obadiah make about Elijah's mysterious behavior in 18:11–12?

_____

See 18:4 and 18:19. Jezebel might easily be called a religious fanatic. In what ways did she try to replace the worship of Yahweh in Israel with her own religion?

_____

_____

4. Read 18:17–40: the contest on Mount Carmel. Ahab meets with Elijah in 18:17–19. What do these verses tell you about Ahab's opinion of the prophet?

_____

What was Elijah's assessment of Ahab's character?

_____

What is Elijah's proposition, or dare, to the people of Israel in 18:20–24?

_____

In their contest with Elijah, how do the prophets of Baal appeal to their god? List the details that show the distress of the Baal priests in 18:25–29.

_____

_____

Elijah was determined to make the Lord's demonstration of power both dramatic and indisputable. In what ways does he underscore the miracle of fire in 18:30–38?

_____

_____

_____

What was the point of the miracle, according to Elijah?

_____

What was the effect of the miracle on the Israelite people? (See 18:39–40.)

_____

5. Read 18:41–46: the drought in Israel comes to an end. There is no doubt that the events of chapter 18 mark the high point in Elijah's career. The triumphant prophet had shown the power of Yahweh to be victorious over the forces of Baal. What athletic feat did Elijah accomplish in his enthusiasm as the drought ended and the rains came? (Mount Carmel is seventeen miles from Jezreel, the site of Ahab's summer palace.)

_____

6. Read chapter 19: the flight of Elijah. Why did Elijah flee the Northern Kingdom?

_____

What evidence can you find that Elijah had plunged into the depths of despair?

_____

What do you think caused his depression?

_____

Where does Elijah end up in 19:8? Why is this site significant?

_____

Look closely at 19:9–12. How does God reveal himself to Elijah?

_____

Why might Elijah have been surprised at the form this revelation took?

_____

List the three things Elijah is commissioned to do in 19:15–16:

_____

Elijah himself accomplished only one of these tasks; the other two constituted a revolution fomented by Elisha, who actually carried them out. How does Elijah call his successor Elisha in 19:19–21?

_____

7. Skip to chapter 21 and read about Naboth's vineyard. What specific injustices do you find in this chapter?

_____

What does the episode reveal about Ahab's character?

_____

What does the episode reveal about Jezebel's character?

_____

What judgment did Elijah deliver to Ahab and his dynasty?

_____

How is Elijah's prophecy concerning Ahab fulfilled in 1 Kings 22:30–40? (The unidentified "king of Israel" in this account is Ahab.)

_____

How is Elijah's prophecy concerning Jezebel fulfilled in 2 Kings 9:30–37?

_____

Discussion Questions

1. Review the miracles Elijah performed through the power of the Lord. How did the people who witnessed these miracles respond to them? What was the relationship between Elijah's deeds (i.e., his miracles) and Elijah's words (i.e., his prayers and proclamations)?

2. What do you consider to be the distinctive characteristics of Elijah the *person*? of Elijah the *prophet*?

THE ELISHA CYCLE: 2 KINGS 1–10

Study Guide

1. Read 2 Kings 1: Elijah's career draws to a close. Ahaziah is a son of the Israelite king Ahab (now deceased) and his Phoenician wife Jezebel (still living). Baal-zebub is a deliberately satirical play on the word *Baal-zebul:* the former means "lord of the flies"; the latter means "baal the prince," and is one of the many names for this pagan god. Why did Elijah declare that Ahaziah would surely die?

_____

_____

2. Read chapter 2: the "translation" of Elijah. Why do you think Elisha refuses to leave his master's side in 2:1–8?

_____

_____

How does Elijah depart from this world?

_____

Later Jewish thought and writings develop the notion that because Elijah never actually died, he will come to earth again and prepare the way for the Messiah.

What proof do you find that Elisha saw the vision and is therefore qualified to succeed Elijah?

_____

See verses 8 and 14. How does Elisha demonstrate that he has inherited Elijah's power? What is meant when we say that someone has "assumed the mantle" of his or her predecessor?

_____

_____

One important difference between Elijah and Elisha is that Elisha worked with a group (the "sons of the prophets") while Elijah always traveled alone. After reading 2:23–24, would you say that Elisha is a lesser or a greater figure than Elijah? Why?

_____

_____

_____

3. Read chapter 4: Elisha's miraculous powers. Briefly describe the miracles performed by Elisha in

A. 4:1–7

_____

_____

B. 4:8–37

_____

_____

C. 4:42–44

_____

_____

4. Read chapter 5: Elisha and Naaman, commander of the Syrian army. Syria and Israel were constantly at war during the ninth century B.C. Nevertheless, the Syrian general Naaman came to visit Elisha. Why?

_____

_____

Why did Naaman at first resist Elisha's advice? What happened when he followed this advice?

_____

_____

What do we learn about the extent of God's power in 5:1 and 5:15?

_____

_____

In what picturesque way did Naaman try to keep hold of his miraculous experience on Israelite soil?

_____

What difficulty did Naaman, who had become a believer in Yahweh, foresee once he returned home and entered the temple of Rimmon, the Syrian god?

_____

_____

Gehazi, Elisha's servant, tried to capitalize on the offer made by Naaman in 5:15. What was Gehazi's sin? How did Elisha know of his wrongdoing? How was Gehazi punished?

_____

_____

_____

What does chapter 5 tell you about the power of the *nabi?* about the impact of Yahweh outside of Israel?

_____

_____

5. Read 8:7–15: Elisha launches a coup in Syria. Why did the Syrian king, Ben-hadad, send Hazael to Elisha?

_____

_____

Elisha was fulfilling God's commission to Elijah (see 1 Kings 19:15). A new king in Syria would punish Israel for its sins. What did Elisha *say* to Hazael? What did he *mean*?

_____

_____

How did Hazael carry out Elisha's prophecy?

_____

6. Read 9:1–37: Elisha brings about the end of Ahab's dynasty. Who was Jehu, and why did Elisha send one of the "sons of the prophets" to him?

_____

_____

What is significant about the place where King Joram's body was cast?

_____

How did Jezebel greet the new king Jehu?

_____

How did Jezebel meet her end?

_____

_____

7. Skim chapter 10: Jehu's purges. Who is massacred in 10:1–11?

_____

_____

What trick did Jehu devise in order to kill all the remaining worshipers of Baal in Israel? (See 10:18–27.)

_____

_____

Read 10:16 and 9:22. What was Jehu's rationale for his bloody purges?

_____

See 10:28–31. Jehu's dynasty in Israel lasted for another four generations, a long time in that politically unstable kingdom. Why do you think Jehu and his house enjoyed this success?

_____

_____

Elisha's death in 13:20 marks the end of the ninth-century prophets. Their attempts to purge Israel of Baal worship were unfortunately short-lived. They are best known for their deeds, rather than for their preachings. The eighth century was to produce a significantly different kind of *nabi*: prophets of the spoken oracle and the written word.

Discussion Question

Reviewing what you have read in First and Second Kings, what would you say are the most important points to remember about Elijah and Elisha in the history of Israel?

CHAPTER 9

Eighth-Century Prophets

SOME MISCONCEPTIONS ABOUT THE PROPHETS

Here is a list of some common misunderstandings concerning the role and the message of the Old Testament prophets. Can you think of other assumptions that should be challenged? Can you challenge the assumptions made in this list?

1. "The Minor prophets are not as important as the Major ones."

The adjectives "major" and "minor" have nothing to do with the significance of the prophet. They refer only to the length of the prophetic books. The Major prophets each took up one scroll; they are Isaiah, Jeremiah, and Ezekiel. The Minor prophets are twelve: Amos, Hosea, Micah, Joel, Jonah, Obadiah, Nahum, Habakkuk, Zephaniah, Haggai, Zechariah, and Malachi. These twelve were all written on one single scroll in Hebrew.

2. "There are two types of prophets: those who spoke, and those who wrote."

Elijah and Elisha, who lived a century before the great age of Hebrew prophecy, were indeed speaking prophets and not literary ones. But is doubtful that Amos, for instance, actually wrote the book by his name. The so-called writing prophets were first and foremost speaking prophets. Their messages were handed down by oral tradition and recorded by disciples.

3. "The Old Testament prophets were merely, or even mainly, social reformers."

Indeed, the prophets provided inspiration for latter-day social reformers. But while they were concerned with injustices, their dominant concern was this: the relationship of a people to their God.

4. "The prophets were mystics."

They were not solitary figures living *outside* the real world. Yes, they had powerful, supernatural experiences. But the prophets were very much *in* the world. Mystics tend to live apart; prophets lived in the very midst of society.

5. "The prophets believed in a heaven and a hell."

In common with all other Old Testament writers, the prophets recognized no real hope in immortality. They believed in no active or intelligent life after death. *Sheol* is not a hell; it is a place of deep sleep but not of awareness. The prophets' concern instead was that this brief life be spent in companionship with God, the giver of life.

6. "The prophets were primarily interested in the future."

First, the heart of prophecy is the relationship to Yahweh, not a crystal ball. Divination, soothsaying, and clairvoyance are all foreign to the Hebrew prophets. Second, when the future is predicted, it is always contingent on the present. Destiny is the consequence of an existing spiritual condition. The future is not set in stone but is conditioned by the *present*: the favorite tense of the prophets.

KEYS TO UNDERSTANDING PROPHETIC LITERATURE

In order to appreciate the prophet as an individual with a particular message, one must ask individual and particular questions of the book. All the questions below except the first can be answered by reading the prophetic book. This outline will be used for the study guides on all the eighth-century prophets: Amos, Hosea, Micah, and First Isaiah.

1. *Historical Context*. Who was the audience? (Southern Kingdom, Northern Kingdom, a particular king, priest, or ruler)

What was the time period? (dates, ruling king, approximate length of prophetic activity)

What was the political situation? (domestic affairs, foreign affairs, the current enemies and allies)

2. *Character Sketch*. What do we know about the prophet himself? What was his background? How do his past experiences affect his message? Was there a particular *call* by God?

3. *Forthtelling*. Forthtelling is the major concern of the prophetic oracles. It means "laying bare" the present, or uncovering the current status of the nation and the people. Forthtelling is concerned with *now*, not *later*. In his forthtelling, the prophet criticizes what he sees going on about him, namely:

A. religious corruption (perverted forms of worship, syncretism, apostasy)

B. ethical corruption (oppression of the poor or helpless, injustices, immorality, sins against humanity)

C. political corruption (kingly or governmental wrongs, foreign policies and alliance systems)

Note the prophet's use of simile, metaphor, and other poetic devices.

4. *Foretelling*. Here the concern is with the future. What will happen if the people don't change? What judgment does the prophet deliver? Is there an element of hope? Note that the future is conditioned by the present; it is rarely set in stone. Again, note the use of metaphor, as well as visions and symbolic actions.

5. *Summary*. Here you are asked to reflect on the primary emphasis of the prophet, and to memorize a key verse.

AMOS

Study Guide

1. *Historical Context*. Amos preached to the Northern Kingdom around 750 B.C., a time of peace and prosperity. Jeroboam II had brought to an end the threat from Syria to the north, and the Assyrian invasions of the ninth century had ceased because of that empire's internal squabbles. It looked like another "Golden Age" had come to Israel. All was quiet; or was it? Would the luxury and security persist?

2. *Character Sketch*. Read 1:1 and 7:10–15. How does Amos describe himself?

_____

_____

What significance do you attach to his hometown (Tekoa is in the southern kingdom of Judah) and to his occupations?

_____

_____

3. *Forthtelling*. Find citations in the book of Amos that apply to Israel's sins:
A. Religious corruptions

_____

B. Ethical corruptions

C. Political corruptions

_____

See 4:6–11. What signs from God has Israel ignored?

_____

_____

4. *Foretelling*. Summarize Yahweh's judgment in these passages:

3:13–15

_____

5:1–3

_____

9:1–4

_____

Read chapters 7 and 8; then give the meaning of the following visions:

A. locusts

_____

B. fire

_____

C. plumb line (first find out what a plumb line does for an architect or builder)

_____

D. the basket of ripe fruit

_____

Is there an element of hope for Israel's future? Read 3:12, 5:14—15, and 5:18—20 before making your decision.

_____

_____

5. *Summary.* What is the primary emphasis of Amos?

_____

Memory verse: Amos 5:24.

AMOS'S ORACLES

Read Amos 1—2 closely. Using the map below, note the order and geographical site for each of the eight oracles in these chapters. Picture the prophet addressing a crowd of Israelites. As he delivers these oracles, Amos circles the Northern Kingdom and blasts the surrounding peoples—enemies of Israel. But all the while he is slowly moving in on his real target, the Northern Kingdom. The final oracle (2:6—8) is powerful in and of itself, but imagine its effect on the crowd. They have heard Amos preach against their enemies, nodding their heads in agreement with him every step of the way. How do you think the crowd, in full accord with the prophet up to this point, reacted to the judgment of Amos 2:6—8?

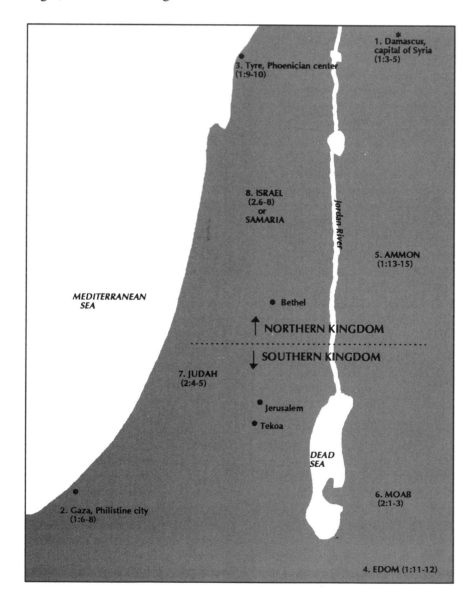

HOSEA

Study Guide

1. *Historical Context.* Hosea preached to the Northern Kingdom just after the time of Amos. He lived through the reign of Jeroboam II, then he saw four Israelite kings assassinated in fourteen years. This was a time of political anarchy in the Northern Kingdom, and Assyria hastened to take advantage of the chaos. In 721 B.C., the Assyrian Empire conquered the Northern Kingdom and deported its inhabitants—the famous Lost Tribes who dwindled into obscurity. Hosea's prophecy spans the years 740–700 B.C.

2. *Character Sketch.* Read chapters 1 and 3. Who was Gomer?

_____

What were Hosea's children named?

_____

Define *promiscuity.*

_____

What analogy is made between Israel and Gomer?

_____

3. *Forthtelling.* Find citations in the book of Hosea that describe these sins:

A. Religious corruption

_____

B. Ethical corruption

_____

C. Political corruption

_____

The prophet's message often takes the form of metaphor. Describe the metaphors used in the following passages:

A. 2:1–13

_____

B. 7:11–12

_____

C. 9:10 and 10:1–2

_____

D. 11:1–4

_____

4. *Foretelling.* Summarize Yahweh's judgment in 10:13–15.

_____

Summarize Yahweh's judgment in 11:5–7.

_____

See 5:15—6:2 and 3:4–5. What is the *value* of suffering?

_____

Now, read and write out one key verse from each passage:
A. 11:8–11

_____

B. 2:14–23

_____

C. chapter 14 (all)

_____

5. *Summary.* What is the primary emphasis of Hosea?

_____

Memory verse: Hosea 6:6.

GOMER*

She was always good company—a little heavy with the lipstick maybe, a little less than choosy about men and booze, a little loud, but great on a party and always good for a laugh. Then the prophet Hosea came along wearing a sandwich board that read "The End is at Hand" on one side and "Watch Out" on the other.

The first time he asked her to marry him, she thought he was kidding. The second time she knew he was serious but thought he was crazy. The third time she said yes. He wasn't exactly a swinger, but he had a kind face, and he was generous, and he wasn't all that [much] crazier than everybody else. Besides, any fool could see he loved her.

Give or take a little, she even loved him back for a while, and they had three children whom Hosea named with queer names like Not-pitied-for-God-will-no-longer-pity-Israel-now-that-it's-gone-to-the-dogs so that every time the roll was called at school, Hosea would be scoring a prophetic bullseye in absentia. But everybody could see the marriage wasn't going to last, and it didn't.

While Hosea was off hitting the sawdust trail, Gomer took to hitting as many night spots as she could squeeze into a night, and any resemblance between her next batch of children and Hosea was purely coincidental. It almost killed him, of course. Every time he raised a hand to her, he burst into tears. Every time she raised one to him, he was the one who ended up apologizing.

He tried locking her out of the house a few times when she wasn't in by five in the morning, but he always opened the door when she finally showed up and helped her to bed if she couldn't see straight enough to get there herself. Then one day she didn't show up at all.

He swore that this time he was through with her for keeps, but of course he wasn't. When he finally found her, she was lying passed out in a highly specialized establishment located above an adult bookstore, and he had to pay the management plenty to let her out of her contract. She'd lost her front teeth and picked up some scars you had to see to believe, but Hosea had her back again and that seemed to be all that mattered.

He changed his sandwich board to read "God is love" on one side and "There's no end to it" on the other, and when he stood on the street corner belting out

How can I give you up, O Ephraim!
How can I hand you over, O Israel!
For I am God and not man,
The Holy One in your midst.

(Hosea 11:8–9)

nobody can say how many converts he made, but one thing that's for sure is that, including Gomer's, there was seldom a dry eye in the house.

(Hosea 1—3, 11)

---

* Excerpted from Frederick Buechner, *Peculiar Treasures: A Biblical Who's Who,* Harper & Row, 1979.

THE LEGEND OF THE LOST TRIBES *

According to tradition the kingdom of Israel consisted of ten of the original twelve tribes, and with the great deportation in 722 B.C. the legend of the Lost Ten Tribes began. It was imagined that the Israelites marched out of their land in one great body and then lost themselves in a far romantic land. Many an explorer coming across some strange people in Central America, or Japan, or Abyssinia, has rushed forth to declare that the Lost Ten Tribes have been found again. But no explorer ever really found them, and no explorer ever will. Those tribes did not wander off together to any distant land, but simply dwindled out of existence right where they were set down

by the Assyrians. Many of the Israelites may have escaped from exile and joined the other two tribes of Hebrews; but quite clearly most of them simply merged with the races dwelling in Assyria and Media, and there faded out of history's picture.

A similar fate met all the other small nations of the ancient orient—all, that is, except Judah. Sargon did not go on from Samaria and seek to destroy Jerusalem too. Though he wiped out the northern kingdom, he spared Judah, for it had paid tribute faithfully. Thus the story of the Chosen People now becomes the story of Judah. That is why from here on we no longer refer to the Chosen People as Israelites, or Hebrews, but as Judeans, or Jews.

* Excerpted by permission of Macmillan Publishing Company from *The Graphic Bible* by Lewis Browne. Copyright 1982 by Lewis Browne, renewed 1985 by Rebecca Tarlow. Page 65.

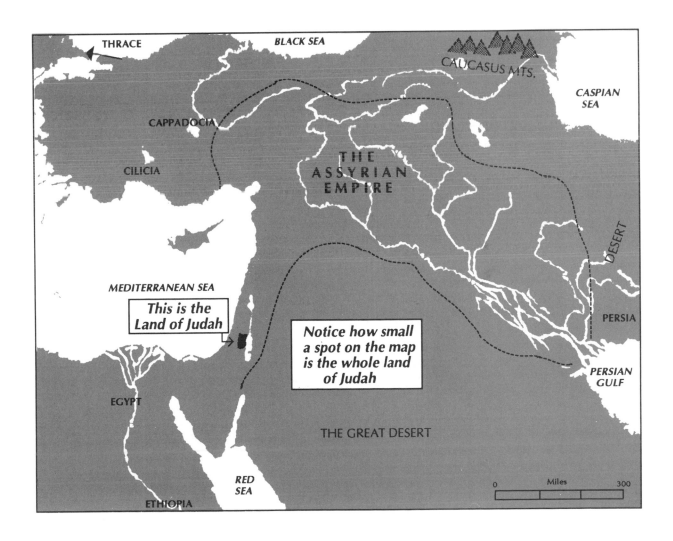

ISAIAH OF JERUSALEM (FIRST ISAIAH)

Study Guide

1. *Historical Context*. Isaiah preached to the Southern Kingdom of Judah between 740 and 687 B.C. These were eventful years: the Northern Kingdom fell to Assyria in 721 and Judah became a vassal state, paying tribute to Assyria each year thereafter. When King Hezekiah sought to free himself from this subjection in 705, retribution followed. The new Assyrian king, Sennacherib, invaded Judah in 701 and surrounded Jerusalem. The seige ended with a miraculous plague (possibly bubonic) which forced the Assyrian army to return home, leaving the countryside devastated but Jerusalem intact. Tribute was again required, but Judah was spared.

2. *Character Sketch*. We know little about Isaiah except that he was married to a prophetess and his children were given symbolic names. What were these names and their meanings? See 7:3 and 8:3.

_____

_____

See Isaiah's call to be a prophet in chapter 6. Where was Isaiah when he was called by God? What does this place tell you about his profession prior to the call?

_____

What signs and wonders accompanied the call?

_____

What was Isaiah's response? God's response?

_____

_____

_____

3. *Forthtelling*. What are the sins of Judah described in chapter 1?

_____

_____

_____

Read the love song of the vineyard in 5:1–7. What are the key features of the allegory? What is the interpretation of the allegory given by Isaiah?

_____

_____

_____

What was Isaiah's advice to King Ahaz of Judah in 7:1–9?

_____

What was Isaiah's opinion of King Hezekiah's alliance with Egypt in 30:1–5?

_____

_____

4. *Foretelling*. What is foretold in 2:1–4?

_____

_____

Define the word *remnant*. What will happen to the remnant according to:

A. 4:2–6

_____

B. 10:20–23

_____

C. 11:11–16

_____

_____

What is foretold in 7:13–17?

_____

_____

Describe the Messiah and his reign after reading 9:2–7 and 11:1–5.

_____

_____

_____

_____

Metaphors for the new age are found in 11:6–9. What do these images indicate about this future time?

_____

_____

5. *Summary*. What is the primary emphasis of Isaiah?

_____

Memory verse: Either Isaiah 2:4 or 30:15.

MICAH

Study Guide

1. *Historical Context*. Micah's prophetic career dates from around 720 to 700 B.C. He was a contemporary of Isaiah in the Southern Kingdom. The international situation in which he worked was the same as that which prompted Isaiah's oracles. Micah saw the fall of the Northern Kingdom to Assyria in 721 and the revolt of the vassal state Judah against Assyria in 705. When the fierce Assyrian king Sennacherib invaded Judah in 701, he stopped short of taking Jerusalem but destroyed the countryside. His warring armies burned a path home, probably through Micah's hometown of Moresheth.

2. *Character Sketch*. While Isaiah was a city man, probably a member of the Jerusalem upper class, Micah was a man from rural Judah (his hometown of Moresheth was twenty-five miles southwest of Jerusalem). What differences in emphasis might you expect between Isaiah's oracles and those of the peasant Micah?

3. *Forthtelling*. Jerusalem is the focal point of Micah's prophecy. Read 1:5, 8, 9 and tell why.

How are the landlords described in 2:1–2?

How are the preachers described in 2:6–11?

What graphic metaphor is used to describe Israel's rulers in 3:1–3?

Why are the court prophets condemned in 3:5–8?

Read 7:2–6 and list some of the ethical problems mentioned here.

4. *Foretelling*. A radical new prophecy is given in 3:9–12. What is the prophecy, and why is it so disturbing?

What image is used to describe Judah in 4:9, 10? Is there any hope to be found in these verses?

Micah prophesies that after the destruction of Judah, Yahweh will inaugurate a new age. Read the vision of the new age in 4:1–8; then list its characteristics.

What are the characteristics of the ruler described in 5:2–4? Is this a messianic oracle?

Read the "courtroom scene" of 6:1–8.

A. Define "plaintiff."

B. Define "defendant."

C. Yahweh, the plaintiff, speaks in verses 3–5. What case does Yahweh make against his people?

D. Israel speaks in verses 6–7. As the defendant, what does Israel say?

E. What is the definition of true religion given by Micah in 6:8?

5. *Summary*. What is the primary emphasis of Micah?

Memory verse: Micah 6:8.

Eighth-Century Prophets at a Glance

	AMOS	HOSEA	ISAIAH	MICAH
Historical Context	c. 750 B.C. King Jeroboam II in N. K. "Golden Age" of peace, prosperity	740–700 B.C. Political anarchy, destruction of the N. K., and after the fall	740–700 B.C. Days of Uzziah, Ahaz, and Hezekiah in S. K. Judah turns to foreign nations for help against Assyria	c. 720–700 B.C. During and after fall of N. K. Judah is vassal to Assyria
Biographical Sketch	Herdsman from Tekoa in S. K.; also a migrant worker Call—7:14–15 Preached in Bethel, N. K.	City-dweller in N. K.; preached to N. K. Married to Gomer; three children	Influential statesman and priest in Jerusalem; preached to S. K. Call—chapter 6	Prophet of the common people—peasant from Moresheth; preached to S. K.
Forthtelling	Primarily ethical Amos sees sacrificial ritual, but not social justice—5:21–24; 2:6–8 Stresses Israel's responsibility as a chosen people—3:1–2	Primarily religious: 4:11–13; 8:11–13; 13:1–2 Israel has *become* "the harlot"—5:3–4 Distinctive use of metaphor—harlot, 2:1–13; parent and child, 11:1–4 The anguish of God in 11:8–11	Primarily political: 30:1–2; 31:1–3; 7:1–4. Trust in God, not power politics or alliances As minstrel, Isaiah sings of the beloved and his vineyard—5:1–7 List of woes in 5:8–23	Primarily ethical: Jerusalem as the center of greed and exploitation—2:1–3; 3:1–3; leaders as butchers False confidence—3:11 Courtroom scene—6:1–8 *Heilsgeschichte*—6:4–5
Foretelling	War and exile for N. K. Visions of locusts, fire, plumb line, basket of fruit—7:1—8:2 *Yom Yahweh* (Day of the Lord): day of judgment and darkness, not light, for Israel—5:18–20	War and exile for N. K. followed by: Purification through suffering—5:15–6:2 New covenant or new "betrothal"—2:14–23; 14:1–8	3 R's: Retribution Remnant Restoration Destruction of Judah—6:11–13 Judean Remnant—10: 20–23 Messianic oracles and the new age—9:2–7; 11: 1–5; 2:2–4; 11:6–9; 35:1–10	Destruction of Jerusalem, the holy city of Zion—3:9–12 Exile, then redemption—4:10 Shepherd-king from Bethlehem—5:2–4 New age (like Isaiah)—4:1–8
Primary Emphasis and Memory Verse	The anger of God: God demands justice Amos 5:24	The anguish of God: God desires love Hosea 6:6	The holiness of God: God is trustworthy Isaiah 2:4 or 30:15	God looks after the outcasts, poor Micah 6:8

WRITING YOUR OWN PROPHECY

Assume that you are a modern day Amos or Hosea. In one or two pages, write a modern prophecy in the style of an eighth-century prophet.

Before you write, think about the following topics and questions. You should try to include information from each topic and answer the questions in your prophecy. Do not worry about treating the topics in order, and do not label the topics. Use your imagination.

I. Historical Context: Who is your audience? What is the setting (time, date, and place)?

II. Biographical Sketch: Are there any events or experiences in your past that affect your message? What were you doing before you were called to prophesy? What are your credentials as a prophet?

III. Forthtelling (the most important topic): What corruptions do you see? Are they religious, ethical, or political in nature? Describe the corruptions using various techniques such as metaphors, analogies, and dramatizations. Make sure your images are modern. Do not simply borrow them from the OT.

IV. Foretelling: What will the judgment be? Can you offer any hope to your audience? Feel free to dramatize this part of your message as well.

Begin your prophecy something like this:

The word came to _____ in the year _____

concerning the people of _____:

Skim over the messages and styles of the eighth-century prophets before you begin writing. Of particular help in your forthtelling section are the oracles in Amos

1–2 ("For three sins of _____ and for four, I will not turn back my wrath . . .").

CHAPTER 10

Prophets of the Fall of Judah and the Exile

THE THEOLOGY OF THE PROPHETS

A few questions about the theology of the prophets are addressed below. Do you have other questions? Do you wish to develop the answers further? After completing this chapter, you might wish to set aside some time for reflecting on these ideas.

• How does prophecy differ from philosophy?

The Greek schools of thought that developed across the Mediterranean during and after the time of Israel's great prophets were abstract rather than concrete. Unlike the Greek philosophers, the prophets did not consciously form a system of thinking. Prophecy is insightful rather than argumentative, intuitive rather than speculative. Greek philosophers grounded themselves in abstract reasoning or empirical observations. They addressed the intellect. The prophets, on the other hand, grounded themselves in the word of God and addressed the covenant relationship between Israel and Yahweh.

• What is the prophetic understanding of history?

While Israel's neighbors thought of time as a never-ending cycle, the prophets thought in terms of linear history. Canaanite religion is based on the rhythm of nature, the repetition of the seasons. In the cycle of spring, summer, winter, and fall, there is no real beginning and no real end. The prophets taught instead that history is "heading somewhere": God initiated it, and God is Lord of history. The fall of Judah and the subsequent exile of the Jews were not due to circumstance or accident. The hand of God is seen in these events. God reveals himself in historical action. He is in supreme control over events, and God will eventually establish God's sovereignty.

• How is sin defined?

Sin is defined according to the nature of the god one sins against. If the god demands ritual ceremony, one sins by witholding rituals from the god. If the god demands material sacrifice, one sins in witholding offerings from the god. But if God demands righteousness, as the prophets insist, then any form of cruelty, injustice, callousness, or even indifference toward another person is sin. Sin is a state of rebellion against God's nature. The actions themselves are merely the manifestations and consequences of a sinful heart. Sin itself is the condition of estrangement from God that leads to these acts.

• What is the nature of God?

God is living and personal; God is not an abstract force. The prophets are convinced of the immanence of God—of God's nearness to his people and his care for them. They use concrete metaphors to describe God's activity. Jeremiah speaks of the scribe who writes upon the heart, or the potter who works the clay. Second Isaiah speaks of the redeemer who pays a ransom to liberate the enslaved, or the man who has branded "ISRAEL" on the palm of his hand. Ezekiel speaks of the Good Shepherd. The prophets attribute human emotions to God: indignation, anger, impatience, jealousy, compassion, sorrow. Yet God is also the Holy One. The Holy One is utterly beyond that which can be known and experienced. The paradox of God's nature is this: God is both close to us and remote, both immanent and transcendant, both intimate and ultimately mysterious.

TIMELINE: JEREMIAH'S LIFE AND TIMES

721 The Northern Kingdom falls to Assyria and the Israelites are scattered abroad. Judah is made a vassal state to Assyria.

701 Siege of Judah by Sennacherib of Assyria. Jerusalem is miraculously spared, but the countryside is razed.

Judah is at peace, but under vassalage to Assyria, for another seventy-five years.

687–642 Reign of Manasseh, most evil and compromising of Judean kings. He mandates the infiltration of Assyrian practices in Yahwist worship.

c. 650 Jeremiah is born in Anatoth, outside the gates of Jerusalem, to a priestly family.

640–609 Reign of Josiah in Judah.

c. 626 Jeremiah is called to be a prophet.

621 Josiah's Reform. Josiah did more than any Judean king to abolish heathen practices, including the worship of Assyrian deities in the temple and human sacrifices. For a complete list of his reforms, see 2 Kings 23:1–25. His reforms were based on a scroll found while cleaning out the temple; this scroll contained parts of the book of Deuteronomy. This so-called Deuteronomic Reform, though at first encouraged by Jeremiah, proved to be hollow in the end. Jeremiah saw that it dealt merely with temple laws and not with the hearts of the people. The Reform was also a political expression of disgust with Judah's Assyrian master. Josiah took advantage of Assyrian weakness, asserted his independence, and annexed the former Northern Kingdom to Judah.

612 Nineveh, the capital of Assyria, is destroyed by Babylonia (called "Chaldea" in the biblical text). Henceforth Jeremiah is convinced that the Babylonian conquest of Judah is inevitable, not for political reasons, but because God will use Babylon to mete out his judgment on sinful Judah.

609 Pharaoh Necho of Egypt invades Judah in an effort to aid his ally, Assyria, and gain safe passage to Babylonia. Josiah is killed by the Egyptians at the Battle of Megiddo (see 2 Kings 23:29–30).

605–562 Reign of Nebuchadnezzar (also called Nebuchadrezzar) in Babylonia.

605 Pharaoh Necho sets Jehoiakim on the Judean throne. Jehoiakim abandons Josiah's Reform and reinstates foreign cults. The Babylonians rout Egypt; Necho's forces fall to Nebuchadnezzar at the Battle of Carchemish. Jeremiah predicts the destruction of the temple and declares that opposition to Babylon is rejection of Yahweh's will. Jehoiakim uses his famous pen knife to shred Jeremiah's prophetic scroll, then burns the scroll. Jeremiah and his secretary Baruch go into hiding. At this low point in his career, Jeremiah writes the Confessions.

602 Jehoiakim refuses to pay tribute to Nebuchadnezzar.

597 Nebuchadnezzar, after a four-year delay, finally takes his revenge on Judah. On his arrival in Judah, he finds Jehoiakim already dead. His young son Jehoiachin is taken into captivity along with the leadership of the land in the "first deportation." Nebuchadnezzar places Jehoiachin's uncle, Zedekiah, on the throne as a puppet king in Judah.

597–588 The reign of Zedekiah in Judah. The "new men" in positions of leadership in Jerusalem thought themselves preferred by Yahweh (why else were they spared the deportation of the old guard?) and the prophetic guild says "all is well." Jeremiah vehemently opposes this folly and advocates non-resistance to Babylonia.

588 Pharaoh Hophra ascends the throne in Egypt. Zedekiah, hoping for Egyptian support, breaks his treaty with Nebuchadnezzar. The war party in Jerusalem has Jeremiah imprisoned, thrown into a cistern, and finally placed under house arrest in the palace.

586 This time Nebuchadnezzar reacts with great speed. He invades Judah and destroys Jerusalem (including the temple). Zedekiah is blinded and taken in chains to Babylon. The last and final deportation of the Jews to Babylon occurs; they are resettled by the River Chebar. For the account of this siege and who is left behind in Judah, see 2 Kings 25:1–12 and Jeremiah 39:1–14. As Jerusalem falls, Jeremiah purchases the field at Anatoth. His entire message changes from oracles of doom to oracles of hope, return, and a new covenant. His last letters, written to the exiles in Babylon, are known as the "Book of Consolation" (Jer. 30–31).

577 (?) It appears (from chapter 44 of his book) that Jeremiah was carried off to Egypt by his countrymen. Tradition holds that he was stoned to death there by the angry Judean exiles.

JEREMIAH

Study Guide

1. *Historical Context.* See the Timeline. Jeremiah is the great prophet of doom (before the fall of Judah) and later the great prophet of hope (to the exiles in Babylon after the fall). Because his career spans so many years (c. 630–580) and such momentous events, and because the book is hopelessly out of chronological sequence, reading straight through is confusing. Refer to the Timeline as we skip through selections of the biblical text.

2. *Biographical Sketch.* We know more about Jeremiah than any other prophet. He is a complex and fascinating figure. Called on to condemn the country that he dearly loved, he suffered on behalf of Judah as a sort of prefiguration of the suffering that he knew Judah would endure. He terrified in order to save. He identified himself personally with the doom of the nation. At the same time he identified himself with Yahweh; the anguish and sorrow of God is mirrored in Jeremiah's own experience. In his oracles, he shifts from God's heartache to his own heart-

ache frequently. Like Hosea before him, Jeremiah was made to know the innermost feelings of God.

A. Read 1:4–10: the call of Jeremiah. What verse indicates that Jeremiah was reluctant to become a prophet?

_____

Jeremiah has a twofold mission. See verse 10; then give the steps in this mission.

_____

How does this call compare with that of Isaiah in Isaiah 6?

_____

_____

_____

B. Summarize the feelings of Jeremiah for his people as they are revealed in the following verses:

    1. 4:19–21

_____

    2. 8:18–9:1

_____

    3. 13:15–17

_____

_____

C. Read about Jeremiah's "treason" and subsequent suffering at the hands of his people. Jeremiah was convinced that the victory of Babylon over Judah and the destruction it would bring were the will of Yahweh. He saw in Nebuchadnezzar's conquest the one hope of reconstruction for his people. Note the reactions of those in authority to Jeremiah's "traitorous" advice.

    1. 20:1–2

_____

    2. 37:11–15

_____

_____

    3. 38:1–13

_____

_____

D. On the eve of the first deportation to Babylon and late in his career, Jeremiah was beset with doubt, despair, and loneliness. His "Confessions" are actually prayers in which Jeremiah pours out his misery and describes the horror of being a prophet of doom. The six Confessions are not given in any logical sequence textually, but it ap-

pears from 17:14–18 that Jeremiah finds, in the end, a deeper source of strength than human approval.

1. Read 11:18–12:4. The popular misconception of the day was that if the prophet were silenced, his prophecy could not come to pass. Thus we find the assassination plots against Jeremiah's life. Remember the twofold mission in 1:10. So far, Jeremiah had preached the first part of his mission, but not the second. Why then did he pray that his enemies be destroyed?

_____

Jeremiah raises the issue of theodicy in 12:1–4. Define *theodicy* using a good dictionary:

_____

_____

See 12:1. What are the pressing questions which theodicy must address?

_____

2. Read 15:15–18. How did Jeremiah describe the ostracism and rejection he had experienced as God's *nabi*?

_____

_____

3. Read 17:14–18. How did Jeremiah feel about the doom that he was compelled to prophesy?

_____

_____

What indication(s) do you find that Jeremiah still trusted in Yahweh?

_____

4. Read 18:18–23. Again, Jeremiah cries out for vindication against his enemies.

5. Read 20:7–12. Why does Jeremiah say that Yahweh has "deceived" him (literally, "taken him by force")?

_____

_____

What happens to Jeremiah when he tries to stop prophesying?

_____

_____

6. Read 20:14–18. Who and what are cursed in this Confession? Why?

_____

_____

_____

3. *Forthtelling*. No doubt Jeremiah studied the eighth-century prophets, particularly Hosea, after his call. He lashed out at social injustices, as Amos did, and false alliances, as did Isaiah. He pinpointed the areas of false confidence, as Micah did. The situation in Judah was little different from that of the Northern Kingdom before its fall to Assyria a century earlier.

A. Read and then describe the metaphors used in:

1. 2:1–3; 2:31–32; 3:1–2; 3:20

_____

_____

_____

2. 3:19; 4:22

_____

_____

What eighth-century prophet used these same images found in questions 1 and 2?

3. 2:20–25

_____

B. Read chapter 5. Note the vain search for one just and faithful person in Jerusalem. What corruptions are described in the following verses?

1. 5:1, 7–8, 26–28

_____

_____

2. 5:12–13, 30–31

_____

_____

C. What is Jeremiah's message to King Jehoiakim in 22:13–19?

_____

_____

D. What is his message to the prophetic guild (i.e., false prophets) in 23:9–22?

_____

_____

E. Jeremiah's temple sermon appears twice, in 7:1–15 and again in summary form in 26:1–6. What basic message does Jeremiah give in this sermon?

_____

_____

See 26:7–19. How do the people react immediately after the sermon was delivered?

_____

_____

Why was Jeremiah's life spared?

_____

F. Note that Jeremiah, like Hosea, reveals the suffering and anguish of God. We see God's humility, tenderness, and sadness. We see the pain caused to God by his chosen people. Describe the feelings found in the following verses:

1. 2:29–32

_____

2. 9:17–18

_____

3. 12:7

_____

4. 31:2–3

_____

4. *Foretelling*. Once again, remember the twofold mission. Before the fall of Judah, Jeremiah's message was one of destruction. After the fall, his message concerns rebuilding and renewal.

A. Jeremiah dramatizes the future. When a prophet acts out his prophecy, it is understood to have a doubled power. The spoken word plus the symbolic act together indicate that the future is set; there is no turning back. Give the symbolic acts and their meanings in:

1. 16:1–4

_____

_____

2. 19:1–2, 10–13

_____

_____

3. 27:1–15 and chapter 28

_____

_____

_____

_____

B. What is the fate of Jerusalem according to 7:33–34 and 9:10–11?

_____

_____

_____

C. Jeremiah's advice to the last king of Judah, Zedekiah, is found in 21:1–10 and 38:17–23. Summarize the advice.

_____

_____

_____

Why do you think his message was ignored?

_____

_____

D. The judgment of Judah involves suffering. Read 9:7 and 6:28–30. The images found here come from metallurgy. In the smelting process, fire is applied to the raw ore; liquid dross, or refuse, then rises to the top. The dross is skimmed off and the result is refined or pure metal. In these verses, who (or what) is the refiner's fire, and what is the result of the refining process?

_____

_____

E. Read about the destruction of Jerusalem in 39:1–14. What methods were used on the city? on its leaders? (Note that Jeremiah and the poorest citizens were left behind in Judah.)

_____

_____

_____

_____

Now let us turn from the messages of doom to the words of hope. At last, after the destruction, Jeremiah is allowed to complete the second part of his prophetic mission. The picture he paints of restoration and renewal is a powerful and poignant one. The exile is not the last word!

F. Read the story of the potter and the clay in 18:1–11. What points are made by this "living parable"?

_____

_____

_____

G. Read all of chapter 24. What metaphors are used here? What is the meaning of the vision?

_____

_____

_____

H. Read 32:1–15, another of Jeremiah's symbolic enactments. He purchased a plot of land in his hometown at the very time the walls of Jerusalem were being stormed by the Babylonians. What is the significance of this act?

_____

_____

_____

I. To the exiles in Babylon, Jeremiah sent messages from Judah, which are now known as the "Book of Consolation." Read the following selections from the "Book," noting what is foretold in:

1. 29:10–14

_____

_____

2. 30:18–22

_____

_____

3. 31:1–20

_____

_____

_____

J. Jeremiah's message of hope concerns the heart, the seat of life in Hebrew thought. What has happened to the hearts of the chosen people since the time of the covenant with Moses? See the following passages:

1. 7:22–26

_____

2. 9:12–13

_____

3. 9:25–26

_____

4. 11:6–8

_____

5. 4:4

_____

K. Read 31:31–34 and 32:36–41 in the "Book of Consolation." Herein we find a description of the new covenant. What promises does Yahweh make here? What are the features of the new covenant? Give citations to support your points.

5. *Summary.* What are the primary emphases of Jeremiah?

Memory verse: Either Jeremiah 31:31 or 31:33.

THE NEW COVENANT

Looking closely at Jeremiah 31:31–34 and 32:37–41, we find the features of the new covenant, the powerful message of hope that Jeremiah sent to the exiles in Babylon. Christians refer to these passages as "the gospel before the gospel." In the context of Hebrew history, what is the relationship between this new covenant and the old Mosaic covenant? What is "new" about the message found in the book of Jeremiah?

The new covenant is like the old Mosaic covenant in two respects. First, both covenants rest on the initiative and authority of Yahweh. It is God who sets the covenants in motion; it is God who sets the terms of the relationship with his people. Second, the goal of both covenants is the same: "I will be their God, and they will be my people" (Jer. 31:33; cf. Exod. 6:7). This as we have seen is the characteristic formula for God's choice of Israel. But the Mosaic covenant had failed. The history of Israel is the history of repeated violations of this covenant. What will God do in order to change the course of this history? How will the new covenant be a fulfillment of the old?

This new covenant will not be like "the covenant which they broke" (Jer. 31:32). It will not fail in its intent. While the Mosaic covenant was conditional, this new thing will be unconditional. While the old was transient and limited by Israel's response (or lack thereof) to God, the new will be eternal: "an everlasting covenant" (32:40). The old had the character of a legal agreement. The suzerain Yahweh sought to bind the vassal Israel to him through the keeping of the torah. The new has the character of a personal relationship: Ephraim [Israel] is "my darling child" (31:20). The new covenant is also new in extent. All, from the least to the greatest, will be open to the covenant promises. The covenant envisions a new community of God's people. "They shall all know me," Yahweh says in 31:34, without exception or distinction.

The key to understanding the new covenant is its message concerning the heart, the seat of life in Hebrew thinking. The heart of Israel has become calloused and indifferent since the Exodus. In Jeremiah 4:4 Yahweh calls on the Israelites to "circumcize yourselves to the LORD; remove the foreskin of your hearts." Their hearts need to be open to God—sensitized to God's goodness. Herein lies the failure of the Mosaic covenant. The people are unable to open their hearts up to God. So God will give them this new thing: "I will give them a heart to know that I am the LORD, and they shall be my people and I will be their God, for they shall return to me with their whole heart" (24:7).

The new covenant will bring about a change in the innermost self. Knowledge of God will be inward and personal, not written on tablets of stone (as in the Exodus) or in books (as in Deuteronomy). The goal of the covenant is the inner identification of the believer with God's will. Henceforth that which was merely external (i.e., the torah, the temple, the teachers) will become internal. The law will be written on the heart (31:33). The temple as God's dwelling place is not even mentioned, for God will dwell in the heart. Teachers will not be needed, for God will lead and direct people in the knowledge of the Lord (31:34). God will put the "fear" (worshipful attitude) in their hearts forever (32:9).

What God will do, and *why* God will do it, are very clear for Jeremiah. However it is not clear *how* or *when* the new covenant will occur. As for when, the only clue we are given is that "behold, the days are coming" (31:31); but the time is not specified. Sometime in the post-disaster future, God will redeem these people. God will gather them and bring them back, and make them dwell in safety (32:37).

As for how the new covenant will be enacted, we must remember the history of the old: the law was not kept, the prophets were ignored, and the people of God went into exile. Their suffering was immense, although the prophets make it clear that nothing less was deserved. But suffering is not the last word. Looking back to Hosea, whom Jeremiah surely studied, we have both a foreshadowing of the new covenant (see Hosea 2:16–23) and the means by which it will be brought about:

> I will return again to my place,
>   until they acknowledge their guilt and seek my face,
>   and in their distress they seek me, saying,

"Come, let us return to the LORD;
   for [the LORD] has torn, that [the LORD] may
    heal us;
[the LORD] has stricken, and . . . will bind us up."

(Hos. 5:15—6:1)

It is out of grief and distress that the movement toward God occurs. Or, in Jeremiah's terms, God puts the people through the "refiner's fire" of judgment (i.e., the Exile) and in their affliction they will turn to him, in readiness for the new covenant.

Last and most important, the new covenant will be brought about by the complete and total forgiveness of sin. In the climax of Jeremiah's prophecy, we see that the transformation of the chosen people rests on Yahweh's forgiveness: "I will forgive their iniquity, and I will remember their sin no more" (31:34). Forgiveness makes all things new. While the Mosaic covenant was based on Israel's obedience, the new covenant is based on the love and forgiveness of God.

In summary, this covenant is new, not in intent, but in form and in extent. Written on the heart, and open to all for eternity, it heralds the time when God "will rejoice in doing them good with all my heart and soul" (32:41).

AMONG THE EXILES

After the destruction of Jerusalem and the temple in 586 B.C., the inhabitants of Judah were divided into three groups. There were those left behind in Judah who were leaderless, helpless, and dispirited. There were those who fled to Egypt and lived in scattered settlements along the Nile. Then there were the Judeans who were deported by Nebuchadnezzar, roughly some 12,000 to 16,000 persons. Our focus shifts to this last group, the Judeans (henceforth called Jews) who were brought to Babylon and resettled along the banks of the Chebar canal.

The Chebar canal, which flowed eastward out of Babylon toward the shrine of Nippur, was a fertile region. It was also well situated for commerce. Many of the exiled Jews took to trading and commercial ventures as they waited for the time when Yahweh would bring them back to their promised land. While Nebuchadnezzar allowed them free rein in their business endeavors, and many grew rich, this was still a foreign land: magnificent, strange, and "unclean."

In an effort to separate themselves from their captors, the exiles reminded themselves of those practices which set them apart from the other nations and adhered to them with renewed fervor. Circumcision and Sabbath observances, strange to the Babylonians, became ways by which the Jews could maintain their identity in a foreign land. Having no temple, and therefore no proper place for sacrifices, they gathered instead in synagogues (or "assemblies") for prayer and study. In this small community, in an effort to make sense out of what had befallen the Jews, many of the oral traditions which had circulated independently in Israel for centuries were gathered together and written down on scrolls. The great anonymous "editors" of the exilic period were at work, taking what they knew to be true of Israel's history and setting it down for the future. What would become much of the Old Testament was now being read and studied. These texts would remind future generations of their origins and the meaning of God's covenant with Israel.

Thus the Jews did not go into exile feeling that their suffering was accidental. They learned instead that God was at work, forging a "remnant" into a people capable of understanding what had happened to them, and why. Meanwhile the prophets of the exilic period—Jeremiah, Second Isaiah, and Ezekiel—pointed the way to the future. And so the Jews survived. When the time came to return to the homeland, those who had learned from the past made their way back to Jerusalem, ready to rebuild the city and renew their covenant with Yahweh.

The psalms became important sources of strength and renewal during the Exile. No doubt psalms were at the heart of synagogue worship, taking the place of sacrifice as a means of affirming the covenant with Yahweh. A number of the psalms were probably composed during the Exile, and reading them can give us an idea of how this deported community felt. We see their nostalgia for their homeland and their distress as strangers in a strange land, as well as their desire for vengeance on their captors. We also see a new way of viewing the past forged out of the exilic experience, and a new way of viewing the future.

The following psalms were probably written during the Exile in Babylonia: Psalms 74; 79; 102; 137. Read them closely. As you read, take notes on what you understand to be the passions, complaints, hopes, and realizations which the exilic community experienced. Imagine yourself to be among the exiles in Babylon. Then write a "letter" to a relative in a Jewish community in Egypt. Explain to this relative how you feel about Jerusalem, the Exile, and God.

SECOND ISAIAH

Study Guide

1. *Historical Context.* King Nebuchadnezzar had made Babylon the greatest power in the Near East, but his empire rested on shaky foundations. After he died in 562 B.C., three kings reigned in a space of six years. Nabonidus, who began his rule in 556, was destined to be the last of the Babylonian emperors. Caring little for the responsibilities of his office, he left his son Belshazzar in charge while he went off to Arabia to explore some ancient temple ruins.

Meanwhile, to the east, Persia was on the rise. King Cyrus, who had by 550 conquered his neighbors, the Medes, was in a position to threaten Babyonia. Cyrus preferred, however, to expand north and west through Asia Minor. When Cyrus finally attacked Babylonia, the irresponsible Nabonidus had lost the support of his priesthood and his populace. He was forced to flee, and Babylon opened its gates to Cyrus. The Babylonian Empire fell to Persia in 539 B.C.

Cyrus issued his famous Edict of Toleration (538 B.C.) whereby exiled peoples were allowed to return to their homes and the temples of native gods were restored. After almost fifty years of exile, the Jews who had been brought to Babylon as captives were freed; their captivity was over.

2. *Biographical Sketch.* We know almost nothing about the so-called Second Isaiah, the anonymous author of chapters 40–55 in the present book of Isaiah. His poetry is so masterful, and his message so grand, that the prophet himself is eclipsed by his writing. He lived among the Jewish exiles in Babylon and wrote around 540 B.C., on the eve of the fall of Babylon to King Cyrus of Persia. His audience, the diaspora (or "dispersed") Jews, felt that God had forsaken them in this strange land. Second Isaiah was called not to chasten these people, but to comfort them with the good news that God is about to end the Exile. While the task of earlier prophets was to threaten and shock, Second Isaiah's task was to strengthen and encourage. In perhaps the most eloquent poetic oracles in the Old Testament, he called on the Jews to sing and rejoice over what God was about to do. (Many scholars identify chapters 56–66 of this book as the work of yet another poet/prophet, "Third Isaiah." The material at the end of the present book of Isaiah appears to have been written *in* Jerusalem, *after* the Exile.)

3. *Consolation and Hope.*

A. Read 40:1–11. List the phrases that would be most likely to touch the hearts of the captive Jews.

_____

_____

B. Summarize the messages of comfort found in these passages:

1. 41:8–10

_____

2. 43:1–7

_____

3. 44:21–22

_____

C. List the phrases used to describe Isaiah's doctrine of God in 40:12–31. What kind of God does this prophet tell us about? How does Yahweh compare to other gods?

_____

_____

_____

_____

D. Central to Isaiah's theology is the understanding that God is the creator. Because God had shown the power of his word in the first creation of the universe, this same God could form a "new thing" out of the stuff of the universe. How would God show his power over nature in the new creation? See 41:17–20 and 51:2–3.

_____

_____

_____

E. Because God is lord of history, and because he had shown his mighty acts in the Exodus from Egypt, this same God could lead his people out of captivity yet a second time. List the phrases which describe the "new Exodus" which God was about to perform in:

1. 43:16–21

_____

_____

2. 49:8–13

_____

_____

3. 51:9–12

_____

_____

F. The prophet told the exiles that God would use Cyrus, king of Persia, to accomplish God's purpose for the Jews. What would Cyrus do? See 45:1–6, 45:11–13, 48:14–15.

_____

_____

_____

_____

4. *Foretelling.* As we have seen, the immediate future held the promise of return and restoration. But the return was not to be the last word; it was but a prelude to the grand design which God had formed for Israel and the world.

A. The Divine Oath. What is the goal of God's design in history? See:

1. 45:22–23

_____

2. 40:5

_____

3. 51:4–6

_____

B. Israel's Mission. In God's threefold promise to Abraham, God swore that by (or through) Abraham, all the families of the earth would be blessed (see Gen. 12:2; 22:18). Of all the Old Testament prophets, it is Second Isaiah who develops this promise, declaring Israel's mission to the whole world. Either write out or summarize the following verses:

1. 41:8–10

_____

2. 42:6–7

_____

3. 49:6

_____

C. The Everlasting Covenant. Read 54:7–10 and 55:3–5. What promises does Yahweh make here? How do these passages compare with Jeremiah's new covenant?

_____

_____

_____

D. The Suffering Servant Psalms. The prophet saw that Israel's great service to the world could be accomplished only at a great sacrifice. In the following passages, a "servant" is described who will suffer vicariously, or on behalf of others, in order to accomplish God's design in history. Read the following "Suffering Servant Psalms" and use the commentary on the next page to help you form a picture of this figure. Then write a paragraph describing the Servant, and the Servant's mission in the future.

1. 42:1–4
2. 49:1–6
3. 50:4–11
4. 52:13—53:12

_____

_____

_____

_____

_____

_____

_____

_____

_____

_____

5. *Summary.* What is the primary emphasis of Second Isaiah?

_____

Memory verse: Isaiah 42:6.

THE SUFFERING SERVANT PSALMS IN SECOND ISAIAH

There are four poems in Second Isaiah identified as the "Suffering Servant Psalms." These psalms are concerned with the future of Israel and of the world. Please note that the identity of the servant, or servants, is not clear. In some cases the servant appears to be the nation Israel, in other cases an individual or a prophetic figure.

Isaiah 42:1–4. The speaker is Yahweh, who presents the servant:

- chosen by God
- given "my Spirit"
- the servant brings forth truth and justice, but does so non-violently

Isaiah 49:1–6. The speaker is the servant, who tells of his call.

- the servant was called "from the womb," or predestined
- the servant functions as God's mouthpiece (like a *nabi*)
- God will be glorified through this servant
- the servant was formed "in order that Israel might not be cut off"
- the servant is given as a "light to the nations," to spread God's salvation throughout the earth

Isaiah 50:4–11. The speaker is the servant; this is a psalm of trust in God.

- the servant sustains the weary
- the servant is tormented and persecuted by the people

- the servant is able to endure all, because God is the servant's helper
- the servant is seen again as the obedient *nabi*

Isaiah 52:13—53:12. This is the key psalm, which is divided into three parts:

A. 52:13–15. The speaker is Yahweh.
- the servant will eventually prosper and be exalted
- first the servant is abused and marred beyond all human appearance

B. 53:1–10. The speaker is Israel or a congregation.
- "We esteemed him [not]. . . . We, like sheep, have gone astray."
- the servant was despised and rejected
- the servant has borne our griefs and suffered on our behalf
- the servant was wounded for our transgressions [an example of vicarious punishment]
- the servant is a scapegoat
- the servant suffers silently, then dies, innocent to the end

C. 53:11–12. The speaker is Yahweh.
- the servant makes the many righteous (vicariously)
- the servant shall be glorified and rewarded by God
- the servant shall see the fruits of his labors
- the servant makes intercession for the sinners

The servant, then, will act as the prophetic mediator for the world. Note that the psalms are not laments (for someone already dead) but foretellings, heralding the coming of the servant in the future.

EZEKIEL

Study Guide

1. *Historical Context.* In 597 B.C. Nebuchadnezzar, king of Babylon, invaded Jerusalem and forced the young king Jehoiachin to surrender. With this first deportation, the king and some 10,000 Jews were carried off into exile. Ezekiel was numbered among this group, the cream of Judean society. Ezekiel's home among the exiles was at Tel-Ábib, a town on the Chebar canal which met the Euphrates River southeast of Babylon.

Socially, the conditions for the exiled Jews were good. Many set up commercial ventures and prospered; they built houses and planted vineyards. Spiritually, however, the exiles felt hopeless and helpless. Many were frustrated. Others were fatalistic, feeling that God had forsaken them.

Meanwhile, back in Judah, the puppet king Zedekiah and his advisers counted on help from Egypt to overthrow Babylon. Along with this smoldering nationalism came a variety of social and spiritual corruptions: pagan worship, slavery, even human sacrifice. The Judeans had learned nothing from the first deportation.

From Ezekiel's call in 593 B.C. until the final destruction

of Judah in 586, he prophesied against the sinfulness of Jerusalem and foretold its fall. Then, when a messenger brought news to the exiles of the disaster of 586, Ezekiel abandoned the oracles of doom. He began to prophesy about the restoration of Judah and the new things God was about to do on behalf of his people.

2. *Biographical Sketch.* Ezekiel's career spans the troubled decades from 593 through 573 B.C. From 593 through 586, his message was addressed to the exiles in Babylon about conditions back in Judah. After 586, he spoke to the exiles about the restoration of homeland and temple.

Ezekiel was a younger contemporary of Jeremiah. While in Jerusalem, his was a prominent family; he was a member of the aristocratic priesthood and intimately associated with the temple. The Exile put an end to his priestly career. When he was thirty, the age at which he should have assumed the full responsibilities of priesthood, he was instead called to be a prophet to the exiled Jews.

He is a peculiar character: an eccentric. It was his bizarre behavior that drove home his message to the exiles. His prophetic career was typified by fantastic visions, fits of ecstasy, striking symbolic acts, and actual bodily suffering.

A. Read 1:1–3:3: the call of Ezekiel. On a separate sheet of paper, make a sketch of the throne chariot vision described in 1:4–28. What difficulties do you encounter as you try to translate the words into pictures?

_____

What is the Lord's commission to Ezekiel in 2:1–3:3?

_____

_____

_____

How does Ezekiel's call compare with that of Isaiah? with that of Jeremiah?

_____

_____

_____

B. God calls Ezekiel a "watchman" in 3:16–21. What is the prophet/pastor's new responsibility, according to this passage?

_____

_____

C. In a strange sequel to the admonition to speak out, Ezekiel is struck dumb in 3:22–26. Read this passage, then read 24:25–27 and 33:21–22. Under what condition(s) was the prophet made able to speak?

_____

_____

D. Instead of preaching, Ezekiel would symbolically dramatize his message.

1. Read chapters 4 and 5. Then list four symbolic acts which Ezekiel performed and the meaning of each one.

_____

_____

_____

_____

_____

_____

_____

2. Read 12:1–20. What is Ezekiel told to do here, and why?

_____

_____

_____

3. Read 24:15–24. The news of the fall of Jerusalem would provoke sorrow too deep for tears. In what striking way was Ezekiel made to know, and to dramatize, this inexpressible grief?

_____

_____

3. *Forthtelling.* The judgment of Judah is found in chapters 1–24 and dates from 593 to 586 B.C. (Chapters 25—32, which we will skip, are oracles against foreign nations.) Many of the themes are already familiar, so we will look at but a few examples of Ezekiel's forthtelling, noting the particular imagery and content of these passages.

A. Read chapter 8: the temple vision. Ezekiel was "transported" back to Jerusalem, where he found himself in a temple which had been profaned by various types of idolatry. The worship of Tammuz, for instance, is described in 8:14–15. Tammuz was a Mesopotamian fertility god, similar in function to the Canaanite Baal. Why did the seventy elders feel free to practice pagan rites (see 8:7–12)?

B. Read 16:1–34: the orphaned child. What images are used here to describe God's love for Jerusalem?

What religious corruptions are described?

What political corruptions are described?

List the particulars of Ezekiel's condemnation of the (1) princes, (2) priests, (3) prophets, and (4) populace.

C. Read 22:23–31: the indictment of the "bloody city." Why was the coming destruction of Jerusalem inevitable? (See 22:30–31.)

4. *Foretelling.* Ezekiel's messages concerning the future are found in chapters 33–48, which date after the fall of Jerusalem (from 586 to 573 B.C.).

A. Read chapter 18: new teaching on individual responsibility. In western societies, we tend to think of ourselves first as individuals, then as family members, finally as citizens of a nation. For the Israelite, the order was reversed. National identity took precedence; then tribal, clan, and family ties; and finally the single being. The individual never stood alone, isolated from his or her nation. Israelites thought in terms of a "corporate personality." Blessings and judgments fell on the society as a whole.

1. Read Ezekiel 18:2 and Exodus 34:6–7. What do these verses, taken together, suggest about the traditional Israelite view of punishment for sin?

2. What is the new standard of responsibility for sin put forth in the rest of Ezekiel 18?

3. In Babylon, the exiled Jews had no established monarchy, no temple, no geographically defined national identity. How does Ezekiel make it possible for the Jew to relate directly to God?

B. Read 37:1–14: the vision of the dry bones. Israel as a nation was dead after 586. If the Exile was a form of death, what is the meaning of this vision?

The Hebrew word *ruah* may be translated in a variety of ways: "breath," "wind," and "spirit" (see also Gen. 1:2 and 2:7). Substitute the word *ruah* for its English equivalents in this passage. Why is the word *ruah* the key to understanding this vision?

C. Read 37:15–28: the oracle of the two sticks. What is the meaning of this oracle?

D. Read chapter 34: the Good Shepherd. What are the characteristics of the bad shepherds (i.e., kings) of Israel's past in 34:1–8?

List the characteristics of God, the Good Shepherd, in 34:10–31. What verses do you find most powerful or important in this passage? Why?

E. Read 43:1–12: the glory of God will return to the temple. Chapters 40—48 constitute a large and detailed vision, a vision of the restoration of Israel and the new temple. God's hand takes Ezekiel out of Babylonia and transports him to the New Jerusalem, which the prophet describes vividly. Chapter 43 marks the real high point of this long section. What would be "new" about the new temple?

_____

_____

What would be "new" about Israel's response to God?

_____

_____

F. Read 36:22–36: the new Israel. Look closely at 36:24–28; then go to 11:17–20 and read. What was Ezekiel's message concerning the heart?

_____

_____

_____

What other promises does God make in 36:22–36?

_____

_____

Why do you think the Garden of Eden is mentioned in 36:35? What associations can you make between the garden in Genesis and the new Israel described in this passage?

_____

_____

_____

Why does God insist that all this will be done "for [God's] name's sake"?

_____

_____

5. *Summary.* What is the primary emphasis of Ezekiel?

_____

Memory verse: Either Ezekiel 18:20 or 36:26.

THE SHEPHERD AND THE SHEEP

The patriarchs of the Old Testament—Abraham, Isaac, and Jacob—were shepherds. Moses in the desert of Midian and David in the hills of Bethlehem were both shepherds by trade before they became rulers by the call of God. Even after they settled in the agrarian society of Canaan, many Hebrews depended on pastoral pursuits for their livelihood. The picture of sheep and shepherd was a familiar one in Old Testament times.

A problem exists for us when we wish to understand the powerful imagery of the shepherd and his sheep used in Ezekiel 34. The image is strange to us today. Perhaps we have had some exposure to the tasks that shepherding involves, but our knowledge is most likely to be limited to Western (rather than Palestinian) practices at best.

God is the shepherd of Israel in two psalms: the beautiful Psalm 23 and Psalm 80:1. Isaiah uses the imagery of the shepherd in 40:11. But the entire chapter of Ezekiel 34 in the Old Testament (and John 10 in the New Testament) develops the description of the shepherd's tasks and the

nature of the beasts that must be tended. Listed below are some facts about shepherding. Much of this information comes from *A Shepherd Looks at Psalm 23* and *A Shepherd Looks at the Good Shepherd and His Sheep*, both by W. Phillip Keller, who spent eight years as a sheep rancher in east Africa. The customs of herders there are similar to those of the Middle East (i.e., Palestine), differing little from the practices familiar to the Old Testament writers centuries earlier.

• In a seminomadic society, sheep were kept for wool rather than killed for food. Sheep were sheared twice a year for their wool, which was an important commodity in the Judean economy. The average lifespan of a sheep is twelve years. The longer the sheep lived, the greater profits it would bring.

• All sheep were highly valued but ewes especially so, for they produced one lamb annually. Ewes also produced milk, which was used to make butter and cheese. Occasionally male sheep were killed and eaten, but only on festal occasions or when honored guests were present. The offering of an unblemished lamb at the temple was indeed a sacrifice.

• Sheep are not known for their intelligence. Instead, they are notorious creatures of habit. If left to themselves they will stray, follow the same trails until they become ruts, or graze the same hills until they become deserts.

• Many animals have a means of establishing dominance or status within the group. Chickens have a pecking order, cattle a horning order, and sheep a butting order. The butting order results in a "top ram" and a "tail-ender." Thus rivalry, tension, and competition are characteristic of sheep. But in the presence of the shepherd, the arrogant ram will stop his search for a member of the herd to butt.

• Sheep follow the mob instinct. A panicky member of the flock can cause the whole flock to run wild. They are timid creatures who are easily scared: even a stray jackrabbit can cause a stampede. But the mere presence of the shepherd puts the flock at ease.

• The shepherd is known to the sheep by his voice. Eastern shepherds developed peculiar whistles and calls that were unintelligible to outsiders but understood by their sheep. Sheep will scatter in panic from a stranger's voice. While not otherwise known for their acumen, sheep do know the true shepherd's call.

• Sheep are easily "cast," and often for simple reasons: they have too much wool, or they are too fat. A cast sheep is a pathetic sight. Lying on its back, unable to get up, it flays frantically. Cast sheep are easy prey for coyotes, dogs, cougars, and mountain lions. If the shepherd does not arrive to set the sheep upright, the sheep will die.

• Sheep must be kept on the move. If left on the same ground too long, they will overgraze the pasture, eating the grass and gnawing at the roots. Itinerant shepherds set up a base camp and fan out from it in wide circles, like a clover leaf, covering new pastures each day and returning to the base camp at night.

• Sheep require large amounts of water daily. The shepherd must find watering holes for his sheep or else they will drink from polluted pot holes. Sheep can also get their daily water supply from heavy dew on the forage in the early morning. The good shepherd will rise early to get his flock out to graze.

• Many of the great sheep countries of the world, including Palestine, are semiarid areas. Dry climate is beneficial to sheep, but pasturelands are uncommon. Green pastures are the product of the shepherd's tremendous labor: rock clearing, deep plowing, special seeding, and irrigation.

• A sheep owner has a distinctive earmark which he cuts into one of the ears of his sheep. It is an indelible, lifelong mark of ownership.

• Because sheep were so valuable in Old Testament days, the flock had to be protected at night from thieves and robbers. The Palestinian shepherd would herd the sheep into a fold, which was simply a square marked off by stone walls on a hillside, through a gate, which was simply an opening in the stone enclosure. Then the shepherd would lie across the gateway to the fold at night, making himself a human door. And so he guarded the flock through the night.

• Finally, the shepherd's task was a dangerous one. He dealt with predators such as lions, wolves, and bears. To fend off wild animals, he carried a sling and a rod, which was simply a wooden club studded at the end with nails. He carried his staff or crook to catch and pull the sheep away from perilous places. With staff in hand, sling in waistband, and rod tied to the waist with a leather thong, he was the picture of one prepared for potential danger.

To summarize, the shepherd's task is characterized by constancy. As Ezekiel writes, the Good Shepherd will seek out the lost, bring back the strayed, bind up the crippled, and strengthen the weak (34:16). He must never cease in his task of caring for the sheep and of seeking them out (34:11). This is because his charges are like us. They are stiff-necked and stubborn. They are oblivious to danger. They are, simply put, unable to take care of themselves. As Isaiah wrote, "All we like sheep have gone astray; we have turned every one to [our] own way" (Isa. 53:6).

CHAPTER 11

Postexilic Literature

AFTER THE EXILE

The two formative events in Old Testament history are (1) the Exodus, culminating in the conquest of Canaan, and (2) the Exile and subsequent Restoration. With the Exodus, Moses led the Hebrews to freedom and forged a covenant community under the guidance and direction of God's laws. Over seven hundred years after the Exodus, the exiled Jews once again entered the promised land. Under the leadership of Ezra, they rededicated themselves to the Mosaic covenant. Like plaster poured into a mold, the features of orthodox Judaism, which we recognize today, were poured into the community back in Judah and became set with the Restoration.

The Exile was a watershed in Israelite history, in terms of both endings and beginnings. What ended with the Exile? The first temple, built by Solomon, was destroyed. The Davidic monarchy was finished. Six hundred years of political independence came to a close. The old history was set at rest; a new era would begin after the Exile. But idolatry and pagan worship, those symptoms of apostasy that were repeatedly condemned by the prophets, ceased as well. Never again would the Jews worship any god other than Yahweh.

What began with the Restoration? Cyrus allowed the Jews to return to their homeland in 538 B.C., but only 40,000 people were willing to make the dangerous trip back. This was less than a half of the population of Judah before the fall of Jerusalem in 586. Many Jews remained in foreign lands: Babylonia, Persia, Egypt. The fact that Jews now lived outside of Judah meant that the faith was no longer tied to a particular geographical site. Synagogues or meeting houses sprang up across the ancient Near East. They became places for diaspora ("dispersed") Jews to gather for worship, prayer, and the study of Scriptures.

Jews no longer depended on the spoken word for instruction after the Exile. Instead, the oral tradition was set down on scrolls, gradually becoming the written books of the Old Testament we have today. Writers and editors set down the important teachings, stories, and prophecies of the past. Judaism would henceforth be a "religion of the book." Rabbis arose as the teachers of the books, and scribes as interpreters and copyists. Because Aramaic gradually displaced Hebrew as the lingua franca, rabbis and scribes were vital as translators of the Hebrew

texts for Jews who could not otherwise read them. Eventually the rabbis would produce *Targums:* Aramaic paraphrases of the Scriptures.

The second temple was built. Sacrifices were offered once again. Priestly religion and cultic ceremony were renewed with great zeal. Indeed, it was the priests who presided over this new theocracy. The leadership of the community passed from the Davidic line of kings to the priestly line of Aaron. Henceforth the priests would lead the community while the scribes and rabbis would teach the legally correct religion and interpret the Torah.

The religious form that emerged after the Exile was not that of the New Covenant, but that of the old Mosaic covenant. With the Restoration, an even greater emphasis was placed on the proper, correct forms of ritual: fasts, dietary laws, unblemished sacrifices, tithes, circumcision, and observance of the Sabbath and such annual festivals as Passover, Yom Kippur, and Purim. The Jews who returned to Jerusalem felt that they must preserve their race and identity. In order to avoid assimilation, the laws and traditions were zealously kept.

You will study the reforms of Nehemiah, governor of Judah, and Ezra, the great priest and scribe of the Restoration. Nehemiah's brick wall around Jerusalem and Ezra's "hedge" of the Torah around the Jews were both ways to maintain Jewish identity. Membership in the covenant community would hereafter be determined by two things: (1) loyalty to the Torah, and (2) birth or Jewish descent. In order to keep the people pure, the Restoration leaders and prophets made a sharp distinction between what was "clean" and what was "unclean." Thus a line was drawn dividing Jew and Samaritan, and another dividing Jew and Gentile. The call to "separate yourselves" from foreigners meant the annulment of mixed marriages when Ezra came to Jerusalem, and no intermarriage in the future. One day, the new age would dawn. As Second Isaiah had written, Israel would serve as "a light to the nations" (Isa. 49:6). But for the time being, Jews were to be exclusive—set apart by birth and by adherence to the Torah.

It was probably during the Restoration that the "short stories" of the Old Testament were set down in writing: the books of Jonah, Ruth, and Esther. Jonah and Ruth, with their message that God's love extends to those outside the community of Israel, shine like little gems in the setting of this era. Esther, on the other hand, reflects the exclusivism seen in the books of Ezra-Nehemiah. How should the Jews relate to foreigners? Conflict and friction were historical realities, but the call for sympathy and congeniality is also heard among the voices of the post-exilic writers.

The last historical book of the Old Testament is Ezra-Nehemiah. Prophecy ceased in this same period after the careers of Haggai, Zechariah, and Malachi. Thus, Old Testament history and prophecy ended around 400 B.C. The spirit of Yahweh has left the prophets, and the period of the rabbis has begun.

To summarize, three major events occurred during the Restoration:

1. The temple was rebuilt.
2. The walls around Jerusalem were rebuilt.
3. The Mosaic covenant was renewed.

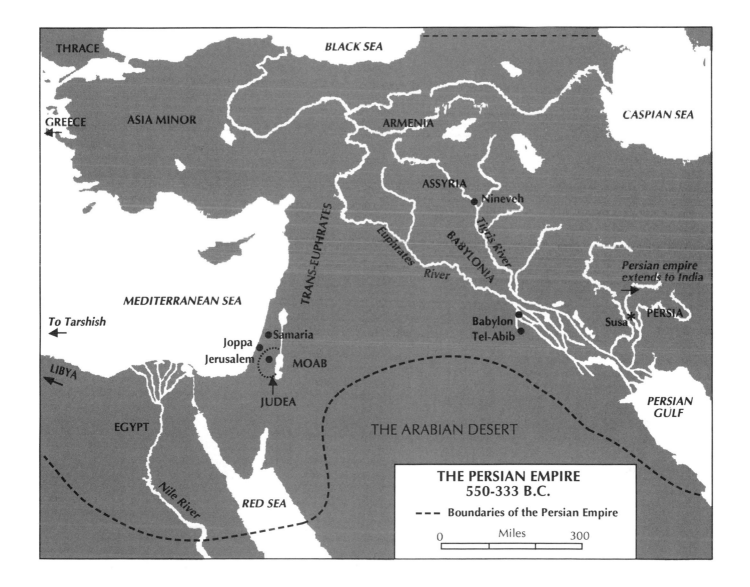

THE PERSIAN EMPIRE
550-333 B.C.

- - - Boundaries of the Persian Empire

0   Miles   300

Timeline
Postexilic Literature

PERIOD	OT SOURCES	EVENTS IN JERUSALEM	PERSIAN RULERS
586 B.C. to 500 B.C.	Ezra 1–6 Haggai and Zechariah 1—8	586: Fall of Jerusalem to Babylon; second and final deportation; diaspora Jews in Babylon 538: First wave of the return to Jerusalem begins (groups continue to drift back over the next century). Zerubbabel begins rebuilding the temple in Jerusalem. Samaritans thwart their efforts; rebuilding project halts. 520: The prophets Haggai and Zechariah call for the rebuilding of the temple to continue; work begins. 515: In March, the second temple is finished.	550–530: Cyrus II (the Great) 539: Fall of Babylonian Empire to Cyrus the Great 538: Cyrus the Great issues Edict of Toleration, allowing Jews to return home 530–522: Cambyses II 522–486: Darius I
500 B.C. to 400 b.c.	[Esther?] Nehemiah's Memoirs: Neh. 1—7 and Neh. 11—13 [Jonah and Ruth?] Malachi	444–432: Nehemiah hears of the plight of Jerusalem while in Persia. He is appointed governor of Judah; the walls around Jerusalem are rebuilt.	486–465: Xerxes I ("Ahasuerus" in the book of Esther) 465–423: Artaxerxes I [Age of Pericles in Athens] 423: Xerxes II 423–404: Darius II 404–358: Artaxerxes II
400 B.C. to 331 B.C.	The "I" narrative—Ezra 7:11—9:15 The "he" narrative—Ezra 10 and Neh. 8—10 The king's letter—Ezra 7:12–26 The lists— Ezra 8:1–14; Ezra 10:18–44; Neh. 10:1–27	398(?): Ezra, priest and scribe, institutes reforms of worship. END OF OT HISTORY, c. 400	331: Alexander the Great conquers the Persian Empire (defeat of Darius III); Age of Socrates, Plato, Aristotle; rise of Hellenism

EZRA-NEHEMIAH

Study Guide

In their present form, the books of Ezra and Nehemiah present a very confused, and therefore confusing, picture of the events of the Restoration. As the introduction to the book of Ezra in the *Oxford Annotated Bible* (Revised Standard Version) reads, the text "has been dislocated in transmission, some of the Nehemiah material appearing in Ezra, and Ezra material in Nehemiah, so that it no longer reads chronologically." No two scholars seem to agree on the exact rearrangement of the various passages that will present the events in a reasonably chronological order.

In preparing this Study Guide, read the passages in the order assigned. Consult the timeline on Postexilic Literature if you find yourself becoming confused.

1. Read Ezra 1: the Edict of Toleration. The Persian king who issued the edict or decree was _____. Summarize the Edict. What is the point of 1:2–3?

_____

2. Read Ezra 2–4: the return begins. The number of people returning to Jerusalem in this first wave after the

Edict was issued was _____(2:64). The leaders of
the return were _____and _____
(3:2). Their first act upon returning home was (3:1–3):

_____

See 3:10—4:5; 4:24. What happened next? Note that
"the enemies of Judah and Benjamin" were probably Sa-
maritans, that is, people from the Assyrian Empire who
had been transported to the area of the former Northern
Kingdom after its fall to Assyria in 721 B.C.

_____

_____

3. The rebuilding continues (520 B.C.). The names of
the prophets who instigated the rebuilding of the temple
were

_____ and _____
(see Ezra 5:1 and 6:14). Why do you suppose they were in
such a hurry to have the temple rebuilt?

_____

Read Ezra 5:3–17. What complaints did Tattenai, governor of Trans-Euphrates ("Beyond the River"), make about
the former exiles in his letter to King Darius?

_____

_____

Read Ezra 6:1–12. What did Darius decide should be
done?

_____

_____

Read Ezra 6:13–18. In March of 520 (the month of
Adar), the second temple was completed. How did the
Jews celebrate this event?

_____

4. Read Ezra 4:7–22: opposition to the rebuilding of
Jerusalem. Summarize the complaints made by the ene-
mies of the Jews to King Artaxerxes (probably Artaxerxes
I, who ruled Persia from 465–423 B.C.).

_____

_____

_____

What did the king decide should be done?

_____

_____

5. Read Nehemiah 1. What prompted Nehemiah to
leave Persia?

_____

_____

6. Read Nehemiah 2:1–8. How did King Artaxerxes
(probably the same king referred to in question 4) receive
Nehemiah's request?

_____

_____

7. Read the autobiographical account in Nehemiah
2:9–18. What is the point of verse 17?

_____

8. Read Nehemiah 2:19, 4:1–3, and 4:7–9. Sanballat
was governor of Samaria at this time. How did he treat
the Jews?

_____

_____

9. Read Nehemiah 4:15–23. The walls around Jerusalem were miraculously built in fifty-two days. What steps
did Nehemiah take to make sure that the walls were completed?

_____

_____

10. List three important reforms of Nehemiah's administration found in

A. Nehemiah 13:1–3

_____

B. Nehemiah 13:15–22

_____

C. Nehemiah 13:23–27

_____

Note: Ezra, whose arrival in Jerusalem is recorded in
Ezra 7:1–6, was probably sent by the Persian king Artaxerxes II, who ruled from 404 to 358 B.C. In other words,
Ezra probably came to Jerusalem around 400 B.C., fifty
years *after* Nehemiah.

11. Read Ezra 7:1–10. How is Ezra described?

_____

How does his office differ from the one Nehemiah held earlier?

_____

12. Read "the king's letter" in Ezra 7:11–26. What powers was Ezra given by King Artaxerxes II?

_____

_____

_____

13. Read Ezra 9: the report to Ezra and Ezra's prayer. What does Ezra say the people in Judah have done wrong?

_____

_____

Can you find the commandment cited in 9:11–12 in the

Pentateuch?_____

14. Read Ezra 10:1–5 and 10:44. What did the people decide to do?

_____

15. The Renewal of the Covenant. Read *Nehemiah* 8:1–12. [Nehemiah's name in verse 9 is a scribal insertion.] When all the people were gathered in Jerusalem, what did Ezra do?

_____

_____

_____

What do you think was the "book of the law of Moses" in 8:2?

_____

What did the Levites do? (Henceforth the priests who claimed descent from Aaron were in charge of sacrifices; the Levites who claimed Moses as an ancestor had the task described here.)

_____

How did the people react?

_____

Read about the people's confession of sin in Nehemiah 9:1–3. Who was excluded from this confession?

_____

Skim Ezra's prayer in Nehemiah 9:6–37. What are the key points of this prayer?

_____

_____

_____

How did the covenant renewal ceremony end in Nehemiah 9:38?

_____

Discussion Question

Why do you think Ezra is called the "father of Judaism"?

POSTEXILIC PROPHETS

Introduction and Study Guide

The postexilic prophets are Haggai, Zechariah, and Malachi. As you read excerpts from these prophets, you will notice a different style and a different set of concerns from that of the pre-exilic prophets. They were interested in the building of the second temple and the role of the priesthood. They prescribed the demands of the temple cultus. In reading the historical narrative of Ezra-Nehemiah and the prophets of this period, we note an increased emphasis on the proper forms of worship. The Jews are to be "clean" and "exclusive."

However, the special status of the Jews is not an end in itself. The prophets look forward with great anticipation to the new age, the time when the Jews will become the teachers and missionaries of God to the whole world. Their expectancy for the messianic age is so keen that the prophets predict its imminent coming, and even contemporary leaders are hastily declared "anointed ones" or kings of the new age. No king came, of course, but the postexilic prophets feverishly awaited the time when Yahweh would bring the old history to a close and inaugurate God's reign on earth.

In the postexilic prophetic writings we find a tension between exclusivism and universalism, a tension which Judaism never fully resolved.

We will examine these prophets as a group, noting characteristic themes of their literature. Thus the questions in the Study Guide are arranged by topics, and you will need to flip through the last three books of the Old Testament to find your answers.

1. The Legally Correct Religion: the prophets raise questions and provide answers on the proper ways to worship.

A. Read Haggai 2:11–14. What makes a person "unclean"?

_____

_____

What makes an offering "unclean"?

_____

_____

B. Read Malachi 1:6–14. What constitutes a proper sacrifice?

_____

_____

C. Read Malachi 3:7–10. What does the prophet say about tithes? (A tithe is a tenth of one's income.)

_____

_____

D. Read Zechariah 8:18–19. How often should the nation fast (that is, refrain from eating from sunrise to sunset)?

_____

_____

E. Read Malachi 2:4–7. What covenant is mentioned here?

_____

_____

What is the role of the priesthood?

_____

_____

F. Read Zechariah 7:8–10 and 8:16–17. Note that right worship must still be accompanied by right living.

2. Exclusivism. When Ezra came to Jerusalem, the Jews were told to separate themselves from the foreigners, or non-Jews, in their midst. This they did. Then the Jews took a vow not to marry foreign women in the future. Read Malachi 2:11–12. What does the prophet say about intermarriage?

_____

_____

Why do you think the postexilic leaders were so concerned about foreign wives?

_____

_____

3. Universalism and Hopes for the New Age.

A. The foundation of the second temple was laid when the first wave of exiles returned to Judah in 538 B.C., but political troubles delayed its completion. In 520, the prophets Haggai and Zechariah called for the rebuilding of the temple. Their reasons were theological. They believed the new temple would be the seat of theocracy and the manifestation of God's kingdom on earth.

1. According to Haggai 1:7–8, what will happen when the "house" (temple) is built?

_____

2. Read Haggai 2:4–9. How will the new temple ("the latter") compare with Solomon's temple ("the former")?

_____

3. Read Zechariah 8:9–13. In what ways will the Jews be blessed once their "hands [are] strong" and they build the temple?

_____

_____

B. The Picture of the New Jerusalem. Read the description in Zechariah 8:1–8. How would you characterize the new Jerusalem?

_____

_____

C. The Conversion of the Nations. What will happen on "the day" when God comes to dwell in the midst of Jerusalem? See Zechariah 2:1–12.

_____

_____

_____

Read Zechariah 8:20–23, a first-rate description of God's universality. What does this passage say about the role of Jerusalem and the Jews in God's plan for the nations of the world?

_____

_____

D. Hopes for the Messiah

1. Read Zechariah 6:9–13. Because he thought the

new age was imminent, pending completion of the second temple, Zechariah foretold the crowning of

_____ .

2 Read Haggai 2:6–7. *When* does the prophet feel that Yahweh will "shake the heavens and earth" to begin the new age?

_____

3. Read Haggai 2:20–23. Haggai foretold the crowning of _____. The "signet ring" mentioned here is God's symbol of authority for the king who will establish God's rule on earth!

[Note: The people mentioned in items 1 and 3, above, failed to fulfill these prophecies. Nevertheless, we see in these prophets their high hopes for the fulfillment of God's purposes in the immediate future.]

4. Read Malachi 3:1–5. What is the significance of God's "messenger"?

_____

_____

5. Read Malachi 3:16–17. What is the significance of the "book of remembrance"?

_____

When will it be used?

_____

6. Read the last verses of the Old Testament—Malachi 4:5–6. Because Elijah the prophet never died, but was "translated" to the heavens (2 Kings 2:11), the idea arose that he would return to this earth. On his return, he will act as the messenger, the one who will prepare the way for the Messiah.

Discussion Question or Creative Writing Assignment

Imagine that you are an elderly priest, or the wife of a priest, who has returned to Jerusalem after the Exile.

Young when the Exile began, you pause to reflect near the end of your life on the lessons you and your people have learned. Your years in Babylon and your experience of the Restoration have taught you much. You have seen the reforms of Ezra and Nehemiah (yes, this makes you incredibly old!). You have heard the messages of the prophets Haggai, Zechariah, and Malachi.

How has your understanding of God and the mission of your people changed over the years? How has your understanding of the requirements of your religion remained the same?

THE SHORT STORIES OF THE OLD TESTAMENT

The books of Ruth, Jonah, and Esther are "short stories," meaning simply that they may each be read in one sitting. They possess unity in plot, theme, character, and tone. They reveal character through a series of actions or under stress. The stories are tightly woven to give a unified effect.

In reading the short stories of the Old Testament we must make a distinction between the time when they were written and the times in which the stories were set. Ruth is set during the era of the Judges, Jonah during the eighth century when the Assyrian Empire was at its height, and Esther during the reign of the Persian king Xerxes I (486–465 B.C.). Thus the settings of these stories span some seven hundred years. Yet they were probably set down in writing during the Restoration. Remember that the major unresolved question of the Restoration was this: Does God's love really extend to all peoples? The authors, using stories set in faraway places and times, are grappling with this very issue. While the settings are remote, the effect of the short stories is either to question the exclusive policies of the Restoration or to demonstrate the necessity of exclusivism.

Are foreigners really worthy of God's love? The books of Ruth and Jonah answer this question with an emphatic *yes*. Ruth was a Moabite woman. One would expect little of her, as the Moabites were long-standing enemies of Israel. Yet Ruth is truly a heroine in her loyalty to her Jewish mother-in-law (and by extension, in her loyalty to Yahweh). The intermarriage of Ruth and Boaz, which would not have been allowed in Ezra's time, actually brought blessings on Israel. The effect of the story is to question the harsh decrees of the Restoration. A foreign woman can in fact be a friend to Israel, and teach the Jews much about true devotion.

In the book of Jonah, the author uses satire to show that a narrow-minded prophet (Jonah) cannot frustrate God's love for foreign peoples. Against his will, Jonah delivers a message that prompts repentance and faith in a foreign land. Again, an ancient national enemy—Assyria—shows finer qualities than one might expect. Even the Gentile sailors and the "great fish" are obedient to God's purposes, while the prophet of Israel is not. In this little book, we see that Yahweh is more merciful than those who proclaim themselves Yahweh's chosen people.

The author uses humor and wit to question the policy of exclusivism.

The book of Esther presents a different picture. It describes a dangerous time, a Gentile world that is hostile to Jews. The tone is nationalistic and defensive. Jews, particularly diaspora Jews, must constantly be on guard against their enemies. Persecution is a real threat. The story gives a nod of approval to the Restoration policies; without Nehemiah's wall around Jerusalem, the enemies of the Jews would wipe out the chosen people. If foreigners are expelled from the community, the community will survive. The Jews must protect their chosen status and remain exclusive, or else their enemies will prevail.

In summary, we see two divergent strands of thought expressed in these short stories. As either potential friends (in Ruth and Jonah) or foes (in Esther), foreigners presented an issue that provoked controversy and debate in the Restoration community. We see these two perspectives on the issue as we read the short stories of the Old Testament.

ESTHER

Study Guide

The book of Esther is set in Susa, capital of the Persian Empire, during the reign of Xerxes I (Ahasuerus). Many diaspora Jews lived in the capital and throughout the Persian Empire. The Persians' laissez-faire attitude toward their conquered subjects is a historical fact. The book of Esther demonstrates how fragile was the thread binding Persian overlords to their foreign populations, and how precarious was the existence of Jews in the diaspora.

Characters in the story are:

KING XERXES, or AHASUERUS—King of Persia, possessor of a large harem, and married to Queen Vashti as the story begins

ESTHER—a beautiful, orphaned Jew. Her Hebrew name was Hadassah.

MORDECAI—Esther's older cousin and guardian

HAMAN—grand vizier (prime minister) to King Xerxes, married to Zeresh

Before you read, define the following words:

1. pogrom

_____

2. irony

_____

1. Read chapters 1 and 2. What do you learn of Persian court life in these chapters?

_____

_____

Why is Esther brought into the royal court?

_____

_____

Did the king know her true identity?

_____

See 2:21–23. How did Mordecai save the king's life?

_____

2. Read chapter 3. Why does Haman hate Mordecai?

_____

_____

The *pur* is a lot or die which was cast to determine the right time for an event to take place. What plot does Haman make against the Jews in 3:7–15?

_____

_____

3. Read chapter 4. What risk must Queen Esther take if she is to enter the king's court?

_____

_____

4. Read chapter 5. How does Haman react to Esther's plans for a banquet?

_____

_____

How does he react to Mordecai's behavior in this chapter?

_____

_____

5. Read chapter 6. How is the king reminded of Mordecai's goodness?

_____

_____

What is the irony of Mordecai's triumph?

_____

_____

6. Read chapter 7. What role did Esther play in Haman's downfall?

_____

_____

_____

What is the irony of Haman's death?

_____

_____

7. How is the reversal made complete in 8:1–2?

_____

8. Read chapters 8 and 9. What actually happened on the day that Haman had set for the Jewish pogrom?

_____

_____

9. The holiday established in 9:19–28 is called *Purim,* named for the *pur* Haman cast to determine the day when the Jews would be destroyed. *Purim* is a feast celebrated on the fourteenth and fifteenth of Adar (around the first of March), commemorating the deliverance of the Jews from Haman's pogrom. *Purim* is a lively, even riotous, festival. For instance, the Talmud (the rabbinical commentary on the law) directs that the celebrators of *Purim* should drink so much wine that they cannot tell the difference between the shouts of "Cursed be Haman!" and "Blessed be Mordecai!" If you are not familiar with the feast of *Purim,* interview someone who is and jot down a few features of the celebration that interest you most.

_____

_____

_____

JONAH

Study Guide

The book of Jonah may be divided into two literary units. Chapters 1 and 2 are set on the high seas. Chapters 3 and 4 are set in Nineveh, the capital of Assyria. The units each begin, "The word of the LORD came to Jonah...." In both cases Jonah finds himself among foreign peoples: the Gentile sailors in the first unit, and the Ninevites in the second. In both cases Jonah is a successful missionary in spite of himself. Note the conversion of the sailors in 1:16 and the conversion of the Ninevites in 4:5–9. God's sovereignty over nature is another theme common to both units. God has command over the storm and the great fish in the first unit, and over the shade plant and the worm in the second.

Read the four chapters of this little book through once, then close your Bible and try to answer the questions. After you have finished, open your Bible and check your answers.

1. When Jonah was told to go to Nineveh the first time, he boarded a ship at Joppa, on the Palestinian coast, and headed to Tarshish. Tarshish (probably southern Spain) was the westernmost "end of the world" in ancient Near Eastern thinking. What conclusions can you draw from Jonah's attempted journey to Tarshish?

_____

_____

2. In what ways does the author cast a sympathetic light on the "heathen" sailors in chapter 1?

_____

_____

_____

3. What purpose does the "great fish" serve in the story?

_____

_____

4. What do we know about Nineveh from the story?

_____

What was the city like before Jonah came? afterward?

_____

5. After his arrival in Nineveh, Jonah became angry twice. What were the reasons for his anger?

_____

6. What lesson was the reluctant prophet taught by the shade plant?

_____

God : Nineveh :: Jonah : plant. In what sense is this analogy true?

_____

7. Compare Jonah the prophet with the other prophets you have studied. What was his attitude toward his mission? toward the Lord? toward foreigners?

_____

_____

What do you think was his attitude toward his own people?

_____

8. Scholars call this little book a didactive narrative, meaning that the author intended to teach his readers something from the story. What is the author's attitude toward Jonah? toward non-Jews?

_____

What point(s) do you think the author was trying to make?

_____

_____

RUTH

Study Guide

Read the story in one sitting, then answer these questions using the Bible.

1. What was Naomi's hometown?_____
What brought Naomi and her family to Moab, a country directly east of the Dead Sea?

_____

What was her relationship to Ruth and Orpah?

_____

2. Why did Naomi decide to return to her hometown?

_____

What problem did this present for Ruth and Orpah?

_____

3. Quote Ruth's famous words to Naomi in 1:16–17. Why is it significant that these words are placed on the lips of a Moabite (foreign) woman?

_____

_____

4. Back home, Naomi sent Ruth to glean among Boaz's fields. Read Leviticus 19:9–10 and give the provisions of the law that allowed Ruth to do this.

_____

5. How would you characterize Boaz?

_____

Why was he so attentive toward Ruth?

_____

What special provisions did Boaz make for Ruth?

_____

6. Why was Naomi so interested in Boaz's attention toward Ruth?

_____

7. What plan did Naomi devise for Ruth to carry out?

_____

_____

8. How did Boaz react when he found Ruth on the threshing floor?

_____

_____

9. According to ancient law, if a man died, his nearest kin was to marry the widow. This was known as a "levirate marriage." In a levirate marriage, any children born to the nearest kin and the deceased man's wife were to be raised as the deceased man's own, in order to perpetuate his name and inheritance. Thus, a portion of the nearest kin's inheritance had to be passed on to the children of this levirate marriage. Why did the nearest kin of Ruth's first husband refuse to undertake the levirate marriage?

_____

_____

10. See the genealogy of 4:18–22. Note also the genealogy of Jesus in Matthew 1:5–6 of the New Testament. Ruth and Boaz would become the great-grandparents of

_____. What is the significance of this genealogy for postexilic Jewish readers?

_____

_____

11. How would you characterize Ruth?

_____

_____

_____

What risks did she take in leaving Moab?

_____

What risks did she take in gleaning the fields (see 2:22)?

_____

What risks did she take in "proposing" to Boaz?

_____

Why did Naomi love her?

_____

_____

Why did Boaz love her?

_____

12. What is the significance of this beautiful little story?

_____

_____

_____

Why is Ruth's non-Jewish status central to understanding the story?

_____

_____

_____

WRITING CREATIVELY ABOUT THE OLD TESTAMENT

Essay Topic

All the biblical short stories are told from the third-person point of view. The narrator tells us about the characters by describing their actions; he or she develops character through dialogue and speech. Even though the point of view is called omniscient (knowing everything), we are not allowed to know the inner thoughts and feelings of the characters. There are no interior monologues or soliloquies. We are limited to the events of the exterior world.

How would the story be affected if it were told from the first-person point of view?

Pick a character who interests you from one of the short stories. Some suggestions are listed below. Next, pick a particular scene or episode from that story. Then, tell your character's story from his or her point of view, using the first person. Give plenty of details, emotional reactions, and insights *based on* the short story. Do not rewrite the entire story; limit yourself to a particular part you wish to develop. Your primary concern is your character; the plot is secondary.

Characters in the book of Ruth:

Naomi, Orpah, Ruth, Boaz, the nearest kinsman (unnamed)

Characters in the book of Esther:

Esther, Mordecai, Ahasuerus (Xerxes), Haman, Zeresh

Characters in the book of Jonah:

Jonah, one of the sailors, the captain of the ship, one of the Ninevites, the king of Nineveh (unnamed)

CHAPTER 12

Wisdom Literature and the Psalms

WISDOM LITERATURE—AN INTRODUCTION

Wisdom has its roots in ancient Near Eastern culture. Egyptian and Mesopotamian texts provide evidence that the wisdom movement was important in antiquity long before it came to Israel. In Egypt especially, wisdom was associated with the royal court. Wise men acted as tutors to the royal family and as advisers to pharaohs. These sages compiled texts on "how to succeed," cast in the form of a king's advice to the crown prince. The wisdom movement probably came into Israel during the reigns of David and Solomon. This "golden age" brought foreign nobles and their wise men to the court in Jerusalem. The form and to some extent the content of wisdom literature was then incorporated into Israelite tradition.

The book of Proverbs represents the collected wisdom of the Israelite sages. Solomon's wisdom was said to be so great that tradition ascribes the authorship of Proverbs entirely to him. Actually the book represents a complex, diverse development which took place over centuries. It was compiled in the postexilic period, probably around the time of Ezra (c. 400 B.C.). Proverbs represents the final stage of a tradition that goes back at least to the time of Solomon. It is the end product of a long process of accumulation. The writers probably include the "scribes" of David's reign, the "wise men" of Jeremiah's time, and the sages (who were neither priests nor prophets, but counselors) who flourished in the court setting of the Israelite monarchies. Thus Proverbs, compiled during the Restoration, rests on the traditions of early pre-exilic times.

The book of Proverbs is actually an anthology of aphorisms—a collection of Israelite wisdom literature cast in the form of short, pithy statements. *Mashal*, the Hebrew word for proverb, does not carry the authority of torah, or law. *Mashal* is a truth gained from general experience. The proverbs give advice, counsel, and direction. Most of the aphorisms in the book of Proverbs are short formulas for success and happiness. Like Israelite torah, proverbs make no distinction between secular and religious subject matter. In fact, there is little mention of the temple or the importance of sacrifice, prayer, and worship. Nor are the proverbs concerned with the "salvation history" (*Heilsgeschichte*) of Israel's past. The focus is on the individual rather than the community. In their concern with the various consequences of an individual's conduct, the tone of the proverbs is one of common sense, prudence, and caution. The proverbs instruct as to how to get the job of living done, typically in an expedient and pragmatic fashion.

Most of the proverbs are couplets or "two-liners." They fall into three major literary patterns. (1) In synonymous parallelism, the second line complements or repeats the meaning of the first (e.g., 17:20). (2) In contrasting or antithetic paralellism, we have a balanced pair of opposites in which the second line is contrasted with the first (e.g., 10:3). (3) In synthetic parallelism, the second line completes the thought that is begun in the first line (e.g., 19:20). The form of these two-line proverbs makes them easy to remember. It appears that the first line was spoken by a teacher or parent, whereupon the students or children would respond by completing the proverb with the second line. In this way, the proverbs were the textbooks for the instruction of Jewish youth in proper living.

"The fear of the LORD is the beginning of wisdom" (Prov. 9:10). This, the thesis of the book, may be paraphrased thus: An attitude of worship, awe, and reverence toward God is the basis, foundation, or heart of true wisdom. The Jews, unlike their Near Eastern neighbors, identified wisdom with the will and purpose of Yahweh. They taught that true wisdom comes only to the person who recognizes God's lordship. Thus, the believer is wise. This person is the one who best understands how to get along in this life. The opposite of wise is not ignorant, but foolish. The fool gropes in confusion and fails in life, regardless of how learned and skilled he or she might be.

There are two types of people in Proverbs: the wise and the foolish. The wise are identified by their righteousness and the fools by their wickedness. The fool turns away from the torah and sins, while the righteous person leads a just life and is blessed. The marks of the righteous life are success, well-being, and longevity. The fool, on the other hand, always comes to ruin. This teaching is similar to the Deuteronomic formula, which outlined the consequences of obedience and disobedience in a forceful appeal to the community of Israel. The nation was called to "choose this day whom you will serve," and the consequences of this choice took the form of national blessings or national curses. In the book of Proverbs, however, the Deuteronomic formula is applied to the life of the individual. Either retribution or material prosperity is meted out individually. "No ill befalls the righteous, but the wicked are filled with trouble" (12:21). God rewards the wise person and punishes the fool. The teachings assure us that rewards and punishments take place in this life.

For all its common-sense advice, wisdom as found in the book of Proverbs raises some real difficulties. The wise/righteous are not always materially blessed, whereas the foolish/wicked often prosper in this life. This problem is addressed in two great books compiled after the Exile: Job and Ecclesiastes. These books are composed of long discourses rather than maxims and aphorisms. In them, we see Job and Ecclesiastes wrestling with the perplexing problems of existence and of suffering. God does not always reward the righteous! Job and Ecclesiastes are critical of the easy optimism inherent in wisdom teaching.

Ecclesiastes' wisdom leaves him baffled; he cannot use reason to make sense of life. There are too many unanswered questions and too many paradoxes in human existence. But in the final analysis, the author nevertheless accepts life. His advice is to enjoy whatever good things God brings your way, until death brings oblivion.

Job suffers not only the material losses and physical pain from which the righteous should be exempt, but also the advice of his friends. The friends, who think themselves the sages of wisdom teaching, are clearly inadequate both as comforters and as theologians. It is God alone who can provide Job with meaning in this universe.

The book of Proverbs stands as a monument to Israel's wisdom in the search for order and basic values. Job and Ecclesiastes plumb the depths of faith when this order is taken away. In their views of God, the types of questions they raise, and their conclusions, Job and Ecclesiastes react (each in his own way) to the traditional teachings of wisdom. Remembering that Israel means "he who struggles with God," we see the fruits of this struggle in Proverbs, and the ongoing struggle in Ecclesiastes and Job.

PROVERBS

Study Guide

I.   Some topics are listed below, along with citations from the book of Proverbs. Read the citations, then give a brief paraphrase of the teaching for each topic.

   1.   on laziness: 6:6–11; 12:24, 27

_____

_____

   2.   on pridefulness: 11:2; 16:18; 27:1

_____

_____

   3.   on self-discipline: 14:17; 14:29; 16:32

_____

_____

   4.   on proper speech: 4:24; 11:12; 13:3

_____

_____

   5.   on lying: 12:22

_____

_____

   6.   on one's reputation: 22:1

_____

_____

   7.   on excessive drinking: 20:1; 23:19–21; 23:29–35

_____

_____

   8.   on raising children: 13:24; 22:6; 23:13

_____

_____

   9.   on poverty and wealth: 10:2, 4; 30:7–9

_____

_____

How successful are your paraphrases? What difficulties did you experience in formulating your paraphrases?

_____

_____

II.   Read chapters 24–29. Find a proverb for each of the following topics. Then give the citation (chapter and verse numbers) for each proverb.

1. on one's attitude toward and treatment of enemies:

_____

2. on neighbors:_____

3. on fools:_____

4. on rulers:_____

5. on the righteous:_____

III.   Read chapter 15. The Lord is mentioned nine times in this chapter. What view of the Lord do you get here?

_____

_____

What points are made about God?

_____

_____

_____

IV.   With a few exceptions, women are not sympathetically portrayed in the book of Proverbs. Contentious wives, strange or foreign women, and harlots are the topics of many proverbs, with the accompanying message to "steer clear" of such types. One notable exception is the description of the ideal wife found in 31:10–31. Read this passage; then describe the ways in which the ideal wife spends her day.

_____

_____

_____

What verses do you think would be most significant to ancient Near Eastern readers?

_____

_____

On a separate sheet write a poem or a short prose piece in which you describe the ideal husband (if you are female) or the ideal wife (if you are male) for today's world.

V.   Chapters 1–9 form the introductory section to the book of Proverbs. This unit was probably written last, perhaps as late as the third century B.C. Here we see the final stage in the development of Jewish thought on the role and value of wisdom. Wisdom is set in a religious context; the relationship between wisdom and Israel's theology is explored.

1.   Read 1:2–6. What is the purpose of the book of Proverbs?

_____

_____

2.   Read 1:7 and 9:10. What is the relationship between the worship of God and wisdom?

_____

3.   Read 3:13–18. How is wisdom personified here?

_____

What does she give to those who embrace her?

_____

_____

4.   Read 8:1–36. How is wisdom personified in this passage?

_____

What are her qualities?

_____

When was she created?

_____

What was her role in the creation of the world? (See also 3:19–20.)

_____

What is the basic message of 8:34–36?

_____

_____

Discussion Question

What was the value of the book of Proverbs for ancient readers?

What is the value of the book of Proverbs for contemporary readers?

In preparing for this discussion, make lists for the following topics, jotting down any hunches that come to mind.

A.   The Jews of Old Testament times might have used the teachings of Proverbs in the following ways or in dealing with these situations:

_____

_____

_____

B.   Readers of the Old Testament today might use the teachings of Proverbs in the following ways or in dealing with these situations:

_____

ECCLESIASTES

Introduction and Study Guide

The Greek word *ecclesiastes* is translated "the preacher." The Hebrew name for this book is Qoheleth (ko-HELL-et), which means one who conducts an assembly or school. The authorship of the book is traditionally associated with King Solomon because of 1:1 and 1:12, but the writing dates from a much later time, probably around 250 B.C. Qoheleth is a philosopher rather than a preacher, and his writing shows the influence of Greek thought in the Hellenistic era. He questions the postexilic teachings on the role and value of wisdom. A strong sense of individualism pervades the book, as well as a cyclical view of history (see 1:9–11). Qoheleth shares the Hellenistic idea that our lot in life is to accept and conform to the world, rather than change it (see 1:15 and the fine poem in 3:1–9).

The work as it now stands is complicated by two factors. The first is that it has no formal structure. The book is a mixture of poems, prose, laments, and proverbs, and Qoheleth's arguments are rambling rather than orderly. The second is that we see another hand (or other hands) at work in later additions to the text which attempt to soften Qoheleth's pessimism and make the book theologically acceptable. Scribes or editors added orthodox glosses, or interpretatons, which are found throughout the book, especially in the miscellaneous proverbs and in the appendix (12:9–12). Because Qoheleth's tone and reasoning is quite different from the rest of the Hebrew scriptures, it was one of the last books to be canonized. Were it not for the references to Solomon and the editorial additions, it would probably not have been admitted to the canon at all!

In preparing this Study Guide, you will be asked to systematize arguments which are not made systematic by the text itself, and you will omit most of the scribal glosses.

I. *Qoheleth's Search for Meaning.* What are the experiments or tests that the author performed with his life, and the results of each one?

1.   1:13–18

_____

2.   2:1–11 (two experiments are found here)

_____

3.   2:18–23

_____

II. *Qoheleth's Ambivalence.* In his observations, the author was confronted with many paradoxes concerning human existence. Read each of the following teachings, then state the tension in each paradox using this form:

This is true: _____ ;

yet this is also true: _____ .

1.   2:13–14

2.   2:26

3.   3:17–18

4.   9:13–16

5.   9:18

6.   11:9

III. *The Problem of Theodicy for Qoheleth.* Define the word "theodicy" if you have not already done so.

_____

Today, the problem of theodicy is cast in the form of the question, Why do bad things happen to good people? How did the author describe the problem of theodicy in the following verses?

1. 7:15

_____

2. 8:10—11

_____

3. 8:14

_____

IV.   *The Finality of Death for Qoheleth.* Earlier Hebrew traditions affirmed that the dead continued to exist, not in a heaven or hell, but in their ongoing participation in the community of Israel. The father lived on in the son, and the memory of the deceased was "kept alive" by the community. Qoheleth's strong tendency toward individualism resists this communal "afterlife." Death is the only real certainty. It overrides all the good things in life: wisdom, wealth, pleasure, family.

Summarize the teaching on death in each of the following passages:

1. 2:16

_____

2. 3:19—21

_____

3. 4:2—3

_____

4. 9:1—6

_____

5. 9:10

_____

What conclusion(s) does the author draw from the fact that we all must die?

_____

_____

V.   *God's Role in Human Affairs.* God is a given for Qoheleth; he never doubts God's existence and sovereignty. What he doubts instead is the final and ultimate meaning of life.

1.   Read 8:17; 9:1; and 11:5. What can we know about God's activity in this world?

_____

_____

Does Qoheleth believe that God guides the life of the individual?

_____

2.   Read 3:11. What do you think Qoheleth means when he says that God has "put eternity into man's mind"?

_____

Given what you have read about death in topic IV, how do you think he feels about this fact?

_____

_____

VI.   *On Living Out One's Life.* Read 2:24—25; 3:12—13; 3:22; 5:18; and 8:15. What is the proper way to spend one's days?

_____

_____

What, according to the author, is good and fitting in this life?

_____

VII.   *Qoheleth's Thesis.* At last we are in a position to examine the author's thesis, which is stated in the introduction (1:2) and restated in the conclusion (12:8). The Hebrew word *hebhel,* translated "vanity," means a breath, mist, fog, or vapor. It denotes that which vanishes, as exhaled breath disappears. *Hebhel* is that which is unsubstantial and fleeting.

Read 1:2 and 12:8. What is the author's thesis?

_____

Is the thesis well supported?

_____

In light of Qoheleth's experience, is it true?

_____

Do you agree or disagree with his thesis? Why?

_____

_____

VIII.   Use a dictionary to define the following terms:

1.   skepticism (or skeptic)

_____

_____

2. cynicism (or cynic)

_____

_____

Do you think Qoheleth is a skeptic? a cynic? Why or why not?

_____

IX. Read 12:9–14, keeping in mind that this appendix is a later addition to the book made by an orthodox editor.

1. How is the author described by the editor in 12:9–10?

_____

Is this description consistent with his role in the rest of the book?

_____

2. What does the editor say about books and studying?

_____

Why do you think the editor says this?

_____

_____

3. How does the teaching in 12:13–14 compare with the rest of the book?

_____

_____

Discussion Questions

1. Compare Ecclesiastes and Proverbs as to their tone, advice, outlook on life and God.
2. Why do you think Ecclesiastes was included in the Old Testament canon? Are you glad it was included? Why or why not?

JOB — AN INTRODUCTION

The themes of wisdom teaching, especially the "exact retribution" doctrine wherein one's suffering is equal to one's sin, are prevalent in the book of Job. Yet these themes, as placed on the lips of Job's friends, are questioned. Wisdom's inability to establish the order of the universe is a late development in Jewish thought. The book of Job is dated after the Exile—probably as late as the fourth century B.C.

The first two chapters of the book and the last chapter belong to an ancient prose legend that was common in the Near East. The form and characterization in these chapters are strikingly different from the bulk of the book (chapters 3–41), which is a series of poetic dialogues. Chapters 1 and 2 tell the story of an incredible series of disasters that befall a righteous man named Job. Here the Satan (literally "the adversary"), who is not the Evil One but a member of God's heavenly council, is in charge of investigating the souls of people on earth. The Satan suspects that Job is a fair-weather friend to God, and God allows this prosecuting angel to test his hypothesis. So Job, blessed materially by God, loses all. The last chapter of the book tells of Job's restoration to favor. In return for his faithfulness, Job is granted a long and happy life.

The point between overwhelming disaster and re-warded faith, which is neatly bridged in the prose legend, is the subject of the poetic discourses. Job begins the discourses by cursing the day of his birth. In the poetic sections Job does not passively accept disaster; he passionately questions it. His faith is not abandoned, but it is stretched way past the orthodox "wisdom" limits of his friends. Job is overwhelmingly personal in his prayers to God. His desire is to "see God," not simply hear about God from his friends, for he knows if God would only draw near, God would see Job's righteousness and justify him. But God is not near—and it is the absence of God which makes his misery unbearable.

His friends accuse him of rebelling against God. Job, on the other hand, insists on maintaining his integrity. Job believes God calls him to honesty; his friends virtually tell him to lie, or to profess guilt where there is none. Job also maintains *God's* integrity and freedom. God is absolutely free to do as God pleases. The Almighty is not bound by the friends' pat formulas of exact retribution, where the punishment always equals the crime. Yet God had been Job's friend. What happened to this relationship? God is not with him! This, not the problem of suffering or theodicy, is the real question for Job. He agonizes over the loss of his relationship with God.

Meanwhile, his friends defend God. They are actually giving half-truths; more than that, they are defending not God but their own religion. Instead of sympathizing with Job, they turn against him with increasingly harsh indictments. They uphold their wisdom formulas and religious doctrines at Job's expense.

God's answer is altogether different. God gives Job what he both wanted and needed: a vision of God himself. The experience of God transcends the philosophical problem of Job's suffering. God speaks to him personally. Job's response suggests his new, personal faith over and against traditional teaching, or his prophetic vision over and against the friends' dry wisdom:

> I had heard of thee by the hearing of the ear,
>> but now my eye sees thee.
>
> (42:5)

Then Job repents; he acknowledges his own creatureliness and God's mystery. After thirty-nine chapters of discourse on God's will, God's mystery is left intact. God is to be *believed*, not *known* as fully as Job would have liked, or as his friends pretended to do.

SELECTED READINGS: JOB

If you are preparing this assignment on your own, read all the passages indicated below and mark the passages in your Bible as you read.

If you are preparing this assignment as a class or group, assign the following roles to seven class members: a narrator, Job, Eliphaz, Bildad, Zophar, Elihu, and God. All class members should mark the passages indicated as they are read aloud in class.

Scene I: the prologue: tragedy strikes.

Narrator: chapters 1 and 2

Scene II: the speeches: arguments of the friends and Job.

Narrator: 3:1–2
Job: 3:3–6, 20–26
Eliphaz: 4:2–8; 5:8–18
Job: 6:8–14, 24–30
 (to God) 7:11, 16–21
Bildad: 8:2–7, 20–22
Job: 9:13–24, 32–35
 (to God) 10:1–8
Zophar: 11:2–6, 13–20
Job: 13:1–17
 (to God) 13:18–24
Eliphaz: 15:1–6
Job: 16:18–22; 19:2–7; 19:21–27
Eliphaz: 22:2–11, 21–30
Job: 23:2–17; 27:2–6; 29:2–16
Narrator: 32:1–5
Elihu: 33:12–28; 34:36–37; 35:9–14; 37:23–24

Scene III: the climax: the theophany to Job.

Narrator: 38:1
God: 38:2–21
Job: 40:4–5
God: 40:7–14
Job: 42:2–6

Scene IV: the epilogue.

Narrator: 42:7–17

JOB

Study Guide

Answer these questions after you have completed the assignment on the selected readings from Job on the preceding page. Where chapter references are given, reread the verses that you have already marked.

1. *The Prologue* (chap. 1–2). What is the Satan's wager with God?

_____

_____

What limits does God set on the Satan in his dealings with Job?

_____

How does the prologue indicate that Job remains both faithful to God and accepting of his fate?

_____

_____

List all the verbs that describe the three friends' actions when they first saw Job in his misery.

_____

_____

What did they do for seven days and nights?

_____

2. *The Arguments of Job's Friends.* What theories do the friends offer Job to explain his suffering? List as many as you can. (Use marked passages from chap. 4, 5, 11, 22, 33, 35, and 37.)

_____

_____

_____

_____

_____

_____

_____

3. *Job's Twofold Problem.*

A.   The Problem of the Presence of Job's "Friends": How does Job describe his friends? (chap. 6, 13, 19)

_____

_____

Why does he say that they torment him?

_____

_____

B.   The Problem of the Absence of God: How does Job describe the absence of God from his life? (chap. 23, 29)

_____

_____

What does Job ask God to do? (chap. 13)

_____

_____

What does he say about the following "mediators" between God and Job?

   1. An umpire in 9:32–35

_____

   2. A witness in heaven in 16:18–21

_____

_____

   3. A redeemer in 19:23–27

_____

_____

4. *The Theophany* (chap. 38–41). In what ways does God's appearance to Job mark the climax of the book?

_____

_____

How does Job respond to the theophany? Why do you think Job says that he "repents"? (42:1–6)

_____

_____

5. *The Epilogue* (42:7–17). What does God say concerning Job's friends? concerning Job?

_____

_____

Discussion Questions

1. What is your opinion of the friends as comforters to Job? as advisers?

2. What do you think the friends could have done for Job instead?

PSALMS

Introduction and Study Guide

If we want to know how the chosen people expressed themselves in both public worship and in private prayer, we need only turn to the compilation of 150 poems known as the book of Psalms, or the Psalter. The psalms are a record of the manifold human response to God. They provide us with models for praise and petition in our personal prayer life. They continue to instruct and inspire us in our synagogues and churches today.

The Psalter spans some thousand years of literary activity. Some psalms were composed before the first temple was built. Others date from the time of the first temple, still others after its destruction, and many after the Exile. The book was compiled around 200 B.C. Thus, the psalms span the entire panorama of Jewish history from the united monarchy to the Restoration.

The authorship of the psalms cannot be determined with any certainty. It is best to say we are indebted to many anonymous poets for their contributions to the book. Almost half of the psalms are accredited to King David, but the phrase "of David" could equally well mean "for" or "about" him or another king. The Chronicler of Israel's history makes frequent mention of the singers and musicians appointed by David "to invoke, to thank, and to praise the Lord" (1 Chron. 16:1–7; see also 25:1–8). Because tradition affirmed that music in the tabernacle was instituted by David, the psalms or songs are accredited to him in much the same way Proverbs was accredited to Solomon.

Many of the psalms were liturgical songs used in services of worship. They were set to the accompaniment of instruments. In Psalm 150, we find a list of the whole orchestra: trumpets, lutes, harps, timbrels, strings, pipes, and clashing cymbals. The word *selah* appears frequently in the psalms; it was an instruction to the musicians, probably indicating a musical interlude or a sign to repeat the instrumental phrase at that point. *Amen,* the response of the congregation indicated at the end of some psalms, means "so be it" or "it is certain."

The Psalter is the hymnbook of Israel. It stands as the testimonial to Jewish worship and devotion. In it we find both praise to God and prayers to God, or "calling on the name of the Lord." In it we find the response of the community, and of individuals, to God's covenant.

1. *Israelite Theology As Found in the Psalter.* Reading the psalms constitutes a study of Old Testament theology in itself. How is God's omniscience and omnipresence described in Psalm 139?

How is the timelessness and eternity of God described in Psalm 90?

Read Psalms 33, 103, 121, and 145. Then list the attributes of God described in these psalms.

God's mighty acts in Israel's history are described in Psalm 105. What references to events in Genesis, Exodus, and Numbers do you find?

God's promises to David are the subject of Psalms 89:19–37 and 132. What is the significance of the Davidic covenant according to these psalms?

Read about God's wondrous works in creation and nature in Psalms 33, 65, and 104. How is God's activity in the natural order described?

Read about the theocracy, or rule of God, in Psalms 47, 93, and 96. How is God's kingship described?

2. *Israelite Anthropology As Found in the Psalter.* Read Psalms 10, 14, and 36:1–4. What characterizes the wicked? the foolish?

Read Psalm 8. What view of humanity do you find here?

How does this psalm reflect the creation story in Genesis 1?

_____

3. *Israelite Hamartiology As Found in the Psalter*. Hamartiology is the doctrine of sin. Read Psalm 51. The superscription tells us that this psalm was written after David's sin with Bathsheba. What is the psalmist's understanding of his sin in verse 4?

_____

What does he ask God to do?

_____

_____

The psalmists understood sin as both a moral and a physical sickness. Sin manifested itself in the heart and in the entire body. They understood God's forgiveness to be both a moral healing of the soul and a physical healing of the body. Read Psalms 30 and 32; then describe the psalmists' experiences of God's forgiveness of sin.

_____

_____

4. *Literary Categories in the Psalter.*

A. Hymns. Almost one-fourth of the psalms are hymns, or acts of praise to God. God is never directly addressed in these hymns, but is referred to in the third person. The literary elements of the hymn are as follows:

1. Summons to praise, or call to worship
2. Reasons why Yahweh should be praised:
   a. God's mighty acts in history and/or
   b. God's works in creation and nature

3. Renewed summons to praise

Read the following hymns: Psalms 100, 113, 135, 136, and 146.

As you read the hymns, mark the elements with brackets and identify them with the numbers used above (1, 2a, 2b, 3).

B. Laments. One-third of all psalms are classified as laments. Some are very personal, while others are the expression of the community. Often the specific circumstances that gave rise to the lament are obscure. The lament is simply a petition to God for aid. In the laments God is addressed directly: God is "Thou." The literary elements of the lament are as follows:

1. Invocation, or calling upon the name of the Lord
2. Description of the trouble(s)
3. Petition(s) to God
4. Vow or promise on the part of the psalmist
5. Expression of trust, or conviction that God has heard and will act

Read the following laments: Psalms 13, 22, 31, 38, 43, 54, 71, and 140.

As you read the laments, mark the elements with brackets and identify them with the numbers used above (1, 2, 3, 4, 5). In some laments, one or more of these elements may be missing.

Creative Activity

Compose a hymn and a lament. Decide if you are writing as an individual or on behalf of a group. If you are writing on behalf of a group, decide who the group is. Then, using the elements of each type of psalm, express your feelings to God in poetic form.

PSALM 23

Commentary and Writing Activity

One of the most memorable expressions of faith in the Old Testament, the Twenty-third Psalm is famous for its fine images of God's care. It is a psalm of trust. Looking back on life, the psalmist recognizes God's protection. Then the psalmist looks forward to his continuing fellowship with God in the future. The psalm depends on two major images for its meaning:

1. God is Shepherd; the psalmist is one of God's sheep (vss. 1–4).
Review the qualities of the Near Eastern shepherd in the commentary found after the Ezekiel Study Guide.
In these verses the psalmist focuses on:

- the Shepherd's constant care of the sheep (vs. 1)
- the quiet and tranquility made possible by the Shepherd (vs. 2)
- the Shepherd's healing, restorative powers (vs. 3a)
- the rightness of the psalmist's walk through life under the Shepherd's guidance (vs. 3b)
- the reality of distress and danger: illness, accidents, violence, weakness, the "deep darkness" of experiences that threaten the psalmist's well-being (vs. 4a)
- the trust of the psalmist, who knows the Shepherd's constant presence and is assured by the implements which the Shepherd uses for the safekeeping and protection of his charges (vs. 4b)

2. God is Host; the psalmist is his welcomed guest (vss. 5–6).

Ancient Near Eastern householders were famous for their graciousness. Hosts would go to great lengths to extend hospitality to travelers. For biblical examples, see Abraham's treatment of his three guests in Genesis 18:2–8 and Lot's determination to be a good host in Genesis 19:1–18.

In these verses the psalmist focuses on:

• the banquet prepared by the Host for the weary traveler (vs. 5a)

• the psalmist's recognition that even his enemies cannot disturb his joy at the Host's banquet (vs. 5a)

• the refreshing oil that the Host pours on the traveler's head as he provides the guest shelter from the hot sun, and the cool relief of the Host's abundant hospitality (vs. 5b)

• the psalmist's understanding that he is not merely a welcomed guest, but a member of the Host's household for all the days of his life (vs. 6)

Activity

Paraphrase the Twenty-third Psalm in personal terms.

Start by picking two images that describe God's care for you. List under each image the reasons for your trust in God. For each image, include your experiences of God's activity in the past and your hopes for the future.

Then write your psalm in poetic form.

Daniel, Apocalyptic Literature, and Intertestamental Times

DANIEL—AN INTRODUCTION

The book of Daniel contains two units: (1) six stories about Daniel and his friends, faithful Jews living in Babylonian exile (chap. 1–6), and (2) Daniel's four visions concerning the course of history and the end times (chap. 7–12).

One of the major problems of Daniel is setting a date for the writing of the book. While the stories are placed in Babylonia during the sixth century B.C., many scholars are convinced that the book was written in second-century B.C. Palestine.

Why? The book contains what appear to be errors. The capture of Jerusalem was not in the time of Jehoiakim (Dan. 1:1), but Jehoiachin (2 Kings 24:8–10). Darius was a Persian, not a Mede (Dan. 9:1). The author makes Darius son of Ahasuerus (Xerxes), when Xerxes was actually Darius's son. Belshazzar was the son of Nabonidus rather than Nebuchadnezzar (Dan. 5:11), and he was never king (Dan. 7:1).

On the other hand, as the author gets closer to second-century B.C. events, the historical details become more accurate. The vision of the "little horn" in chapter 8 accurately describes the tyrant Antiochus IV Epiphanes, the last Seleucid king of Palestine before the Maccabean Revolt around 167 B.C. This despot set up an altar to Zeus in the temple and forced Jews to take part in heathen ceremonies. He ordered Jews to eat swine's flesh and killed those who violated his decrees. Many scholars believe that a second-century B.C. audience made up of people suffering under Antiochus could not fail to see how the adventures of Daniel and his three friends held a message of inspiration for them. The author was not concerned with the sixth century B.C. as history but as a representation of a pattern of tyranny that was recurring in his own time.

Perhaps this analogy will help explain the problem. Asking the age of the book of Daniel is like asking the age of a string of pearls. Like the individual pearls in a necklace, the six stories and four visions that make up the book of Daniel were formed separately and at different times. Some of the "pearls" arose out of the Babylonian captivity in the sixth century B.C. But the finished "string" appears to be a product of the second century B.C. The age was characterized by severe religious restrictions and pressure to conform to a foreign, Hellenistic culture. The author of Daniel selected a number of pearls that would hold a message of hope to Jews suffering under the tyrant Antiochus IV Epiphanes.

We need to examine both the sixth-century B.C. and the second-century B.C. historical settings to enrich our understanding of the book. Nebuchadnezzar, king of Babylonia from 605 to 562 B.C., brought Babylonia to the peak of its power. After defeating Assyria and Egypt, he forced the Judean king Jehoiakim to pay tribute in 602 B.C. Judah rebelled and Nebuchadnezzar marched west. He pulled the new king (Jehoiachin) off the throne, vandalized the temple, and deported the leading citizens in 598 B.C. Judah rebelled again, Nebuchadnezzar invaded again, and a second deportation occurred under the puppet king Zedekiah in 586 B.C. This time the Davidic line was wiped out (Zedekiah's sons were slain in his presence before he was blinded), and Jerusalem was destroyed by fire (2 Kings 25:1–12).

As foreigners, Jews like Daniel were allowed some freedom to settle in their own communities in Babylonia and practice their own trades. But their situation worsened after Nebuchadnezzar's death in 562 B.C. His son was murdered by a group of nobles, and Nabonidus eventually was made king in 556 B.C. The son of a high priestess of a pagan god, Nabonidus was intolerant of other religions and used the exiles for forced labor. His defeat by Cyrus in 539 B.C. brought the Babylonian Empire to an end. Persia reigned supreme for the next two hundred years.

Nebuchadnezzar is the subject of Daniel 1–4. But his behavior in these chapters reminds some historians of Nabonidus, the last of the Babylonian kings. Nabonidus was known for his demon possession (chap. 4) and his strange dreams (chap. 2). He was also known for building a large golden image (chap. 3) and for appointing foreigners to high positions (chap. 1).

Alexander the Great toppled the Persian Empire with lightning speed in 331 B.C. but died without an heir. Alexander's conquered lands were divided among his generals at his death, and Palestine eventually came to be controlled by the Seleucid family. The last Seleucid king of Palestine was Antiochus IV Epiphanes, who ruled from 175 to 164 B.C. He wanted the Jews to accept Greek culture and become his loyal subjects. He forbade circumcision. He defiled the holy of holies with a statue of Zeus. He put to death those who possessed the Torah. Antiochus even outlawed Jewish dietary restrictions. See 2 Maccabees 6:18–7:42 in the Apocrypha for accounts of Jews who were killed by Antiochus because they would not compromise the principles of dietary law. If the book of Daniel was compiled during the reign of this cruel king, as many scholars believe, Palestine was groaning under the oppression of a madman who considered himself to be a god. (*Epiphanes* means "God manifest" or "the evident God" in Greek.)

DANIEL 1—6

Study Guide

1. Read chapter 1: the faithfulness of Daniel and his friends in the Babylonian court. (Note: In the book of Daniel, "Chaldeans" are wise men or sages in the service of the Babylonian king.) What was King Nebuchadnezzar's plan regarding these four Jewish youths?

To observe the Jewish dietary regulations in this pagan court meant that Daniel and his friends could eat only vegetables and water. How did they fare physically?

How did God reward them? What was Daniel's extra reward?

After the "Three-year Plan" was completed, how did the Jewish youths' wisdom compare with the court sages' (the "magicians and enchanters") in Babylonia?

2. Read chapter 2: Nebuchadnezzar's dream. What impossible demands did the king make on his wise men (the "Chaldeans") concerning his troubling dream?

How was Daniel made able to meet the king's demands?

Read the dream and its interpretation. What is "the stone cut by no human hand"?

What happens to this great stone?

In what ways does King Nebuchadnezzar react to Daniel's remarkable feat?

3. Read chapter 3: Shadrach, Meshach, and Abednego in the fiery furnace. Why do you think Nebuchadnezzar set up a colossal image of gold?

What does the youths' reply to the king in 3:16–18 say about their view of God? about their obedience to God?

Punishment by burning was well known in the ancient Near East. The kilns or furnaces of that time were shaped like beehives, with openings at the top and side. The furnace was fed fuel from the top. Ashes were removed from the side door at ground level. How do verses 19–22 increase the suspense of the story?

Who was the fourth person in the fiery furnace?

The gold statue and the king's raging fits would remind second-century B.C. readers of Antiochus IV Epiphanes, the despotic king in Palestine at that time. What is the outcome of the story?

4. Read chapter 4: Nebuchadnezzar's madness. Once again, Nebuchadnezzar has a dream that none could interpret. Briefly, what is the meaning of the dream according to Daniel (also known as Belteshazzar) in verses 19–27?

This narrative is told in the first person, as Nebuchadnezzar's autobiographical account, except for verses 28–33. Use a dictionary and define *theriomania*.

_____

Why do you think verses 28–33 are told in the third person?

_____

_____

What does Nebuchadnezzar do once he returns to his senses?

_____

5.   Read chapter 5: the writing on the wall. (Note: Belshazzar is called king of Babylon in this narrative. He was never king, but his father Nabonidus was the last king before Babylon fell to Cyrus the Persian—not Darius the Mede as in 5:31.) What sacrilege did Belshazzar and his party commit at the great feast?

_____

_____

What caused the king to go limp with fear?

_____

_____

Once again, Daniel was brought in to solve the mystery. What words were written on the wall?

_____

How did Daniel interpret these words?

_____

_____

_____

6.   Read chapter 6: the lion's den. A "satrap" was a governor of a province in the Persian Empire. How did Darius use Daniel in his governmental structure?

_____

What was Darius's plan for Daniel in the future?

_____

How did the jealous officials plan to get rid of Daniel?

_____

_____

How does Daniel observe Jewish practices despite the king's decree?

_____

_____

Because Persian laws could not be revoked, Darius reluctantly commanded that the punishment be carried out. How does Daniel explain his safekeeping in the lion's den?

_____

What happens to Daniel's accusers *and* their families?

_____

_____

Discussion Question

In what specific ways would these stories in Daniel 1–6 encourage an audience that was undergoing persecution for its beliefs?

DANIEL 7–12 AND APOCALYPTIC LITERATURE

Apocalypse means "revelation"; apocalyptic literature is the literature of revealed future time. Chapters 7–12 in Daniel constitute the largest and best example of apocalyptic literature in the Old Testament. (Other apocalyptic passages are found in Joel, Isaiah 24–27, Ezekiel 38–39, and Zechariah 9–14.)

Apocalyptic writings were addressed to an audience undergoing suffering and persecution. While the "authorities" would not be able to decipher the writings, the Jews could decode the puzzle and find the real message: God would soon act on their behalf. Dreams, visions, animal symbols, and numerical puzzles are stock features of apocalyptic writing.

The author of Daniel wrote not for some far-off age but for his present age of crisis. His period in history was characterized by severe religious restrictions and the pressure to conform to a foreign, Hellenistic culture. The visions of Daniel 7–12 are like our sermons today. The writer wanted his readers to find practical applications of his message to their situation in life. Be obedient to God! Have courage! God will intervene, soon and catastrophically, on behalf of God's people!

God's power and God's goal are the emphases of apocalyptic literature. Daniel's visions show God literally pulling history toward its end in spite of misguided human efforts. Hope rests not in this world but elsewhere. The writer of apocalyptic literature sees people suffering. The message is one of consolation to help them stand firm in their trials. The writer of Daniel wanted his people to look beyond their suffering to a glorious future in God's hands.

Where is history heading? Toward the kingdom of God, the book of Daniel says. Thus the book serves as a bridge between the Old Testament and the New Testament and provides us with an understanding of Jesus' teaching on the kingdom.

DANIEL 7–12

Study Guide

The last half of the book of Daniel and the interpretations it requires are beyond the scope of our study. Instead, we will look briefly at a few of the chapters in order to sample the features of this piece of apocalyptic literature.

1. Read chapter 7: the vision of the four beasts. The fantastically deformed beasts of this vision symbolize the great empires of the ancient Near East:

• The winged lion is the Babylonian Empire.
• The bear is the Median Empire.
• The winged leopard is the Persian Empire.
• The beast with iron teeth is the empire of Alexander the Great, with its ten horns representing his Seleucid successors, and the little horn with eyes being the tyrannical king of Palestine, Antiochus IV Epiphanes.

How is God (the "Ancient of Days") described in 7:9–10?

_____

_____

What does Daniel learn about the "one like a son of man" in 7:13–14?

_____

The beast with the iron teeth is also called the "fourth kingdom" in 7:19–27. How does this last beast prove to be the worst?

_____

_____

_____

What kind of kingdom will follow the destruction of the fourth beast?

_____

_____

2. Read chapter 8: the vision of the ram and the he-goat. This chapter consists of a dream (vss. 3–12) and its interpretation (vss. 19–26). Here the two-horned ram is the Medo-Persian Empire, the he-goat is the Hellenistic Empire, and the great horn of the he-goat is Alexander the Great. The four horns that arise from the great horn are the four kingdoms of his successors:

A. Macedonia (a region which is now part of Greece, Bulgaria, and Yugoslavia) went to Alexander's general Cassander;

B. Asia Minor (a region that is now Turkey) went to his general Lysimachus;

C. Egypt went to Ptolemy;

D. Syria, Babylonia, and the Near East (including Palestine) eventually went to Seleucus.

Out of the he-goat's four horns arises a "little horn," described in 8:9–12 and again in 8:23–25. This little horn is Antiochus IV Epiphanes. List the verse numbers of the abominable acts of this little horn next to these historical realities of Antiochus's reign:

A. He required unclean swine to be sacrificed on the altar of the temple._____

B. He burned the Torah and decreed the death penalty for those who possessed it._____

C. In 168 B.C., Antiochus sent a tax collector to Jerusalem, ostensibly to calm the fearful people. After gaining their confidence, the official suddenly massacred the trusting crowd by order of the tyrant._____

D. He called himself divine, adding the title Epiphanes ("God manifest") to his name._____

E. He finally died of some strange affliction._____

What angel gave Daniel the interpretation of this vision? (See 8:15–17.) _____

Daniel 9 is concerned with a prophecy of Jeremiah, given around 586 B.C., that seventy years must pass before the desolation of Jerusalem would come to an end (Jer. 29:10–14). Daniel learns from the angel that it is actually seventy *weeks* of years, or 490 years, before the kingdom of God will come. In other words, Daniel is told that this kingdom is imminent!

In Daniel 10, the seer is prepared to receive the vision of the last days, which is revealed to him in chapters 11 and 12.

The rulers and intrigues described in chapter 11 are very detailed. The history of the struggles between the Seleucids and the Ptolemies found here is too complicated for our purposes.

3. Read chapter 12: the final consummation of history. What sort of times will precede the end of history and the coming of God's kingdom? See 12:1.

_____

The angel Michael of this chapter is the patron angel of the Jews.

In Daniel 12:2–3 we find the first mention of the resurrection of the dead in the Old Testament. How is this general resurrection described?

_____

_____

Note that Daniel himself is assured a place in "the end of days," that is, the end of time and the beginning of God's eternal reign (12:4, 13).

Discussion Question

What have you found to be the distinctive *literary* features of apocalyptic writing? What *theological* values are stressed in this type of literature?

INTERTESTAMENTAL TIMES

Old Testament history ends around 400 B.C. with Ezra's reforms and the renewal of the Mosaic covenant. Palestine was under Persian rule from 538 B.C., when Cyrus the Great toppled the Babylonian Empire and freed the Jews from their captivity, until 331 B.C., when Alexander the Great toppled the Persian Empire and ushered in a new, Hellenistic culture. For two centuries then, Palestine was a Persian province, a part of the large satrapy known as "Beyond the River." While not politically independent, the Jews enjoyed a high degree of personal and religious freedom. Communities of diaspora Jews, scattered throughout the ancient Near East, grew and prospered under Persian rule. And while monotheism became the hallmark of Judaism after the Exile, certain Persian religious features were incorporated by the Jews much as compatible branches are grafted on a tree.

The Persian king Darius I (522–486 B.C.) established the religion called Zoroastrianism as the official state cult. The name comes from Zoroaster, its great teacher who lived shortly before the time of Darius. Ahura-Mazda was its deity: god of light, lord of creation, and upholder of morality and truth. Ahura-Mazda waged war against the forces of evil led by Ahriman (the "Lie"). While Zoroastrianism is militantly monotheistic—Ahura-Mazda being the only true God—it actually taught a dualistic view of

the world. The world is under the dominion of two opposing principles: one is true and good, the other evil. Angels and demons allied themselves with these opposing forces, and paradise was promised the followers of truth and light. Evil persons were to be eternally punished after death.

Beginning with the Persian period, we can trace Judaism's gradual inclusion of these religious features. (1) The Jews developed a belief in angels. Four archangels were identified: Michael, Gabriel, Raphael, and Uriel. Under them in the celestial sphere existed a huge hierarchy of lesser angels. (2) The traditional Deuteronomic formula, wherein both good and bad fortune were traced to human actions and ultimately to the will of the Yahweh, was replaced on a popular level by the belief that Satan (or "Belial") played a part in human affairs. "The Satan" of Job, who was originally one of God's heavenly council, became the fallen angel who now headed up the invisible powers or demons who were opposed to God. (3) Also derived from Persian beliefs was the doctrine of afterlife: the resurrection of the dead to eternal judgment or eternal reward. First mentioned in Daniel 12, the doctrine of a general resurrection was well established by the second century B.C.

Alexander the Great toppled the Persian Empire with

lightning speed around 331 B.C. and proceeded to promote his ideal: a cultural union of East and West known as Hellenism. As the first step in this planned assimilation, he settled Greeks in colonies all over the ancient Near East and arranged mass marriages between his troops and the native populations. Alexander and his successors forbade circumcision and wherever possible displaced native religions with Greek worship rites. But Hellenism was subtly pervasive as well as overtly forced. Beautiful and modern cities were built in the Greek fashion. Education and recreation were based on the Greek gymnasium. Music halls and theaters promoted Hellenistic arts. Hippodromes and stadiums for sports events, where pagan opening ceremonies were performed, attracted many Jews. Hellenistic society encouraged a distinctive dress, hair style, and fashion. Compared to this cosmopolitan culture, many Jews felt old-fashioned and embarrassed about their distinctive worship practices. And so many Jews became Hellenized, gradually accepting Greek culture while perhaps maintaining their adherence to the less conspicuous aspects of their Jewish tradition.

At the death of Alexander in 323 B.C., the mighty empire was divided among his four generals. While Syria went to the Seleucid family and Egypt to the Ptolemies, Palestine was claimed by both as the important "bridge" between Africa and the East. The Ptolemies ruled Palestine from 323 to 198 B.C., years about which we know very little, except that warfare with the Seleucids over the Palestinian "bridge" was frequent. The Ptolemies, like the Persians, were lenient in their treatment of the Jews. They made no effort to impose Hellenistic culture on Palestine. Back in Egypt, a large Jewish population grew in Alexandria. These Jews were Greek-speaking, and it is from them that we get the Septuagint (LXX), or the Greek translation of the Scriptures, made around 275 B.C.

The Ptolemies were finally driven out of Palestine by the Seleucids in 198 B.C., and the situation changed radically. Hellenizing pressures began at once. These pressures culminated in the reign of Antiochus IV Epiphanes, Seleucid emperor from 175 to 164 B.C. Ruling Palestine from Damascus, he thought it would be no problem to convert his Jewish subjects to pagan, Hellenistic ways. He forbade the worship of Yahweh and the possession of the Torah. Mothers who had their sons circumcized were killed. His crowning act, "the abomination that makes desolation" in Daniel 11:31, was to profane the temple in Jerusalem with a statue of Zeus in 167 B.C.

It is at this point that a remarkable resistance movement was kindled. Seleucid soldiers were sent into the countryside to enforce Antiochus's decree that sacrifices be made to Zeus. At Modin, a small village near Jerusalem, a Jew named Mattathias was asked to make the first sacrifice. Mattathias was an elderly priest, a member of the Hasmonean family. While Antiochus's deputy

thought this request innocuous, Mattathias thought it repugnant. He flatly refused, and when another Jew stepped forward to the altar to make the sacrifice instead, Mattathias killed both the Seleucid official and the Jewish compromiser. After destroying the altar, he fled for the hills along with his five sons and a zealous band of freedom fighters. This Hasmonean family became known as the Maccabees, or "Hammerers," because of their warlike determination. And so in 167 B.C. Mattathias sparked the Maccabean Revolt.

Already an old man, Mattathias died within a few months (166 B.C.) but was ably succeeded by his son Judas. In December of 164, three years to the month after Antiochus desecrated the temple, Judas cleansed it of foreign influences and restored it as the place for sacrifices to Yahweh. Hanukkah, or "Dedication," is the annual Jewish festival that celebrates this event. While Seleucid kings continued to pour armies into Palestine like cannon fodder over the next two decades, each of the five Maccabees or sons of Mattathias arose in turn to fight them off with brilliant guerrilla tactics. The Syrian army withdrew completely in 142 B.C.

This victory would not have been possible were it not for the Hasidim, the "loyal" or "pious," who joined Mattathias and his sons in revolt. While Hellenized Jews who supported the Seleucids were typically city dwellers from the upper classes, the Hasidim often came from rural backgrounds. Strongly anti-Hellenistic, they formed the resistance movement under Antiochus IV Epiphanes. In the book of Daniel, they are referred to as "the saints of the Most High" (Dan. 7:22, 27).

In 140 B.C., Simon, the youngest son of Mattathias, was proclaimed high priest, military commander, and civil governor of the Jews by popular decree. The last independent Jewish nation had ended in 586 B.C. This new independent nation, officially recognized by Rome, was ruled not by a Davidic king but by the priestly, Hasmonean family. The sad sequel to the Maccabean Revolt is that the reigns of later Hasmoneans were marked by family disputes, costly wars of conquest, and forced conversions of neighboring peoples. The Hasmoneans wanted only to aggrandize themselves and to enlarge their empire.

It was during the Hasmonean era (140–63 B.C.) that the Sadducees arose as the party of power in Judea. The Sadducees were technically a priestly caste, claiming descent from King David's high priest, Zadok. Actually they were Hellenized aristocrats. They were liberal, even compromising, in their political dealings. Their chief concerns were the temple services and maintaining their priestly, and successful, position.

Around 100 B.C. a group called the Pharisees arose in opposition to the Sadducees and the growing corruption of the Hasmonean state. They continued the tradition of the Hasidim in their zeal for the law, their moral earnestness, and the respect they commanded of the populace. They were the true spiritual leaders of Judaism, opposed as they were to Hellenism and its Hasmonean patrons. They were a constant thorn in the flesh to these rulers. Alexander Janneus, one of the last Hasmonean kings, crucified eight hundred Pharisees who displeased him.

Conservative and traditionalist in their political dealings, the Pharisees were liberal theologically. While the Sadducees accepted only the written Torah (or Pentateuch) as authoritative, the Pharisees also recognized the Prophets and the Writings, that is, the entire Hebrew canon. They also accepted a large body of oral law that accompanied the Torah. This oral law was eventually codified around A.D. 200 as the Mishnah. The Pharisees looked forward to an apocalyptic kingdom and the resurrection of the body. They also believed in angels and demons. The Sadducees, on the other hand, rejected all these beliefs. While the Sadducees looked to maintaining their present status quo, the Pharisees looked to the coming of God's kingdom. And while they awaited it, the Pharisees zealously kept Jewish law in both its oral and written traditions.

In 66 B.C., trouble arose between two Hasmonean brothers who appealed to Rome to settle their quarrel. The great Roman general Pompey seized the opportunity and invaded Judea. After a three-month siege, Pompey attacked on the Sabbath (when no Jew would raise a weapon to resist), putting an end to the Hasmonean dynasty and Jewish independence. Hereafter Palestine was technically a part of the province of Syria during the Roman era, but the Jews had their own titular kings who ruled alongside Roman procurators. In 37 B.C., Herod the Great was appointed king of the Jews by the Roman Senate. The New Testament opens with the birth of Jesus during his reign (Matt. 2:10).

A survey of intertestamental times would be amiss not to include some mention of the remarkable community that has been made known to us through the Dead Sea Scrolls. These scrolls were discovered in 1947 by a Bedouin goatherd in a cave high in the cliffs along the northwest shore of the Dead Sea. Subsequent excavations at nearby Qumran have uncovered ruins of a huge fortified monastery which supported some two hundred males, members of the Essene sect within Judaism. While not all Essenes lived at Qumran (they were in fact scattered throughout the eastern Mediterranean world), these monks constituted the spiritual heart of the Essene movement.

It appears that sometime between 150 and 100 B.C., some Essenes withdrew from Jerusalem and began living as monks at Qumran. These men believed themselves to be living "in the last days." Like the Pharisees, they continued the tradition of the Hasidim in their opposition to corrupt rulers (in this case, the Hasmoneans and later the Romans). But their apocalyptic tendencies were extreme. The Dead Sea Scrolls included many apocalyptic manuscripts that were unknown before their discovery in 1947. Approximately one-fourth of the manuscript finds are texts of the Hebrew Scriptures, including all of Isaiah and portions of every Old Testament book except Esther. The most popular scrolls at Qumran, however, concerned the last days. The Essenes believed themselves "the men of the covenant," the remnant of the end time. They looked for two messiahs: one priestly, the other political and Davidic. Their Manual of Discipline shows them to be highly ascetic as they prepared for the cosmic battle and the age of glory. The monastery was destroyed in A.D. 68, the time of the Roman conquest of the Jordan valley. This community was wiped out and their ideas sealed away until our present century.

Reference Material

For Further Study

Using the Library and Building Your Own

Having completed this Study Guide, you are now ready to pursue your own studies and to deepen your understanding of OT subject matter. The next steps you take will involve research, gaining access to materials, and building your own library to facilitate your studies.

First, familiarize yourself with the types of libraries in your area: public, church, school or university, synagogue. Don't hesitate to call various churches or schools and ask about check-out privileges. Often a small deposit or a special pass allows non-members or non-students this right.

Take some time to explore the library. The first things to locate are the card catalog, the reference section, and the places various books are shelved. Find the biography section, the fiction section, and where the non-fiction religion books are kept.

Card catalogs are usually arranged alphabetically by author, title, and subject. These catalogs enable you to find the call number of each of the library's books, recordings, and filmstrips. Every book in the library is represented in the card catalog by an author card and a title card. In addition, there are separate cards for each subject with which the book deals. Each book's subject headings are also listed on the author and title cards. Subject headings in the card catalog are useful for topical studies (such as "Covenant," "Prophets," "Prayer").

Determine your library's classification system, which is the way the library shelves its non-fiction books. The two most popular systems are the Library of Congress and the Dewey Decimal. Ask your librarian for the printed guide used there. This list will steer you to books on the subjects you want to explore. The Dewey Decimal System, for instance, assigns the call numbers 200–299 to religious non-fiction. Go to this section in the stacks with the call number of a book that interests you, and you will find additional useful books that you might have missed in the card catalog.

Now turn to the reference section. *The Reader's Guide to Periodical Literature* is the best single source from which to find references to current and past magazine articles, which you can then locate in a large library. *The Reader's Guide* is a quick way of answering three types of questions: what articles on a given *subject* (e.g., Dead Sea Scrolls, Israel) were published in general magazines in a specific period, what articles by a certain *writer* were published in that time, and exactly where you can find an article if you know only its title and subject matter. The full set of over forty dark green volumes goes back to 1900. For the current year, the library keeps paperbound copies of semi-monthly, monthly, and quarterly issues loose in a box next to the bound volumes. Over 180 periodicals are indexed. Sixty of these are indexed in *The Abridged Reader's Guide to Periodical Literature,* designed for use in smaller libraries.

Familiarize yourself with the abbreviation key found at the beginning of each volume, as all entries in *The Reader's Guide* are made in abbreviated form. Look up the subject "Bible" and note the cross-references (called "see also" references), such as "Creation," "Prophets." Articles under the "see also" references might contain some information on the subject in which you are interested. If you wish to find material on a particular aspect of a broad subject, scan the middle of the column for subheads printed in boldface type. If you look again at the subject entry "Bible," you will see that immediately under the subject heading are entries that treat the general aspects of the Bible. Then come the subheads, arranged alphabetically: "Apocrypha," "Criticism," "Old Testament," and even further subdivisions under these (by biblical book, for instance.)

Once you have found the entries to articles that interest you, copy the magazine name and the numbers following it. The first number is the volume of the periodical, and the numbers after the colon denote the pages on which the article appears. At the end of the entry the date of issue of the magazine is given. Keep in mind that smaller libraries will not carry all 180 magazines and their back issues. Consult the library's list of available periodicals, which is often found near *The Reader's Guide.* "Self-help" libraries will allow you to find your articles yourself; in other libraries you must fill out a "periodical request slip" and hand it to the reference librarian.

Large public libraries will carry *The Biography Index,* with volumes from 1946 to the present. It brings together, under the subject's name, references to biographical material appearing not only in periodicals but in books of biography and chapters within books. This source is excellent for the study of biblical personalities.

Large public libraries, seminaries, and divinity schools will carry *The Index to Religious Periodicals,* designed for scholarly use and technical study.

Now that you know how to track down articles for your studies, look at the types of reference books available. Learn how to find quickly the ones most useful to you. Since books found on reference shelves may not be checked out, you must use them on the spot. Consider acquiring those you find most helpful for your own private collection.

Five categories of reference works are helpful for Old Testament study. Examine and get to know these categories: histories, commentaries, atlases, Bible dictionaries, and concordances. Before using, and certainly before buying, make note of the features offered by the particular reference book at hand. Note the copyright date, for atlases as well as some commentaries, if you desire up-to-date information. Skim the table of contents to discover quickly what the book is about. Examine the book for its arrangement, looking for convenience. Look for a bibliography, which will refer you to sources used or further reading on a subject. Search for appendices and glossaries toward the back of the book—often useful charts, definitions, and short articles are found there. Then see the index and cross-references at the end. Note the comprehensiveness of these lists for your subject. Finally, look up a topic with which you are familiar and read the article critically. Read several articles carefully. Note whether articles are popular or scholarly, signed or unsigned, impartial or biased. In reference works, try to attain a balance of interpretations. Often this means consulting two or more reference books in the same category.

Histories of biblical times are valuable aids. *Everyday Life in Old Testament Times,* by H. W. Eaton (Scribner, 1956), gives factual but informal description of all aspects of life in Israel and the Mediterranean world. The National Geographic Society publishes two beautifully illustrated volumes: *Everyday Life in Bible Times* (1967) and *Great Religions of the World* (1971). John Bright's *A History of Israel* (Westminster Press, 1981) is extremely useful and thorough as a reference text.

Commentaries give explanations of each biblical book by chapter and verse. Fine single-volume commentaries are *The Abingdon Bible Commentary* (Doubleday, 1979), by F. C. Eiselen and others, and *The Interpreter's One-Volume Commentary on the Bible* (Abingdon Press, 1971), edited by Charles M. Laymon. *The Interpreter's Bible* (Abingdon Press, 1951–57), a twelve-volume set, is an expensive but useful reference work for individual collectors. Other highly readable sets are *The Layman's Bible Commentary* (John Knox Press, twenty-five volumes), and the *Daily Study Bible* (Westminster Press), edited by John C. L. Gibson (Old Testament) and William Barclay (New Testament).

Atlases provide not only maps, but photographs and drawings to enrich your mental picture of biblical locations. See the *Reader's Digest Atlas of the Bible* (1982); *The Oxford Bible Atlas,* edited by Herbert G. May (Oxford University Press, 1985); and the classic *Westminster Historical Atlas to the Bible,* edited by G. E. Wright and F. V. Filson (Westminster Press, 1956). All of these atlases provide articles, charts, and historical notes.

Bible dictionaries are encyclopedias of people, places, objects, events, and theological concepts found in the Bible. *The Interpreter's Dictionary of the Bible,* edited by George A. Buttrick and Keith R. Crim (Abingdon), is a five-volume set. The best single-volume dictionaries are *The New Westminster Dictionary of the Bible* (Westminster Press, 1982), edited by H. S. Gehman, and *Harper's Bible Dictionary* (Harper & Row, 1985), edited by Paul J. Achtemeier.

Concordances are hefty but handy reference tools for word studies, finding major themes in the Old Testament, or simply locating names of places and people in the Bible. Exhaustive concordances list almost every word found in the Old Testament. *Nelson's Complete Concordance* is keyed to the Revised Standard Version, while *Strong's* and *Young's* are keyed to the King James Version. *Harper's Topical Concordance* is designed for the person looking for texts or quotations on a given subject. *Nave's Topical Bible* cross-references 100,000 verses under 20,000 topics for conceptual studies.

How does the Old Testament student who wishes to build a private collection get hold of certain titles? Your neighborhood bookstore is sure to help. Bookstores keep certain reference books to help them order and sell books—even books they do not regularly stock. The *Subject Guide to Books in Print,* published annually, lists book titles currently available from 13,900 book publishers. These titles are indexed under nearly 62,000 subject headings with numerous cross-references. Don't hesitate to ask bookstores to order books for you. Some bookstores will even try to track down books that are no longer "in print" (available from the publisher).

Selected booklists will provide you with good descriptions of available titles. The Church and Synagogue Library Association compiles an excellent pamphlet entitled "Helpful Books for Bible Readings and Study." They also have annotated bibliographies on "Reference Books" and "Interesting People (A Biographical Booklist)." For this information, write CSLA, P.O. Box 1130, Bryn Mawr, PA 19010.

Finally, keep this *Guide* as a record of your interaction with the Old Testament texts. It will serve you well as a foundation and starting point. As you continue your studies, you will find that the texts speak to you with different emphases and in new ways as you become more familiar with them. You have begun a journey that will cover a lifetime.

Glossary

'Abiru—wanderer, outsider, displaced person; similar to "Hebrew."

'Adam—Hebrew word for mankind, humanity, humans. Used as a man's first name in Genesis 2—3.

'Adamah—Hebrew for dust, dirt, the earth or ground.

Amen—Hebrew for so be it, truly.

Amphictyony—a loose confederacy. Political organization of the twelve tribes before the monarchy; a loosely organized tribal system.

Ancient Near East—the bridge of land between the Mediterranean Sea and the Persian Gulf. During biblical times, the ancient Near East comprised the empires of Canaan and Israel, Babylon, and Persia. Modern nation states are Israel, Jordan, Syria, and Iraq.

Anthropology—the doctrine of human beings: our nature, origin, destiny. In this *Study Guide,* anthropology as the study of human nature is contrasted with theology, or the study of the nature of God.

Anthropomorphism—a literary device by which human features (physical and/or emotional) are attributed directly to God.

Apocalyptic—writings concerned with the end times: the consummation of history and the beginning of God's kingdom.

Apocrypha—books labeled "hidden" or "secret" by Jews and Protestants and bound separately from the canon, but accepted as authoritative Scripture by the Roman Catholic and Eastern Orthodox churches.

Apodictic law—unconditional, absolute law; cast in the form of "Thou shalt not . . . ."

Apostasy—the act of turning away from one's faith; abandoning or forsaking belief.

Atonement—reconciliation of two parties; the restoration of a relationship. Atonement is usually associated with sacrifice, by which the obstacle (sin) that separates the two parties is purged, covered, or wiped away.

Baal—Canaanite male deity; literally the lord, master, or owner of the land, usually written in the plural (baals) to refer to fertility gods.

Babylonian captivity—586–539 B.C. Period of Jewish history when part of the population of Judah was sent into exile by Nebuchadnezzar, king of Babylon.

Canon—authoritative list of sacred books, accepted as Holy Scripture.

Casuistic law—case law, conditional law, cast in the form of "If . . . , then . . . ."

Circa—Latin for "around"; used for dates that are approximate, uncertain.

Circumcision—at one time, a practice unique to the Israelites, and thus a sign of their chosen status before God.

Cosmology—a picture or view of the universe.

Council of Jamnia—synod of rabbis which met in A.D. 90 in Jamnia, a town on the coastal plain of Israel, to discuss Hebrew Scriptures. After the council, the Hebrew canon was closed.

Covenant—(1) an unconditional promise, or a unilateral treaty; (2) an agreement made between two parties for the accomplishment of a task. Covenants are always relational in nature. The Hebrew word for covenant, *berith,* appears over 280 times in the Old Testament; *berith* is central to the OT understanding of the nature of God.

Decalogue (Greek); Debarim (Hebrew)—literally "ten words"; designation for the Ten Commandments of Exodus 20:1–17.

Deuteronomic formula—a system of blessings and curses first outlined in the book of Deuteronomy. The formula stresses that the nature of rewards and punishments is concrete, material, earthly. Blessings are tied to obedience to the Torah, while curses are the result of disobedience to the Torah.

Deuteronomic Reform—short-lived (c. 620–605) reform of cultic practices and temple worship made by King Josiah of Judah; based on a book found in the temple which contained parts of the present-day book of Deuteronomy. See 2 Kings 23. The reform called for the removal of pagan shrines and the centralization of worship in Jerusalem.

Diaspora—Greek for "scattered abroad." Beginning with the Babylonian captivity of 586 B.C., diaspora is applied to any Jew who lives outside of the Holy Land.

Elohim—Hebrew for god or spirit.

Etiology—a story that explains the origins of a phenomenon: a practice, a custom, a name, or anything else.

Exclusivism—the notion or belief that God's choice of people is limited to a few. Simply put, the attitude of "I'm chosen; you're not."

Fractricide—the murder of one's brother or sister.

Genealogy—"family tree"; a list that accounts for the descendants of a person, family, or group.

Genre—category of written composition characterized by a particular style, form, or content.

Geschichte—German for "history," concerned with the meaning of past events.

Gilgamesh, Epic of—Babylonian myths set down in writing c. 1750 B.C.; includes an account of a flood.

Gregorian calendar—introduced by Pope Gregory XIII in A.D. 1582; the system of dating used in the West. The calendar uses A.D. (Anno Domini, "the year of our Lord") for dates after the birth of Christ, and B.C. (before Christ) for dates prior to Jesus' birth.

Haggadah—commentary on those Hebrew Scriptures that are

not legal in character. The *Haggadah* contains stories that supplement, in an imaginative way, the history of the Old Testament. It includes a commentary used for the ritual of *Pesach,* or Passover, which was used as early as 200 B.C. and has been revised over the centuries.

Hamartiology—the study of sin: its nature, causes, results. From the Greek *hamartia,* missing the mark.

Heilsgeschichte—German for the history of salvation, the story of God and God's chosen people.

Herem—Hebrew for the sacrificial ban placed on all pagan captives and booty; a feature of Israelite holy war.

Hesed—Hebrew for steadfast love, also translated grace, mercy, and loving-kindness. Used over 240 times in the Old Testament, God's *hesed* is the constant element in the history of the covenant with Israel. This love, unique to God, is expressed in God's choice of Israel and God's commitment to this choice.

Historie—a German word for "history," which denotes the factual data of the past; a listing of events.

Isaiah—actually two books; chapters 1–39, or "First Isaiah," were written in Jerusalem in the late eighth century B.C. Second Isaiah, beginning with chapter 40, dates from the sixth century B.C. and originated in Babylon. Some scholars identify chapters 40–66 as one "book," while others identify chapters 40–55 as Second Isaiah and chapters 56–66 as Third Isaiah, dating from the Restoration period in Jerusalem.

Kosher—pure food laws; dietary regulations. Many kosher practices reflect a separation from Canaanite sacrificial rites. For example, Canaanites boiled a young kid in its mother's milk as a sacrifice to the nature gods. This practice, and by extension the mixture of dairy and meat products, is forbidden in Leviticus.

Levirate marriage—provision is made in the OT for a widow to marry the closest kin of her deceased husband.

Lex talionis—from Exodus 21:23–25, the teaching that the punishment must equal (and not exceed) the crime.

LXX—Roman numerals for "seventy"; abbreviation for the Septuagint. The LXX is the Greek translation of Hebrew Scriptures made c. 275 B.C. in Alexandria, Egypt. The LXX includes both the Hebrew (Palestinian) canon and apocryphal or deuterocanonical literature.

Mashal—Hebrew for proverb; a truth gained from general experience.

Messianic oracle—prophetic poem that foretells the coming of a messiah, or an "anointed one," of the Davidic line.

Millennium (singular), millennia (plural)—a thousand-year unit. The first millennium B.C. runs from the year 999 to year 1 B.C. The second millennium B.C. runs from 1999 to 1000 B.C.

Mishnah—Hebrew collection of laws concerning tithes, feasts, marriage, ritual purity, and sacrifices. This code of law emerged c. A.D. 200.

Nabi—Hebrew for mouthpiece; also designates a prophet.

Noachian covenant—God's unconditional promise that never again would God destroy the earth. The sign of this covenant is the rainbow.

Patriarch—forefather/progenitor. The patriarchs of the Hebrew faith are three: Abraham, Isaac, and Jacob.

Patriarchal history—Genesis 12–50, from the call of Abraham to the settlement of Jacob's twelve sons and their families in Egypt.

Pentateuch—Greek for five books; denotes the first five books of the Old Testament: Genesis, Exodus, Leviticus, Numbers, Deuteronomy.

Pesach—Hebrew for Passover, commemorating the Exodus event. A family holiday, *Pesach* consists of a seder dinner in which symbolic foods are eaten and a liturgy is read.

Polytheism—belief in many gods. A variant is henotheism: the worship of one god without denying the existence of other gods.

Polygamy—having more than one spouse. It is clear from the Pentateuch that polygamy was common in patriarchal times. By the time of the monarchy, however, polygamy was limited to the royal family (e.g., David and Solomon) and served as a sign of wealth and status in the ancient Near East.

Primeval history—Genesis 1–11, containing epics that are concerned with the origins of things.

Restoration—the time marked by the end of the Exile and the return of diaspora Jews to Judea, dated from 538 B.C. on. High points are the reforms of Ezra and Nehemiah and the completion of the second temple in 515 B.C.

Ruah—Hebrew for breath, wind, or spirit.

Satan—"the adversary," the member of God's heavenly council in charge of investigating the affairs of humans on earth. See Job 1–2. In postexilic period (c. 300 B.C.), Satan came to be identified with the serpent in Genesis 3 and the leader of the forces of evil.

Semitic peoples—from Shem, son of Noah (Gen. 10), peoples who first dwelled in Mesopotamia and later migrated west into Canaan. Semitic peoples share a common language group, which includes Assyrian, Babylonian, Aramaic, Canaanite, Hebrew, Moabite, Arabic, and Ethiopian dialects.

Shema—Hebrew for "hear" and the first word of Deuteronomy 6:4–5; this important credal statement is known as "the *shema.*"

Sheol—Hebrew for the underworld; a place of deep sleep for the dead.

Superscription—the title or heading written above a psalm, giving information on the origin of that psalm.

Suzerain—the initiator of a covenant treaty.

Suzerainty treaty—covenant in which the lord or king lays out obligations to the vassal. First used by the Hittites in the second millennium, suzerainty treaties were adapted by the Hebrews with the understanding that Yahweh is suzerain and the chosen people are God's vassals.

Synagogue—Greek for assembly; place for prayer and study (but not for sacrifices). Synagogues probably arose during the Babylonian captivity as meeting places for the exiled Jews.

Syncretism—the combination of two or more different forms of belief or religious practices.

Tabernacle—portable sanctuary of the Hebrews, built and described in Exodus.

Targums—Aramaic paraphrases of the Hebrew Scriptures produced between 250 B.C. and A.D. 300; used for readings in the synagogues.

Temple—the "house of Yahweh" located in Jerusalem as the place for sacrifice and worship, attended by the Levitical priests. The first temple was built by Solomon in the tenth century B.C. and destroyed by the Babylonians in 586 B.C. The second temple was built between 520 and 515 B.C. and destroyed by the Romans in A.D. 70.

Theocracy—rule by God; government either under immediate divine guidance or by mediators who are divinely guided.

Theology—the study of God; discourse on the nature, existence, and meaning of God.

Theophany—a manifestation or appearance of God.

Torah—(1) capitalized and with the definite article, the Torah designates the first five books of the Old Testament, or the Pentateuch; (2) without the definite article and in lower case, torah is Hebrew for law, teaching, or instruction, originating with God and mediated through Moses to all Israel. Torah is the basis for the Mosaic covenant. Thus, in later Judaism, all Jewish tradition (both written and oral law) is referred to as torah.

Tribal Confederacy—political organization of the twelve tribes during the conquest of Canaan (books of Joshua and Judges) before the monarchy; an amphictyony or loosely organized political system.

United Monarchy—the period during which the twelve tribes of Israel were ruled by one king. The United Monarchy includes the reigns of Saul, David, and Solomon. It splits into a Northern Kingdom and a Southern Kingdom with Solomon's death in 922 B.C.

Universalism—doctrine that stresses God's love for all people or God's inclusiveness, in contrast to exclusivism.

Vassal—a person under the protection of a suzerain or lord.

Yam suph—Hebrew for the sea of reeds or marshy lake through which the Hebrews escaped during the Exodus from Egypt; mistranslated "Red Sea" in the Greek Septuagint.

YHWH—the sacred name for God; translated "I am who I am," "I will be who I will be," or "I cause to happen." Because the name itself is too holy to utter, the word "Lord" (in Hebrew, *Adonai*) was substituted whenever the text was read. YHWH is translated LORD God in the Revised Standard Version.

Yom Kippur—Hebrew for Day of Atonement, celebrated annually ten days after the new year in the Hebrew calendar. In biblical times, the annual fast day was when the scapegoat was driven into the wilderness, symbolizing the death of the sins of the nation. See Leviticus 23.

Ziggurat—religious temple built in ancient Mesopotamia for the worship of the gods. These terraced towers provided ancient Near Eastern worshipers with a stairway to the heavens.

Sources and Suggested Readings

Ackerman, James S., senior author. *Teaching the Old Testament in English Classes*. Bloomington, Indiana: Indiana University Press, 1973.

Anderson, Bernhard W. *Understanding the Old Testament*, 4th edition. Englewood Cliffs, New Jersey: Prentice-Hall, Inc., 1986.

Bright, John. *A History of Israel*, 2d edition. Philadelphia: Westminster Press, 1976.

Browne, Lewis. *The Graphic Bible*. New York: Macmillan Publishing Company, 1928.

Buechner, Frederick. *Peculiar Treasures: A Biblical Who's Who*. New York: Harper & Row, 1979.

Childs, Brevard S. *Introduction to the Old Testament as Scripture*. Philadelphia: Fortress Press, 1979.

Harvey, Van A. *A Handbook of Theological Terms*. New York: Macmillan Publishing Company, 1964.

Henderlite, Rachel. *Exploring the Old Testament*. Atlanta: John Knox Press, 1945.

Heschel, Abraham J. *The Prophets*. New York: Harper & Row, 1962.

Laymon, Charles M., ed. *The Interpreter's One-Volume Commentary on the Bible*. Nashville: Abingdon Press, 1984.

May, Herbert G., ed. *Oxford Bible Atlas*, 2d edition. London: Oxford University Press, 1974.

Pritchard, James B., ed. *Ancient Near Eastern Texts: Relating to the Old Testament*, 3d edition. Princeton: Princeton University Press, 1969.

Smith, Huston. *The Religions of Man*. New York: Harper & Row, 1958.

Von Rad, Gerhard. *Old Testament Theology*. New York: Harper & Row, 1962.

Young, Robert. *Young's Analytical Concordance to the Bible*. Grand Rapids, Michigan: Eerdmans Publishing Co., 1975.